The Tyndale Old Testament Commentaries

General Editor:
PROFESSOR D. J. WISEMAN, O.B.E., M.A., D.Lit., F.B.A., F.S.A.

JOEL and AMOS

For

PAUL (†1979), JOHN, LAURA and BOB
Brothers and sister in
blood and Spirit

JOEL and AMOS

AN INTRODUCTION AND COMMENTARY

by

DAVID ALLAN HUBBARD,
B.A., B.D., Th.M., Ph.D., D.D., L.H.D., Lit.D.

*President, Fuller Theological Seminary,
Pasadena, California*

INTER-VARSITY PRESS
LEICESTER, ENGLAND
DOWNERS GROVE, ILLINOIS, USA

Inter-Varsity Press
38 De Montfort Street, Leicester LE1 7GP, England
P.O. Box 1400, Downers Grove, Illinois 60515, U.S.A.

© *1989 David Allan Hubbard*

Inter-Varsity Press, England is the book-publishing division of the Universities and Colleges Christian Fellowship (formerly the Inter-Varsity Fellowship), a student movement linking Christian Unions in universities and colleges throughout the United Kingdom and the Republic of Ireland, and a member movement of the International Fellowship of Evangelical Students. For information about local and national activities write to UCCF, 38 De Montfort Street, Leicester LE1 7GP.

InterVarsity Press, U.S.A., is the book-publishing division of InterVarsity Christian Fellowship, a student movement active on campus at hundreds of universities, colleges and schools of nursing. For information about local and regional activities, write Public Relations Dept., InterVarsity Christian Fellowship, 6400 Schroeder Rd., P.O. Box 7895, Madison, WI 53707-7895.

Distributed in Canada through InterVarsity Press, 860 Denison St., Unit 3, Markham, Ontario L3R 4H1, Canada.

All Scripture quotations, unless otherwise indicated, are from the Holy Bible, New International Version. Copyright © *1973, 1978, International Bible Society. Used by permission of Zondervan Bible Publishers.*

Text set in Great Britain by Parker Typesetting Service, Leicester

Printed in the United States of America ∞

UK ISBN 0-85111-642-6 (cloth)
UK ISBN 0-85111-844-5 (paper)
USA ISBN 0-8308-1428-0 (cloth)
USA ISBN 0-87784-274-4 (paper)
USA ISBN 0-87784-880-7 (set of Tyndale Old Testament Commentaries, cloth)
USA ISBN 0-87784-280-9 (set of Tyndale Old Testament Commentaries, paper)

British Library Cataloguing in Publication Data

Hubbard, David Allan
 Joel and Amos
 1. Bible O.T. Joel. Critical studies
 2. Bible O.T. Amos. Critical studies
 I. Title II. Series
 224'.06

Library of Congress Cataloging-in-Publication Data

Hubbard, David Allan.
 Joel and Amos: an introduction and commentary/by David Allan Hubbard.
     p.   cm.—(The Tyndale Old Testament commentaries)
   Includes bibliographical references.
   ISBN 0-8308-1428-0.—ISBN 0-87784-274-4 (bpk.)
   1. Bible. O.T. Joel—Commentaries. 2. Bible. O.T. Amos—
 Commentaries.   I. Title. II. Series.
 BS1575.3.H83 1989
 224'.707—dc20   89-36877
                                                       CIP

17   16   15   14   13   12   11   10   9   8   7   6   5   4   3   2   1
99   98   97   96   95   94   93   92   91   90   89

GENERAL PREFACE

THE aim of this series of *Tyndale Old Testament Commentaries*, as it was in the companion volumes on the New Testament, is to provide the student of the Bible with a handy, up-to-date commentary on each book, with the primary emphasis on exegesis. Major critical questions are discussed in the introductions and additional notes, while undue technicalities have been avoided.

In this series individual authors are, of course, free to make their own distinct contributions and express their own point of view on all debated issues. Within the necessary limits of space they frequently draw attention to interpretations which they themselves do not hold but which represent the stated conclusions of sincere fellow Christians.

The messages of the so-called 'minor' prophets Joel and Amos should be as relevant for the reader today as for their original hearers. Dr Hubbard helpfully brings this out as he guides us through the text by which their words come down to us. Joel's call to repentance and salvation by faith through grace still registers, and his promise of the gift of God's holy Spirit reminds us that God's presence and power are available today to every believer. Amos stresses that crimes against humanity will certainly bring the judgment of God and that we should be more concerned with present spiritual commitment than with past experience, influential though that may be.

In the Old Testament in particular no single English translation is adequate to reflect the original text. The version on which this commentary is based is the Revised Standard Version, but other translations are frequently referred to as well, and on occasion the author supplies his own. Where necessary, words are transliterated in order to help the reader who is unfamiliar with Hebrew to identify the precise word under discussion. It is assumed throughout that the reader will have ready access to one, or more, reliable rendering of the Bible in English.

5

GENERAL PREFACE

Interest in the meaning and message of the Old Testament continues undiminished and it is hoped that this series will thus further the systematic study of the revelation of God and his will and ways as seen in these records. It is the prayer of the editor and publisher, as of the authors, that these books will help many to understand, and to respond to, the Word of God today.

D. J. WISEMAN

CONTENTS

JOEL

AMOS

CONTENTS

8

AUTHOR'S PREFACE

JOEL and Amos are books for our times. Nothing in the past 2,500 years has made their messages passé. Amos still calls moribund congregations to turn their liturgies into loving actions. He still beckons the wealthy and powerful of our lands to do right by the poor and disadvantaged. Joel still teaches peoples beleagured by plague, drought, or other disasters to seek relief through repentance. His words still provide magnificent perspective on the work of God the Holy Spirit.

No-one who writes a commentary starts from scratch. Origen himself would doubtlessly agree with that. By my side have been the works of Hans Walter Wolff, James Mays, Hammerschaimb, Arthur Weiser, S. Amsler, Robert Martin-Achard, W. Rudolph, Leslie Allen, Arvid Kapelrud, G. W. Ahlstrom and W. S. Prinsloo. When my debt to them is especially deep or my difference from them is especially wide I have cited their names. But even where they are not mentioned their help may well be present.

This commentary has sought to make its own contribution by treating the books as unified compositions artfully shaped by their authors and/or editors. The final form of the work is the only one of whose structure and content we can be sure. Interpretations based on theories of stages in the production of a work must ever remain tenuous. The approach to unity adopted here means also that context is as crucial as content to the message of any part of a book. I have tried, therefore, to help the reader keep track of what leads into a given passage as well as what flows out of it. In addition I have kept an eye on the literary forms that have been so skillfully combined in both of these books. They are clues to the nuances that the prophets wanted their hearers to grasp, as they addressed the emotions as well as the intellect of the people. The Revised Standard Version, whose readings are usually italicized in the text, served as the basis for my comments, while the other

9

versions were consulted frequently.

Special thanks are due to Vera Wils, Elsie Evans and Shirley Coe, who saw to the production of the typescript while also carrying out their other duties in my office. Dr Dawn Waring and Dr John McKenna assisted immensely with the final editing. I am more than grateful to Professor Donald Wiseman, to the external readers and to the Reverend David Kingdon for their gracious patience, thoughtful suggestions and meticulous care in the preparation of the book.

The dedication is a small token of my gratitude to, and affection for, my brothers and sister whose Christian witness in word and life shaped the faith and calling of their youngest brother in more ways than he can express.

DAVID ALLAN HUBBARD

Note

Where reference is made to comments on Hosea (for example, on pages 43 and 57), this relates to the Tyndale Old Testament Commentary on *Hosea* by David Allan Hubbard, to be published in the autumn of 1989.

CHIEF ABBREVIATIONS

AB	The Anchor Bible.
ANEP	*The Ancient Near East in Pictures* edited by James B. Pritchard (Princeton University Press, ²1969).
ANET	*Ancient Near Eastern Texts Relating to the Old Testament* edited by James B. Pritchard (Princeton University Press, ³1969).
ANVAO	Avhandlingar utgitt av Det Norske Videnskaps-Akademi i Oslo.
AOAT	Alter Orient und Altes Testament (Neukirchen-Vluyn).
BASOR	*Bulletin of the American Schools of Oriental Research.*
BDB	F. Brown, S. R. Driver and C. A. Briggs, *Hebrew and English Lexicon of the Old Testament* (Oxford University Press, 1906).
Bib	*Biblica.*
BZAW	*Beihefte zur Zeitschrift für die alttestamentliche Wissenschaft.*
CAT	Commentaire de l'ancien testament.
CBC	Cambridge Bible Commentary.
CB.OT	Coniectanea Biblica. Old Testament Series (Lund, Sweden: Gleerup).
CBQ	*Catholic Biblical Quarterly.*
CHALOT	W. L. Holladay, *Concise Hebrew and Aramaic Lexicon* (Grand Rapids: Eerdmans, 1971).
DOTT	*Documents from Old Testament Times* edited by D. Winton Thomas (London: Nelson, 1958).
E.T.	English translation.
ETR	*Etudes Théologiques et Religieuses.*
EvTh	*Evangelische Theologie.*
HAT	Handbuch zum Alten Testament.
HTR	*Harvard Theological Review.*
IB	Interpreter's Bible.
IBD	*The Illustrated Bible Dictionary* (Leicester: IVP, 1980).
ICC	International Critical Commentary.

11

CHIEF ABBREVIATIONS

IDB	*Interpreter's Dictionary of the Bible* (Nashville: Abingdon Press, 1962).
IDB Supp.	Supplementary volume to *IDB* (Nashville: Abingdon Press, 1976).
Int	*Interpretation.*
ISBE, rev.	*International Standard Bible Encyclopedia,* fully revised (Grand Rapids: Eerdmans, 1979–88).
ITC	International Theological Commentary.
JBL	*Journal of Biblical Studies.*
JETS	*Journal of the Evangelical Theological Society.*
JSOT	*Journal for the Study of the Old Testament.*
JTS	*Journal of Theological Studies.*
KAT	Kommentar zum Alten Testament.
KB	L. Köhler and W. Baumgartner, *Lexicon in veteris testamenti libros* (Leiden: E. J. Brill, 1951–53).
NBC rev.	*New Bible Commentary,* revised (Leicester: IVP, 1970).
NCB	New Century Bible.
NICOT	New International Commentary on the Old Testament.
OTL	Old Testament Library.
OTS	*Oudtestamentische Studien.*
TDNT	*Theological Dictionary of the New Testament* edited by G. Kittel and G. Friedrich (Grand Rapids: Eerdmans, 1946–76).
TDNT abr.	*Theological Dictionary of the New Testament* abridged by G. W. Bromiley (Grand Rapids: Eerdmans, 1985).
ThZ	*Theologische Zeitschrift.*
TRE	*Theologische Realenzyklopädie.*
TynB	*Tyndale Bulletin.*
VT	*Vetus Testamentum.*
VT Supp.	*Vetus Testamentum,* Supplements.
WBC	Word Biblical Commentary.
WMANT	Wissenschaftliche Monographien zum Alten und Neuen Testament.
ZAW	*Zeitschrift für die alttestamentliche Wissenschaft.*
ZDPV	*Zeitschrift der deutschen Palästina-Vereins.*

Texts and versions

AV	Authorized (King James) Version, 1611.
BHS	*Biblia Hebraica Stuttgartensia,* 1967/77.

JB	Jerusalem Bible, 1966.
LXX	The Septuagint (pre-Christian Greek version of the Old Testament).
MT	Massoretic Text.
NAB	New American Bible, 1970.
NASB	New American Standard Bible, 1960.
NIV	New International Version, 1978.
RSV	Revised Standard Version, 1952.
Vulg.	The Vulgate (the late fourth-century Latin translation of the Bible by Jerome).
Moffatt	J. Moffatt, *A New Translation of the Bible,* 1935.
Syr.	Syriac.

SELECT BIBLIOGRAPHY

These are the works frequently referred to and which are cited in the text by the last name of the author.

Old Testament introductions

Childs, B. S., *Introduction to the Old Testament As Scripture* (SCM, 1983. US ed. Philadelphia: Fortress Press, 1979).

Crenshaw, J. L., *Story and Faith: A Guide to the Old Testament* (New York and London: Macmillan Publishing Co., 1986).

Gottwald, N. K., *The Hebrew Bible: A Socio-Literary Introduction* (Philadelphia: Fortress Press, 1985).

Kaiser, O., *Introduction to the Old Testament: A Presentation of Its Results and Problems* (E.T., Blackwell, 1980. US ed. Minneapolis: Augsburg Publishing House, 1975).

Robert, A. and Feuillet, A., *Introduction to the Old Testament* (E.T., New York: Desclee Co., 1968).

Soggin, J. A., *Introduction to the Old Testament*, OTL (E.T., SCM, 1988. US ed. Philadelphia: Westminster Press, 1976).

Weiser, A., *The Old Testament: Its Formation and Development* (E.T., New York: Association Press, 1961). (Cited as Weiser, *Old Testament.*)

Old Testament histories

Bright, J., *A History of Israel* (SCM, 2nd rev. ed., 1981. US ed. Philadelphia: Westminster Press, [3]1981).

Donner, H., 'The Separate States of Israel and Judah' in *Israelite and Judaean History*, ed. by J. H. Hayes and J. M. Miller, OTL (Philadelphia: Westminster Press, 1977), pp. 381–434.

Herrmann, S., *A History of Israel in Old Testament Times* (E.T., Philadelphia: Fortress Press, [2]1981).

Miller, J. M. and Hayes, J. H., *A History of Ancient Israel and*

14

Judah (SCM, 1986. US ed. Philadelphia: Westminster Press, 1986).

Old Testament theologies

Jacob, E., *Theology of the Old Testament* (E.T., London: Hodder, 1958. US ed. New York: Harper and Brothers, 1958).

Rad, G. von, *Old Testament Theology*, 2 vols. (E.T., Edinburgh: Oliver and Boyd, 1962, 1965. US ed. New York: Harper and Row, 1962, 1965).

Vriezen, Th. C., *An Outline of Old Testament Theology* (E.T., Oxford: Blackwell, ²1970. US ed. Newton, Mass.: C. T. Branford, ²1970).

Zimmerli, W., *Old Testament Theology in Outline* (E.T., n.e., Edinburgh: T. and T. Clark, 1983. US ed. Atlanta: John Knox Press, ²1978).

Works on the prophets

Blenkinsopp, J., *A History of Prophecy in Israel* (SPCK, 1984. US ed. Philadelphia: Westminster Press, 1983).

Buber, M., *The Prophetic Faith* (New York: Harper & Brothers, 1949).

Clements, R. E., *Prophecy and Tradition* (Blackwell, 1975. US ed. Atlanta: John Knox Press, 1975).

Coggins, R., 'An Alternative Prophetic Tradition?' in *Israel's Prophetic Tradition: Essays in Honour of Peter Ackroyd*, ed. by R. Coggins, A. Phillips and M. Knibb (Cambridge University Press, 1984), pp. 77–94.

Gordis, R., *Poets, Prophets and Sages: Essays in Biblical Interpretation* (Bloomington and London: Indiana University Press, 1971).

Hanson, P. D., *The People Called: the Growth of Community in the Bible* (San Francisco: Harper & Row, 1986).

Heschel, A. J., *The Prophets* (New York and Evanston: Harper & Row, 1962).

Hunter, A. V., *Seek the Lord! A Study of the Meaning and Function of the Exhortations in Amos, Hosea, Micah and Zephaniah* (Baltimore: St Mary's Seminary & University, 1982).

Koch, K., *The Prophets: vol. 1. The Assyrian Period* (E.T., SCM, 1982. US ed. Philadelphia: Fortress Press, 1983).

Kuhl, C. *The Prophets of Israel* (E.T., Edinburgh and London: Oliver and Boyd, 1960).

Murray, R., 'Prophecy and the Cult' in *Israel's Prophetic Tradition*, pp. 200–216.

Nicholson, E. W., *God and His People: Covenant and Theology in the Old Testament* (Oxford: Clarendon Press, and New York: Oxford University Press, 1986).

Phillips, A., 'Prophecy and Law' in *Israel's Prophetic Tradition*, pp. 217–232.

Sawyer, J. F. A., 'A Change of Emphasis in the Study of the Prophets' in *Israel's Prophetic Tradition*, pp. 233–249.

Van der Woude, A. S., 'Three Classical Prophets: Amos, Hosea and Micah' in *Israel's Prophetic Tradition*, pp. 32–57.

Vuilleumier, R., *La tradition culturelle d'Israël dans la prophétie d'Amos et d'Osée*, Cahiers Théologiques 45 (Neuchâtel: Editions Delachaux & Niestlé, 1960).

Whybray, R. N., 'Prophecy and Wisdom' in *Israel's Prophetic Tradition*, pp. 181–199.

Joel: commentaries

Allen, L., *The Books of Joel, Obadiah, Jonah and Micah*, NICOT (Grand Rapids: Eerdmans, 1976).

Bewer, J. A., *Joel et al.*, ICC (Edinburgh: T. & T. Clark, 1911).

Bič, M., *Das Buch Joel* (Berlin: Evangelische Verlaganstalt, 1960).

Delcor, M., 'Joel' in *Les Petits Prophètes*, La Sainte Bible (Paris: Letouzey & Ané, 1961).

Driver, S. R., *Joel and Amos*, The Cambridge Bible for Schools and Colleges (Cambridge: The University Press, 1898).

Kapelrud, A. S., *Joel Studies*, Uppsala Universitets Arsskrift 1948: 4 (Uppsala and Leipzig: A. B. Lundequistska Bokhandeln and Otto Harrassowitz, 1948).

Keil, C. F., *The Twelve Minor Prophets*, vol. 1 in *Biblical Commentaries on the Old Testament* by C. F. Keil & F. Delitzsch (E.T., Reprint: Grand Rapids: Eerdmans, 1949).

Keller, C. A., *Joel*, CAT (Neuchâtel: Editions Delachaux & Niestlé, 1965).

Robinson, T. H., *Die Zwölf Kleinen Propheten*, HAT (Tübingen: J. C. B. Mohr [Paul Siebeck], 2 1954).

Rudolph, W., *Joel, Amos, Obadja, Jona*, KAT (Gütersloher Verlaghaus Gerd Mohn, 1971).

16

Sellin, E., *Joel*, KAT (Leipzig, 1930).
Smith, G. A., *The Book of the Twelve Prophets*, Expositor's Bible (New York and London: Harper & Brothers, 1928).
Thompson, J. A., *Joel*, IB (New York: Abingdon Press, 1956).
Watts, J. D. W., *The Books of Joel, Obadiah, Jonah, Nahum, Habakkuk and Zephaniah*, CBC (Cambridge and New York: Cambridge University Press, 1975).
Wolff, H. W., *Joel and Amos*, Hermeneia (E.T., SCM, 1977. US ed. Philadelphia: Fortress Press, 1977).

Joel: special studies

Ahlström, G. W., *Joel and the Temple Cult of Jerusalem*, VT Supp. 21 (Leiden: E. J. Brill, 1971).
Plöger, O., *Theocracy and Eschatology* (E.T., Richmond, Virginia: John Knox Press, 1968).
Prinsloo, W. S., *The Theology of the Book of Joel*, BZAW 163 (Berlin and New York: Walter de Gruyter, 1985).

Amos: commentaries

Amsler, S., *Amos*, CAT (Neuchâtel: Delachaux & Niestlé, 1965).
Cripps, R. S., *A Critical and Exegetical Commentary on the Book of Amos* (SPCK, ²1955).
Delcor, M., 'Amos' in *Les Petits Prophètes*, La Sainte Bible (Paris: Letouzey & Ané, 1961).
Hammershaimb, E., *The Book of Amos: A Commentary* (E.T., Blackwell, 1970. US ed. New York: Schocken Books, 1970).
Martin-Achard, R., *Amos*, ITC (Edinburgh and Grand Rapids: The Handsel Press Ltd. and William B. Eerdmans Publ. Co., 1984). (Cited as Martin-Achard, ITC.)
Mays, J. L., *Amos* (SCM, 1978. US ed. Philadelphia: Westminster Press, 1969).
Motyer, J. A., *The Message of Amos: The Day of the Lion* (Leicester: IVP, 1984).
Robinson, T. H., *Die Zwölf Kleinen Propheten*, HAT (Tübingen: J. C. B., Mohr [Paul Siebeck], ²1954).
Rudolph, W., *Joel, Amos, Obadja, Jona*, KAT (Gütersloher Verlaghaus Gerd Mohn, 1971).
Weiser, A., *Die Prophetie des Amos* (Giessen: Alfred Topelmann, 1929).

17

Wolff, H. W., *Joel and Amos,* Hermeneia (E.T., SCM, 1977. US ed. Philadelphia: Fortress Press, 1977).

Amos: special studies

Auld, A. G., *Amos,* OT Guides (Sheffield: JSOT Press, 1986).

Coote, R. B., *Amos Among the Prophets: Composition and Theology* (Philadelphia: Fortress Press, 1981).

Kapelrud, A. S., *Central Ideas in Amos* (Oslo University Press, 1971).

Martin-Achard, R., *Amos: L'homme, le message, l'influence* (Geneva: Labor et Fides, 1984).

Neher, A., *Amos: Contribution à L'étude du Prophétisme* (Paris: Librairie Philosophique J. Vrin, 1950).

Reventlow, H. G., *Das Amt des Propheten bei Amos* (Göttingen: Vandenhoeck & Ruprecht, 1962).

Vollmer, J., *Geschichliche Rückblicke und Motive in der Prophetie des Amos, Hosea und Jesaia, BZAW* 119 (Berlin: Walter de Gruyter, 1971).

Ward, J. M., *Amos & Isaiah: Prophets of the Word of God* (Nashville and New York: Abingdon Press, 1969).

Watts, J. D. W., *Vision and Prophecy in Amos* (Grand Rapids: Eerdmans Publishing Co., 1958).

Wolff, H. W., *Amos the Prophet: the Man and His Background* (E.T., Philadelphia: Fortress Press, 1973). (Cited as Wolff, *Prophet.*)

JOEL

INTRODUCTION

THE word of God came to Joel in the heat of an emergency. What prompted Joel to preach and then record his words was an *invasion of insects*, a devastating plague of locusts. So widespread and so death-dealing was their assault that every aspect of human life was put in jeopardy, especially the daily offerings in the Jerusalem temple, which were ordered to maintain communion between God and the people. Joel's understanding of the creation drove him to see the insects as agents of the Creator, carrying out the task of judgment on a disobedient nation. The severity of the judgment, described twice – first in literal, then in figurative terms – proved to Joel that he had begun to witness nothing less than the Day of the Lord. Amos and Zephaniah had spoken of that Day in terms of inescapable darkness and intolerable suffering. The clouds of locusts that obscured the sun and devoured the food supply were the heralds of that Day. Yahweh marched with them, the death of his incorrigible people on his mind.

But also on his mind was their rescue in response to their repentance. The very temple that had been stripped of its offerings could be the site of a return to him. The very priests who wrapped themselves in sackcloth to wail at the altar could be the leaders of that return. Yahweh was ready for change and now the prophet urged the people of God also to be ready.

Pity, not wrath, was his response to their penitence, and with that pity came full restoration of all the insect damage. Beyond that, the whole episode of judgment and deliverance brought with it a new understanding of Yahweh's uniqueness. It had a revelatory quality that marked it as the harbinger of the days to come, when all Israelites, not just prophets, would experience personal communion with God

21

and fresh revelations of his power and glory. The era of Yahweh's spirit was on the way, an era so world-shaking that it signalled the final judgment, when the neighbour nations would pay for their savagery and Israel's covenant faith would be confirmed by God's abiding presence in their midst.

Amos had said that the Day was darkness *not* light (5:18, 20); Joel says that it is darkness *before* light. The Lord in covenant love had spared the people in the plague and preserved the honour of his name before the nations. Now he has a Day beyond the Day, when the vengeance that is his prerogative alone, and the grace that flows from his unique person, will be manifest to the whole world. On behalf of all God's people, Joel saw that Day and sang of it. From him we can learn the tune which we are to be ready to sing whenever the sovereign Lord is ready to give the cue.

II. THE PLACE IN THE CANON

With the Jews through the centuries, we need to look at the Minor Prophets not only individually but as one book, The Book of the Twelve. Hosea was placed first, not only because of the early date (mid-eighth century), but because of the length of his message and comprehensive treatment of the great prophetic themes of judgment and hope. Why was Joel placed second in the Hebrew list that has carried over to our English versions (the LXX has it in fourth place after Hosea, Amos and Micah)? The best answer will not be chronology alone since the Twelve are arranged in only rough chronological order, and Jonah, Obadiah and Joel are hard to fit into any historic framework. Joel seems to use Amos' view of the Day of Yahweh as a foil, both to reinforce his interpretation of the plague and to move beyond it to a radiant understanding of the ultimate victories of the Day, which amplifies Amos' brief note on future prosperity. As much as any single component, it is the common emphasis on the Day that probably accounts for Joel's position before Amos in the collection.[1] The thematic similarity is reinforced by verbal correspondences, especially Joel's use of Amos 1:2 in 3:16 and of Amos 9:13 in 3:18, and by the parallels between Joel's announcements of doom to Tyre, Philistia and Edom (3:4, 19) and Amos' threats to the

---

[1] See G. T. Sheppard, 'Canonization', *Int*, 36, 1982, p. 24.

same nations (Amos 1:8–12).

Even more important in determining Joel's place in the Canon of Scripture was the movement in his work from doom to hope, from judgment to salvation. In a sense, Joel, replete with ideas and terms drawn from many prophets, encapsulated the basic movement not only of individual prophetic books (*e.g.* Hosea, Isaiah) but of the prophetic corpus as a whole: 'for manifest in Joel is a comprehensive view of prophecy . . .' that prompted the arrangers of the Twelve to invite us to 'read Amos and the following prophets in the light of Joel's proclamation' (Wolff, p. 4).

III. THE DATE OF THE BOOK

Dates proposed for Joel's ministry and the composition of his book range from the early ninth century BC to the Maccabean era, some seven hundred years later. The broad diversity of scholarly opinion is evidence of the book's scarcity of information to help us pin-point the date. The fact that the book's centre-piece, the locust invasion, has left no other tracks in biblical history compounds our problem. Happily, most of what Joel has to teach we can grasp without the precise knowledge of his times, though we could read between his lines more keenly if we knew when he lived.

The most common theory of an *early date* would place Joel in the period of Joash's youth (*c.* 835–825 BC). That regency period (see 2 Ki. 12:1–21 for the role of Jehoiada the priest in guiding young Joash) would help to account for the absence of mention of a monarch in the book. The most common arguments for this early date are these: (1) the place in the Canon between two eighth-century prophets (but see above); (2) Joel's possible role in Judah's on-going struggle against the incursion of Baal worship (*cf.* Bič, pp. 106–108). The pivotal argument for the early date has usually been Joel's position in the Canon. If other sound ways of accounting for that position can be brought forward, then the case for a ninth-century date is greatly weakened. (3) The table of enemies, condemned for their ill-treatment of Judah: Tyre (dealing slaves to Edom, Am. 1:9), Sidon (the home of Jezebel, Ahab's pagan wife, 1 Ki. 16:31), Philistia (a constant thorn in Judah's western side, Am. 1:6; 2 Ch. 21:16–17), Ionians (Greeks who lived on both sides of the Aegean Sea and were renowned as slave-traders; the

Assyrians, Sargon II and Sennacherib had dealings with them in the late eighth century), Egypt (whose raid against Jerusalem in Rehoboam's day was well remembered, 1 Ki. 14:25–28), Edom (in constant tug-of-war with Judah for control of the southern regions, 2 Ki. 8:20–22; Am. 1:6, 9, 11); not a word is heard of Assyria, Babylonia and Persia, the dominant powers from the eighth through to the fifth centuries BC.

Those who advocate a *late post-exilic date* (c. 400–180 BC) have based their claims on a number of lines of evidence: (1) a two-stage composition of the book (see on Unity below) which assigns a late date to the apocalyptic outlook of 2:28 – 3:21, with its supernatural heavenly portents and its seemingly simplistic view of Judah's vindication and the subjugation of the neighbour nations; (2) the heavy use of what appear to be quotations from other books:

Joel passages:

> Joel 1:15, *cf.* Is. 13:6; Ezk. 30:2–3; Zp. 1:7;
> Joel 2:2, *cf.* Zp. 1:14–15;
> Joel 2:3, the reverse of Is. 51:3; Ezk. 36:35;
> Joel 2:6, *cf.* Na. 2:10;
> Joel 2:17, *cf.* Ps. 79:10;
> Joel 2:27, *cf.* Is. 45:5–6, 18; Ezk. 36:11;
> Joel 2:28, *cf.* Ezk. 39:29;
> Joel 2:31, *cf.* Mal. 4:5;
> Joel 2:32, *cf.* Ob. 17;
> Joel 3:4, *cf.* Ob. 15;
> Joel 3:10, the reverse of Is. 2:4; Mi. 4:3;
> Joel 3:16, *cf.* Is. 13:13; Am. 1:2;
> Joel 3:17, *cf.* Ezk. 36:11;
> Joel 3:18, *cf.* Am. 9:13;[1]

(3) mention of the wall of Jerusalem (2:7, 9), presumably rebuilt by Nehemiah (c. 445 BC); (4) reference to the Greeks (or Ionians, see above), often interpreted, especially by earlier commentators, as evidence of a Hellenistic date (post 332 BC); (5) if the heavenly portents are eclipses of sun and moon, dates based on astronomical calculations would be

---

[1] For a table of these quotations, see H. G. M. Williamson, *ISBE*, rev., II, p. 1078.

after 357 or 336 BC.[1]

None of these arguments can be deemed conclusive: (1) though apocalyptic literature is generally to be dated later than prophetic, the two genres are often so close, especially in the early stages of apocalyptic, that the border-line between the two is not clearly marked and the differences in literary motifs between Joel 2:28 – 3:21 and Daniel are more significant than the similarities; (2) even if the flow of quotations is one-way, with Joel as the recipient, none of them needs necessarily be later than 500 BC and several of them may reflect common use of a traditional saying rather than direct borrowing; furthermore, the scholarly consensus has come down heavily on the side of Joel's unity in recent years;[2] (3) Jerusalem's wall prior to Nehemiah's reconstruction does not seem to have been completely levelled; there could well have been substantial parts standing, as the brief rebuilding time (52 days, Neh. 6:15) may intimate;[3] (4) contacts between Greek traders and merchants and their counterparts in the Levant, several centuries prior to Alexander's time, are now well documented;[4] (5) the darkened sun (2:30–31) need not be understood literally as an eclipse but figuratively as a mark of *theophany* (cf. 2:10; 3:15; cf. Am. 8:9).

The *middle range of dates* (cf. 630–500 BC, just before to just after the Exile) seems to offer the most promise in our effort to narrow the options. Composition during this period seems best to accord with the close parallels cited above between Joel

---

[1] F. R. Stephenson, 'The Date of the Book of Joel', *VT*, 19, 1969, pp. 224–229.

[2] G. W. Ahlström (p. 91), arguing from Joel's prophetic perspective that the future arises out of the present, from the absence of threat from world powers, from the lack of any connection between Joel and an historic figure under whose name he speaks, from the literary style, which is remarkably free of allusions to secret knowledge, puzzling riddles, or allegorical pictures of the world's end, concludes: 'Thus, Joel is not an apocalyptic book.' All the same, Ahlström acknowledges that Joel 'May have contributed to the beginning of apocalyptic' by 'the strong emphasis on the paradisaical future', *cf*. also Kuhl (p. 177) who sees Joel, as a 'transition' to apocalyptic, and Plöger (p. 104) who finds in Joel 'the beginnings of the path which leads to the later apocalyptic'.

[3] See W. S. LaSor, 'Jerusalem', *ISBE*, rev., II, p. 1017.

[4] Kapelrud, pp. 153–158; J. M. Myers, 'Some Considerations Bearing on the Date of Joel', *ZAW*, 74, 1962, pp. 177–195; D. Auscher, 'Les relations entre Grèce et la Palestine avant la conquête d'Alexandre', *VT* 17, 1967, pp. 8–30. Bič (pp. 90–91) has gone so far as to remove the reference to Greeks (Ionians; 3:6) by reading the Heb. *yāwān* (Ionian) as *yāwēn* 'sediment', 'mire' (*cf*. Pss. 40:2; 69:2). 'Sons of mire' he then understands as the Egyptians (*cf*. 3:19), so named thanks to the yearly flooding and silting of the Nile.

and Zephaniah, Jeremiah, Ezekiel and Obadiah. The affinities with Zephaniah, as well as Amos, are particularly striking in the passages that deal with the Day of Yahweh (see below). Joel's attention to the cult and his tantalizingly brief mentions of its role and functions seem to resemble the pictures of temple-worship preserved in Jeremiah and Ezekiel.[1] There is not an insoluble problem with any of the names of cities or nations in such a sixth-century dating, as Kapelrud (his conclusion is Zedekiah's day; 598–587 BC; p. 191), Rudolph (597–587 BC) and Keller (his projected date is 630–600 BC; p. 103) have clearly shown (*cf.* also Koch, pp. 158–159). The arguments from language, word-usage, syntax, spelling, *etc.* can be pressed only with considerable tentativeness but tend to weigh against an early pre-exilic date (Ahlström, pp. 1–22).

The only major data which may help to narrow further the time-spread are the descriptions of the havoc wrought against Judah by the nations (3:1–8): parcelling out the land and giving it away, casting lots for the people, selling children into slavery for a pittance, stripping the people of their silver and gold, auctioning the citizens to the Ionians as slaves and thereby scattering them throughout the Mediterranean basin. The text sounds literal not hyperbolic and appears to leave us with only one period in Judah's history where all this could have happened on the scale that Joel implies: the *Exile*, with its total disruption of life in Judah and Jerusalem. The Old Testament clearly remembers how viciously opportunistic were the Edomites (3:19) at Jerusalem's fall (586 BC; Ps. 137:7; La. 4:21; Ezk. 25:12–14; 36:5; Ob. 10–14) and how impotent at best and treacherous at worst were the Egyptians on whom Judah relied in her futile rebellion against Babylon (2 Ki. 24:1–7; Je. 46:1–26). That the people of Tyre, Sidon and Philistia may also compound Judah's suffering both by direct involvement (Ezk. 25:15 – 26:7) or by buying slaves from Edom (*cf.* Edom's stellar role in slave-trade; Am. 1:6, 9) will not surprise any one acquainted with the vaunted cruelty and insatiable ambition which the Old Testament and other historical records attribute to them.

Judah has been exiled, so we surmise: no king is summoned (*cf.* Ho. 5:1), only citizens and elders (1:2, 14; 2:15–16). Yet the temple ritual is in full operation, so Joel states. This

[1]See Ahlström, pp. 35–61, for detailed arguments to this effect.

26

combination of inferences suggests a date for Joel roughly contemporary with Haggai and Zechariah but after the completion of the second temple, rebuilt by Zerubbabel at the urging of the two prophets and completed about 515 BC. Malachi's picture (c. 450 BC) of the abuses of public worship and his style of prophetic declaration, heavily influenced both by the catechetical techniques of the wisdom teachers and the *tôrâ* disputes of the priests and scribes, are sufficiently different in tone and content to suggest that Joel's work must have been some decades earlier. Worth noting here is that Joel (3:19) sees Edom's devastation as yet in the future, while Malachi (1:2–5) describes it as past. When all is said, a date for Joel in the vicinity of 500 BC may not be too wide of the mark.[1]

IV. THE SETTING OF THE BOOK

We have so little personal information about Joel (no more than his father's name) that we can only guess at how he lived, where he worked and what lay behind his prophetic utterances. There are no historical notes about his ministry (cf. Ho. 1:2; Am. 7:10–17) and no record of his call or commission.

Some lines of evidence combine to suggest that he may have had an official attachment to the temple. His familiarity with temple practices and procedures, his knowledge of liturgical formulas, his featuring of the role of priests both in the suffering and recovery from the plagues, his concern for Jerusalem in her present distress as well as her future deliverance, his focus on Mount Zion as the dwelling place of Yahweh mark him, at the very least, as a pained yet hopeful citizen of the capital and probably as a participant even in the temple services. Worth special note is what seems to be Joel's role as spokesman for Yahweh in describing the setting of the salvation oracle (2:18) and delivering the oracle itself (2:19 –

---

[1]Among recent commentators, there is a strong tendency to settle for a late 6th-century to mid-5th-century date: Ahlström (p. 129), 515–500 BC; Watts (p. 13), 'period of the second temple between the revival of Haggai and Zechariah and the reforms of Ezra'; Myers, *loc. cit.*, c. 520 BC; L. C. Allen (p. 24) agrees with Ahlström and Myers; Williamson, *loc. cit.*, places the book between 515 and 345 BC; W. S. Prinsloo (pp. 5–9) surveys the various theories without adding to them, except for his brief 'after the exile' in the concluding chapter (p. 127). H. W. Wolff (p. 5) settles for 'the first half of the fourth century' and thus departs somewhat from the current concensus. *Cf.* also Hanson, pp. 313–314.

3:21). It is the combination of the *temple setting*, so expressly prescribed, and the *oracle itself* that marks off Joel's prophecy from other salvation oracles.

Clearly fashioned with material from Judah's liturgical literature, especially her communal complaints (often called 'laments'),[1] the prophecy of Joel is not itself a liturgy but a call to participate in one (1:2 – 2:17) accompanied by a record of what happens when the people do (2:18 – 3:21).[2] As to whether the book or its parts were ever put to liturgical use during the centuries immediately after its composition, we have no information though we assume from Micah 7, Habakkuk 3 and other prophetic passages that liturgical editions of prophetic materials were not uncommon.

Joel's interest in the temple worship may show itself in his repeated attention to the Day of Yahweh, which as Amos (5:18–20, 21–27) informs us was a theme associated with the cultic assemblies of Israel. The new and the familiar turns which Joel gives to the Day (*cf.* on 3:14) may reflect both his continuity with Judah's joyful expectations of divine protection and restoration under the aegis of the covenant, and his certainty that none of this would happen without the judgment on God's people foreseen by Amos and Zephaniah.

This leads us to the major point. If Joel was a temple prophet, as he may well have been, he was no routine functionary, no mere mouthpiece for the priests and their teaching of Torah. His close acquaintance with prophetic writings (see above for list of quotations) and his eschatological vision mark him as much more than a cultic herald.[3] The close attention given to the cult and its imminent collapse, thanks to the grasshopper hordes, may well signal that the cult itself was

---

[1]I find it useful to distinguish *complaints* (*e.g.* La. 3; 5) where rescue is yet possible from *laments* (La. 1; 2; 4) where death or total destruction have set in and grief is outpoured without any hope of redress.

[2]G. S. Ogden, 'Joel 4 and Prophetic Responses to National Laments', *JSOT*, 26, 1983, pp. 97–106, has noted a number of connections between the four oracles of ch. 3 (Heb. 4) and the psalms of national complaint, describing *military* disaster. Kapelrud (pp. 7, 44, 55, 72–74, 90, 132, 159, 167) finds the setting of Joel in the liturgies of the New Year Festival which purportedly included royal enthronement ceremonies connected with the Day of Yahweh. Such a liturgical setting seems to assume more than can be proved.

[3]See Coggins, pp. 88–93, for a balanced interpretation of Joel's ministry that links him to the Jerusalem cult without implying that he is distanced in form and shape of ministry from the other prophets of his time.

corrupt. Without overtly singling out the sins of the religious leaders and their compromises, perhaps even to the point of idolatry, Joel almost subliminally may be calling for a renewal and purification that can be found only with a full return to Yahweh. The attention paid to Yahweh's uniqueness, especially in the recognition/self-introduction formulas (2:27; 3:17), would seem to underscore the religious syncretism or pluralism that lay at the heart of Judah's problems. Since the disaster had already occurred at the point where the prophecy begins, Joel's crisis is unlike that of most prophets, who can focus on the sins of the people while there is still time and sharpen that focus by the threats of judgment yet to come; Joel's attention is fully occupied by the disaster all around him, so the normal pattern of a judgment speech (*cf.* Am. 1:3ff.) is not available to him. He has to point the way out and he does that with a brilliant and passionate call and summons in 1:2 – 2:17. But into these calls and their accompanying descriptions of disaster he folds hints of the religious corruption which was costing the cult its life.

The calls issued to *drunkards* (1:5), *farmers* (1:11) and *priests* (1:13) may contain more than meets the eye. Drinking to excess within the cult was a crime that more than once drew prophetic fire (Ho. 4:11; 9:2; Am. 1:8). Not surprisingly, drunkards are *not* singled out for blessing in the restoration (2:21ff.), even though wine is promised among the divine blessings. For the farmers, confoundment and wailing have replaced joy and gladness. The reason may be more than agricultural; it may be religious. The farmers, most of all, were vulnerable to Canaanite fertility practices. Their threshing floors and wine vats (2:24; Ho. 9:1–2) were the arenas where the power of their fertility cults was proved or disproved. When crops failed, thanks to Yahweh's judgment, their work places were inevitably turned from sites of joy to scenes of lamentation (1:11; *cf.* Am. 5:16–17). The priests (1:13) may be earmarked not only as those who suffered keenly because the offerings ceased but as those who merited suffering through failure to keep the cult pure. The weeping to which they were summoned may have included tears of contrition as well as petition (2:17). The failures for which Hosea held them explicitly culpable (Ho. 4:1 – 5:7) Joel may have been alluding to implicitly, in a subtle form of matching punishment to crime.

The clearest case that Judah's failing, for which the locust plague was retribution, was a cult-gone-wrong is found in the language that calls for *return* and displays the results of that return (2:12–14). Return implies defection, disobedience, covenant-rebellion. Return is the reversal of waywardness. The call is not general but specific – 'unto me' (2:12); 'to Yahweh, your God' (2:13). And the return is to be effected in and through the cult, the official, public worship: its *signs* are fasting, weeping, mourning (2:12); its *site* is the temple; its *spokespersons* are priests (2:17); its tangible *result* is material blessing, the means of presenting cereal offerings and libations of wine to Yahweh (2:14); its *climax* is the recognition of the truth of Yahweh's self-proclamation – 'I am your God and there is none else' (2:27; *cf*. 3:17). The reminder that 'there is none else' coupled with a seven-fold use of 'your God' (1:14; 2:13, 14, 23, 26, 27; 3:17) is calculated as rebuke and reassurance. Along with the call to return, the stress on Yahweh's exclusive relationship to his people is strong evidence that *idolatry* had not been completely purged from the second temple. Like their ancestors in Josiah's day (*c.* 621BC), the men and women of post-exilic Judah had succumbed to syncretism and compromised the exclusivity of Yahweh's sovereignty and their covenant commitment to him.

Their cult had become as corrupt as it was crucial. Its activities continued at full pelt, but its focus had been badly blurred. Hence, the locusts, commissioned by an offended Sovereign. Hence, the call to return, uttered by an aggrieved prophet. Hence, the cries of penitence, addressed by a contrite congregation to their one Lord, whose uniqueness became dazzlingly clear in the midst of their deprivation. Hence, the spirit, outpoured on the entire people to make endemic the knowledge of the one true God through manifold means of revelation (2:28–29).

If this reconstruction of Joel's setting is reasonably accurate, the purpose of his book becomes plain. He saw in the locust-plague God's means of correcting, of purifying, the cult and, beyond that, of preparing the way for the full blessing of Yahweh on the people through the gift of his spirit, the defeat of his enemies, and the permanent prosperity of Judah and Jerusalem. None of this would have happened without the divinely induced return to the chief stipulation of the covenant: 'You shall have no other gods before me' (Ex. 20:3). That the Exile with all its agony and dislocation did not permanently purge the people of their idolatrous inclinations is a potent reminder of the truth of the old hymn, 'Prone to wander, Lord I feel it; prone to leave the God I love.' Through Joel's plague and the thousands of catastrophes that followed it, God has prompted his people of both covenants to return to him.[1]

V. UNITY AND STRUCTURE

The strongest evidence for the unity of Joel is found in its tight-knit structure and its pattern of repeating key words and phrases throughout the book. These marks of unity have impressed recent scholars more strongly than have the earlier arguments for disunity based in the main on supposed differences in tone between 1:1 – 2:27, where the locust-plague and the recovery from it dominate, and 2:28 – 3:21, with its eschatological picture of the Day of Yahweh.[2]

The arguments for structural unity have been discussed and even diagrammed in various ways. Representative of these efforts would be Williamson's tabular revision (*ISBE*, rev., II, p. 1079) of Allen's analysis (pp. 39–43):

Part I. 1:2 – 2:17

A. 1:2–20 parallel with	B. 2:1–17
1. 1:2–12	1. 2:1–11
2–4	1–2
5–7	3–5
8–10	6–9
11–12	10–11
2. 1:13–20	2. 2:12–17
13–14	12–14
15–18	15–16
19–20	17

---

[1]For a thorough, though at times overdrawn, picture of the cultic background of Joel, see Ahlström, pp. 23–61. Markedly different is the reading of G. S. Ogden, *op. cit.* He views the locusts, the fire and the drought all as images of military invasion and, in sharp contrast to Ahlström and the approach of this Commentary, contends that Judah's suffering is undeserved (as in certain psalms where protests of innocence are found) and that Joel, therefore, 'does not regard repentance as necessary' (p. 105).

[2]B. Duhm, 'Anmerkungen zu den Zwölf Propheten', *ZAW*, 31, 1911,

JOEL

Part II. 2:18 – 3:21

A. 2:18–32 parallel with	B. 3:1–21
1. 2:18–27	1. 3:1–12
18–20	1–3
21–23	4–8
24–27	9–12
2. 2:28–32	2. 3:13–21
28–29	13–14
30–31	15–17
32	18–21

The symmetry and artistry apparent in this schema argue for an integrating hand, whether the prophet's or one of his disciples. Efforts to find layers or insertions in the book will not prove nearly so productive as energy spent in understanding the work's overall unity of theme and purpose.[1]

---

pp. 184–187, viewed 2:28 – 3:21 as Maccabean additions reflecting the apocalyptic views of a synagogue preacher. Among these influenced by his bifurcated view of Joel have been Bewer, Sellin, Robinson, R. E. Wolfe, 'The Editing of the Book of the Twelve', *ZAW*, 53, 1935, pp. 90–129, H. Birkeland, *Zum hebräischen Traditionswesen. Die Komposition der prophetischen Bücher des Alten Testaments* (Oslo: ANVAO, 1938), pp. 64–66, and Soggin.

[1]An alternative structure based on chiasma (or arches) is proposed by D. A. Garrett, 'The Structure of Joel', *JETS*, 28, 1985, pp. 289–297. Garrett focuses on the contrasts between punishment and forgiveness which he finds in both halves of the book:

A (1:4–20), Punishment: the locust plague

  B (2:1–11), Punishment: the apocalyptic army

    C (2:12–19), Transition: repentance and introduction to Yahweh's response

  B¹ (2:20), Forgiveness: the apocalyptic army destroyed

A¹ (2:21–27), Forgiveness: the locust damage restored

His schema for the second half of the book runs like this:

Introduction to Yahweh's response (2:18–19; note the intentional overlap with the first schema)

A (2:20), Judgment: the apocalyptic army destroyed

  B (2:21–27), Grace: the land restored

  B¹ (2:28-32), Grace: the Spirit outpoured

A¹ (3:1–21), Judgment: the nations destroyed

The weakness of the second schema is that the destruction of the nations which triggers the peace and prosperity of Judah (3:16–21) would have been reckoned by Joel and his hearers as a word of *grace* not *judgment*.

The relationship between the two halves of the book should be read in terms of growth and development as well as parallelism and symmetry. The second account of the locust attack (2:1–11) builds on the first and surpasses it in vividness of detail and degree of penetration into the lives of the people. Moreover, the Day of Yahweh theme (1:15; 2:1–2, 10–11, 31; 3:14) is treated more fully as the book moves forward. Most importantly the picture of divine blessing moves through stages of crescendo from the restoration of locust damage (2:18–27), through the outpouring of the spirit and its attendant portents (2:28–32) to the judgment of the nations and the vindication of Jerusalem and Judah (3:1–21). The step-like character of the book, with each section building on the previous, is set down like this by Prinsloo (p. 123):

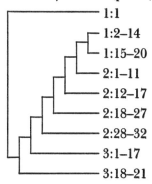

1:1
1:2–14
1:15–20
2:1–11
2:12–17
2:18–27
2:28–32
3:1–17
3:18–21

Further argument for that unity is found in the correspondences of terminology between the two parts of the book: 1:2 – 2:27 and 2:28 – 3:21.[1] Wolff (p. 8) lists a number of words or phrases that help to knit the book together: (1) sanctify . . . proclaim (1:14; 3:9); (2) for the Day of Yahweh is close (1:15; 2:12; 3:14); (3) Yahweh's Day is coming (2:1; 2:31); (4) darkness (2:2; 2:31); (5) an escape (2:3; 2:32); (6) heavens and earth quake (2:10; 3:16); (7) darkening of sun, moon, stars

---

[1] Childs' approach (pp. 391–392) seems to project a sharper break between Joel the prophet and an editor 'who took up this prophecy and fashioned it into a message for future generations' than the structural and verbal similarities between the two halves of the book would suggest. For a similar approach, see O. Plöger, pp. 96–105.

JOEL

(2:10; 3:15); (8) Yahweh utters his voice (2:11; 3:16); (9) Yahweh's Day, great and fearful (2:11; 2:31); (10) gather (2:16; 3:2); (11) my people and my heritage (2:17; 3:2). The combined evidence of structure and language has produced a growing consensus among modern commentators as to the book's unity. Ahlström (p. 137) posits two possibilities and draws similar conclusions about the integrity of the work from each: (1) Joel is the author whether in person or by dictation: 'From this point of view, everything in the book can be ascribed to Joel'; (2) another cult prophet, perhaps Joel's disciple, memorized the message verbatim and recorded it: 'Also, in this case, there is no reason to advocate that any verse be considered as secondary.'[1]

VI. THE MESSAGE

'Joel is a *theocentric book*'. So concludes a recent study of its message (Prinsloo, p. 124). The plague, the call to lament, the instructions to return, the restoration, the gift of the spirit and the assurance of final victory are all God's acts.

Yahweh's sovereignty over creation is one of Joel's strong emphases. There is no hint of any other source of the locust invasion. Yahweh is responsible both for the sending (2:11) and the withdrawing of his army (2:20). In both judgment and restoration Yahweh holds sway over the creation in such a way that the Hebrews can hold no view of nature as a set of laws or pattern that operate on their own, independent of the Lord's control.

Joel's picture of sovereignty has a definite polemic thrust. It reminds his hearers that there is not a vestige of truth in the Canaanite fertility cults which hold such fascination for Hosea's contemporaries, nor in the trust in Assyrian astral deities against which Amos warned (5:21–27). The locust plagues were not only acts of judgment, they were words of revelation of the unique power of Yahweh and they were cogent calls to return to the true and living Lord.

The whole creation, framed by Yahweh's word and shaped to achieve his purposes, is seen as a unity by Joel along with

[1]Among those who have espoused the book's unity are these: Kapelrud, Thompson, Keller, Rudolph, Wolff, G. S. Ogden, *op. cit.*., Prinsloo, and D. A. Garrett, *op. cit.*

34

the psalmists and prophets. The literary personifications that depict the pain and shame of scorched land and starved animals (1:10, 17–18) are more than artistic devices: they demonstrate the vitality of a creation designed not just as a stage for redemption's drama but as players in it, sharply affected by the changing scenes of judgment and grace. From Eden forward, human beings and the rest of creation have been wrapped in one bundle of life. What touches one reaches the other, whether in bane or blessing (*cf.* Am. 4:6–10; 9:13–15).[1]

Yahweh's compassion in forgiveness is the ground on which is based the hope of relief and recovery from the plague. Confidence in the constancy of the divine character was what motivated the prophets and informed their message. Without presumptuously assuming that Yahweh *had* to grant forgiveness (note the 'who knows' of 2:14; *cf.* Am. 5:14–15), Joel's call to return to full loyalty to Yahweh and to an obedient exercise of the means of grace offered in the cult (2:12–17) is anchored in his understanding of Yahweh's covenant love (*ḥesed*, 2:13) which cannot be contained or cabined and which regulates the volume and duration of the divine wrath. So dominant is this loyal love, so steeped in grace (*ḥannûn*, 2:13) and mercy (*raḥûm*, 2:13), that it encourages Yahweh to stay open to changes in his plans, when those plans centre in disaster for his disobedient people. It is that compassion, mediated through the whole-hearted use of the prayers of repentance in the cult, that paves the way for the outpouring of the spirit and the concomitant blessings of security, and fellowship with the Lord that compose Judah's future as Joel sees it.

The positive use of the cult is a theme that helps to unify Joel's book. We have suggested that the chief cause of the plague was the cult-gone-wrong, perverted by the excesses of drunken participants and slack-handed priests, who allowed pagan practices to dilute the purity of worship that should have centred in Yahweh's name alone and in his unique, exclusive lordship over the people. To highlight these abuses, the plague attacked the cult itself in a way that jeopardized its very existence. But the answer to the threat was not a call to

[1]For this perspective on creation, see W. S. LaSor, D. A. Hubbard, F. W. Bush, *OT Survey* (Grand Rapids: Eerdmans, 1982), pp. 442–443.

abandon the cult (*cf.* Ho. 9:1–6; Am. 5:21–27) but to use it properly – to engage in its acts of humiliation, to respond to the calls of its priesthood, to assemble physically at its site, to give voice to its prescribed liturgies of complaint, to seek an oracle of salvation, to wait in it for its promised blessings (2:14; *cf.* Ps. 24:5).

Physical, material, corporate acts of worship have played a part in God's programme for his people at all stages of their history and will continue to do so into the eschatological future. Gathered, structured, patterned worship is implied in the Lord's prayer (Mt. 6), the experience of the early church (Acts 2; 1 Cor. 11, 14), and the book of Revelation (chs. 4, 7, 11, 15). The biblical understandings of creation, history and community require these kinds of expression and celebration – Joel knew that. He understood that prophetic condemnations of the cult had reform not rejection as their goal, even though the language was necessarily hyperbolic. The real answer to wrong cult was not no cult, but right cult. Joel's final picture of Yahweh abiding in Jerusalem, on Mount Zion, the site of Solomon's and Zerubbabel's temples, is clear proof of that.

The terror and hope of the Day of Yahweh stitches the parts of Joel together like an uncuttable thread. Its diverse uses mirror something of its diverse background in Israel's religious life. Its connections with *cultic life* (see Ps. 118:24–25; Am. 5:18–20) echo in the woe-cry to be uttered in the temple (1:15). Its ties to Yahweh's intervention in *holy war* (*cf.* Jdg. 7:19–23; Is. 9:4) are apparent in the description of the nation of locusts rumbling like an army through the land (2:1–11). Its *eschatological dimensions*, which reach to the horizons of the future and encompass the preservation of Israel and the defeat of her enemies (2:31; 3:14), become the dominant and final theme.

The earlier notes that Joel sounds must have been calculated to evoke shock and surprise among the hearers. He saw the Day not as a time of blessed celebration or divine rescue (as in Ps. 118:24–25) but of woe and devastation. The cultic cry was not 'Aha' but 'Alas' (1:15). Yahweh's victims in holy war were not the Gentiles but the covenant people who surrounded the holy mountain (2:1) and were citizens of its promised regions and its protected capital (*cf.* 2 Ki. 19:35–36). The great arches of Israel's cathedral of faith were collapsed on the people by the prophetic word: celebration turned to woe; confidence in inviolability, to the dismay of utter desolation.

This was a reminder that the Lord's Day was *his* Day. He wrote the script and acted it out. Where the darkness of judgment was called for, that was his response. If the public worship misunderstood the Day, presumed on divine grace and blessing, the worship itself had to be cut off. If popular faith counted blandly on God's protection despite covenant disloyalty, Yahweh would march with enemy forces to teach his people the lessons of obedience.

Joel's approach to the Day, influenced by Amos' (5:18–20) and Zephaniah's (1:14–18) dark and dire descriptions, is to see it in two stages: (1) a Day of judgment presaged by the locust hordes and designed to drive the people to repentance and reform, and (2) a Day of vindication predicated on a new obedience of, and communion with, Yahweh made possible by the outpouring of the spirit (2:28–32). The ramifications of the return, presumed to take place between 2:17 and 2:18, flow to the end of the book like eddies from a massive stone dropped in the middle of the pond: (1) the material restoration of plague damage (2:18–26); (2) the realization of Yahweh's uniqueness in their midst (2:27); (3) the effusion of the spirit on the whole nation with its accompanying revelation of Yahweh's will and power (2:28–29); (4) ominous signs and portents that signal the coming of the second Day, the Day beyond the Day which promises rescue to God's people (2:30–32); (5) the judgment of the nations for their abuse of Yahweh's people (3:1–14); (6) the prosperity of the people as the Lord dwells in Zion (3:15–21; *cf.* Zc. 14:1–9).

The components of the Day of Yahweh are of a piece. None can be separated from the others without distorting the whole. *Return* (2:13–14) is essential to all of this. Whatever blocks covenant fidelity must be dealt with, as Malachi also warned (4:5–6). Joel is no mere puppet mouthing nationalistic jingoes. There is nothing automatic about Judah's vindication. Preservation and victory are possible only because judgment has done its work and the people have penitently responded to its painful prodding (contrast with Am. 4:6–12).[1]

---

[1] On the Day of Yahweh in Joel, see Ahlström (pp. 62–97); Allen (pp. 36–39); Wolff (pp. 33–34); Koch, pp. 159–163.

37

VII. JOEL AND THE NEW TESTAMENT

Joel's use as scripture is readily attested in the New Testament. Among the words, phrases, or motifs which have helped to shape *the picture of the end-times* are these: (1) the blast of the trumpet to signal the Day (2:1; *cf.* 1 Cor. 15:52; 1 Thes. 4:16; Rev. 8:6 – 11:19); (2) the use of *near* to express the imminence of the Day (1:15; 2:1; 3:14; *cf.* Mt. 24:32; Mk. 13:29; Jas. 5:8); (3) 'You shall eat in plenty and be satisfied' (2:26; *cf.* Lk. 6:21 and the accounts of the feeding of the multitudes, Mt. 14:13–21; Mk. 6:32–44; Lk. 9:10–17; Jn. 6:1–14); (4) judgment of the Gentiles (3:1–14; *cf.* Mt. 25:31–46); (5) darkening of sun and stars as signs (2:30–31; 3:15; *cf.* Lk. 21:25; Rev. 8:12); (6) shaking of earth and heaven (3:16; *cf.* Heb. 12:26); (7) 'Put in the sickle, for the harvest is ripe' (3:13; *cf.* Mk. 4:29); (8) the locust army compared to horses (2:4–5; *cf.* Rev. 9:7, 9).[1] Dodd's conclusion on the basis of this evidence is that chapters 2 and 3 of Joel 'played a significant part in moulding the language in which the early Church set forth its convictions about what Christ had done and would yet do.'[2]

Joel's other major contribution to Christian understanding of God's redemptive activity is *the prophecy of the Spirit's coming* (2:28–32; *cf.* Acts 2:14–41). Peter made double use of Joel's verses and their context: (1) he refuted the ludicrous conclusions that the Christians were drunk (Acts 2:13–16) by declaring that the last days were at hand, triggered by the Spirit's activity; (2) he laid the foundation for his gospel proclamation and invitation by the use of Joel's key promise, 'whoever calls on the name of the Lord shall be saved' (Acts 2:21) and the parallel clause, 'whom the Lord our God calls to him' (Acts 2:39; *cf.* Joel 2:32). 'Pentecost was a clear indication that the Messianic age had dawned. Its consummation, whether near or remote, was rendered certain.'[3]

---

[1]For most of these illustrations, see C. H. Dodd, *According to the Scriptures: The Sub-Structure of New Testament Theology* (James Nisbet, 1952), pp. 62–64.
[2]*Ibid.*, pp. 63–64.
[3]E. F. Harrison, *Acts: The Expanding Church* (Chicago: Moody Press, 1975), p. 58.

ANALYSIS

I. INTRODUCTION (1:1)

II. THE LOCUST PLAGUE AND THE DAY OF THE LORD (1:2 – 2:17)
   a. The awful plague (1:1–20)
      i. Its unique nature (1:2–4)
      ii. Its effects upon the people (1:5–14)
      iii. Its relation to the Day of the Lord (1:15–20)
   b. The imminent Day of the Lord (2:1–17)
      i. The army of destruction (2:1–11)
      ii. The hope of deliverance (2:12–17)

III. THE COMING VICTORY (2:18 – 3:21)
   a. Restoration of the plague-damage (2:18–27)
   b. Outpouring of the Spirit (2:28–32; Heb., 3:1–5)
   c. Threshing of the nations in judgment (3:1–14; Heb., 4:1–14)
   d. Rescuing of Judah (3:15–21; Heb., 4:15–21)

COMMENTARY

I. INTRODUCTION (1:1)

1. The book is introduced by one of the prophetic revelatory formulas, 'The word of the Lord that came' (literally 'that was, or came to be'). Compare Hosea 1:1; Micah 1:1; and Zephaniah 1:1; see also Zechariah 1:1. While these books also fix the date of the revelation, Joel (which most likely means Yahweh is God), like Obadiah, Jonah, Nahum, Habakkuk and Malachi, contains no chronological reference. The names of the prophet (one of a number of Joels in the Old Testament; *cf.* Williamson, *ISBE*, rev., II, p. 1076) and his father Pethuel are listed without any personal history. The brief introduction directs the reader's attention away from the prophet to the prophecy, and underscores its divine character, whether it is actually spoken by Yahweh in 'I' form (*cf.* 2:12, 19–20, 24–30; 3:1–12, 21) or by the prophet, who received the word with strong assurance, either by audition (Is. 6:8) or vision (Am. 7:1ff; 8:1ff.; 9:1).

II. THE LOCUST PLAGUE AND THE DAY OF THE LORD (1:2 – 2:17)

a. The awful plague (1:2–20)

After this very brief introduction the prophet rushes into the problem at hand – the devastating locust plague, what it means, and what the people must do about it. Though his descriptions of its ravages are vivid, his real aim is to *call the people*, whether 'drunkards' (vv. 5–7), the general populace (vv. 8–10), or 'farmers' (vv. 11–12) *to lament*, with the hope that Yahweh will send relief.

i. Its unique nature (1:2–4). In verse 2 Joel calls the entire nation to give strictest attention to his rhetorical question.

41

Hear includes both listening and remembering, as frequently in the Old Testament (*e.g.* Gn. 4:23; Is. 1:2, 10; Mi. 1:2). *Aged men* (*zᵉqēnîm*) is probably not used here in the technical sense of 'elder' (*cf.* 1:14) but in the more general meaning where age, not position or rank, is emphasized. They are singled out because their long experience and their acquaintance with the traditions of their ancestors concerning locust plagues would eminently qualify them to give an accurate answer to the question (*cf.* Ex. 10:6, 14; La. 1:12, for other instances of unprecedented destruction). *All inhabitants of the land* (*i.e.*, Judah) are addressed in order to get the prescribed negative answer from the widest possible audience and also to guarantee that the command of verse 3 will be executed. *Give ear* (*haᵃzînû*) is a synonym of 'hear' (*šāmaʻ*) and is used almost exclusively in poetry in parallel to the more common word (*cf.* Ho. 5:1).

3. The incomparable event, as yet unnamed, is to be 'recounted' (*sappērû*), suggesting a detailed enumeration to generations following. Driver (p. 36) points out that 'usually, it is the memory of Jehovah's deliverances, which is thus to be handed on from father to son . . . here it is the memory of an unprecedented disaster.'[1] In the Hebrew text emphasis is placed upon the disaster by the fact that *of it* stands at the beginning of the sentence. It is not only the physical disaster but its connection with the Day of Yahweh (*cf.* 1:15; 2:1) that makes the event so permanently memorable.

4. Until this point the prophet has deliberately kept us in suspense as to the nature of this unparalleled phenomenon. He has referred to it vaguely as 'it' or 'this'. Having caught the interest of his hearers, he now enlightens them as to the meaning of his message.

Two lines of interpretation have dominated the study of verse 4 and its parallel in 2:25. One (Credner) has held that the four words for locust denote successive stages in the development of the locust – larva, pupa, *etc.*[2] Against this comes the argument that although four words are used in the text, only three stages of development – larva, pupa and

---

[1] In support of his statement, Driver cites, among other passages, Jdg. 6:13; Pss. 44:1; 78:3.

[2] This view was first proposed by K. A. Credner, *Der Prophet Joel übersetzt und erklärt* (Halle: 1831).

winged insect – are discernible to the ordinary observer. Furthermore, *'arbeh*, the generic word for locust, occurs second in the list here (first in 2:25) and would have to denote the immature insect if these words describe stages of development. Another factor is that the order of words in 2:25 differs from that of 1:4. A final argument against the theory of stages is that locust swarms tend to move from place to place with the result that the successive stages do not develop on the same ground. The second line of interpretation seems closer to the mark. It infers that these four words for locust (the Old Testament knows five others) indicate successive waves of insect attack and highlight the intensity of destruction as the poetic chain (*sorites*) would suggest (*cf.* on Ho. 8:7; 9:11–12). Repetition is a standard means of emphasis in Hebrew literature: note the triple use of the noun 'the left-overs' and the verb 'has eaten' (*cf.* Ho. 2:12; 5:7; 7:7, for Heb. *'kl* meaning to 'devour' in judgment).

The first insect (*gāzām*), to judge from its Semitic root, is a *cutting* (or shearing) *locust* capable of incredible devastation (*cf.* Am. 4:9). *Swarming locust* (*'arbeh*, the usual name for locust in Hebrew, well attested in Ugaritic and Akkadian) is so translated because of the probable connection between *'arbeh* and the Semitic root 'to multiply' (*rbb/rby*; *cf.* Ho. 4:7). The third name (*yeleq*) seems to mean 'leaper' or 'hopper' (*cf.* the Arabic root which means 'to hasten', 'to walk swiftly'), although some have connected it with the root *lqq* and thus translated it 'lapper', a term unsuitable to the way locusts eat. The suggestion that *yeleq* may have denoted the ordinary locust in its wingless larva or pupa stage (Driver, p. 36) does not seem to take into consideration Nahum 3:16 where the *yeleq* is said to fly away. The fourth term (*ḥāsîl*) means 'destroyer' or 'finisher' (*cf.* Dt. 28:38 for use of *ḥsl* to describe the destructive activity of locusts).[1]

ii. Its effects upon the people (1:5–14). Having caught the attention of the citizenry and portrayed the thoroughness of the devastation, Joel now addresses various groups or classes within the nation and shows how the plague directly touches

---

[1]For a thorough discussion of the locusts, see Driver, pp. 82–91; Wolff, pp. 27–28; Allen, pp. 49–50.

them. Joel was a poet. He could not be satisfied with a mere prosaic statement of the calamity. With dramatic power he calls on the various classes of the people to lament over the awful catastrophe (Bewer, p. 77). More than a poet, Joel was a worshipper of Yahweh who knew that the only deliverance lay in contrite penitence and humble petition. The purpose of this section is to provide motivation for those necessary acts.

5. Dramatically, he calls on the *drunkards* first, not to condemn them but to indicate that they would be the first to suffer because their happiness is dependent on the fruit of the vine. *Awake*, not from sleep but from drunken stupor. The LXX adds 'from their wine', probably under the influence of Genesis 9:24: 'When Noah awoke from his wine.' *Sweet wine* ('āsîs) was made by drying the grapes in the sun for a short time and then allowing the juice to ferment for five to seven days instead of the more usual nine (Driver, p. 225; Am. 9:13; *cf.* the 'new wine' of Acts 2:13, 15). *Wail* (*cf.* Ho. 7:14) supplants the usual merriment which accompanies drinking.

6–7. These verses emphasize the numerical strength and the amazing destructive powers of the locusts. They are like a *nation* in number (*cf.* Pr. 30:25–27).[1] The singular pronoun in the phrase *my land* probably refers to the prophet as representative of the people, because in this chapter the Lord is usually mentioned in the third person (vv. 9, 13, *etc.*), though we may see here a snatch of divine speech designed to show Yahweh's sovereign ownership of what is being destroyed. (See *my vines* and *my fig trees*, v. 7.) *Powerful* ('āṣûm) is used several times by Joel to describe both the numerical and physical strength of the locusts (2:2, 5, 11; *cf.* Am. 5:12). This word occurs frequently in the Old Testament to describe mighty nations (*e.g.* Dt. 26:5; Is. 60:22; Mi. 4:7). The phrase *without number* is used of the locust plague of Exodus in Psalm 105:34.

The descriptions of travellers who have observed locust swarms are legion. E. B. Pusey,[2] Driver (*loc. cit.*) and other commentators have given lengthy descriptions of locust attacks in the Levant. Driver cites a report of a locust-swarm covering 2,000 square miles and comprising an estimated

[1] For a similar comparison between locusts and a vast army in Ugaritic see the Legend of Keret I, ii, 35–51. G. R. Driver, ed., *Canaanite Myths and Legends* (Edinburgh: T. & T. Clark, 1956), p. 31.
[2] E. B. Pusey, *The Minor Prophets: A Commentary* (Grand Rapids: Baker Book House, 1950), I, pp. 148–154.

24,420 billion insects. Some thirty years ago, a grasshopper horde attacked California and was described in the newspapers in terms reminiscent of Joel. In one county 200,000 acres were covered with insects 'over every inch and in some places stacked on top of each other'.

The ferocity of the locusts' bite is compared with that of the *teeth* of a lion ('*arȳēh*; *cf.* Am. 5:19) and the *fangs* (*cf.* Ps. 58:6; Pr. 30:14) of a lioness (*lābî*', a word used only in poetry; *cf.* Nu. 23:24; Dt. 33:20). So voracious is the locusts' appetite and so strong their jaws that no fruit, leaf, twig or bark can survive their attack; even the larvae can join in the devastation (Wolff, p. 27). The Revelation has drawn upon this verse for part of its picture of apocalyptic locusts (9:8).

Vines and *fig trees* which often grew in the same field, are singled out (v. 7) as the finest fruit-producers, the symbols of Palestinian prosperity (1 Ki. 4:25; 2 Ki. 18:31; Mi. 4:4; Zc. 3:10). Both crops can be preserved and thus used all year whether in alcoholic or sun-dried form. The vine is mentioned in most lists of staples (Ho. 2:12) because its crop is the more important, especially in this context which deals with the plight of the heavy-drinkers. The devastation does not stop with the laying waste (*cf.* Ho. 5:9, for *šammâ*, a favourite term in Jeremiah; *e.g.* 2:15; 4:7; 18:16; 19:8) of grapes and leaves, but includes also the splintering (*cf.* same root *qṣp* in Ho. 10:7) of the fig tree; the bark itself is peeled off and thrown down so that the denuded branches appear white. A California agricultural official reported that 'what they (the grasshoppers) don't eat they cut off for entertainment.' He also noted that in the wake of the insects, fields are left 'bare as the floor', apple trees are stripped of every leaf and rose bushes are consumed through the green bark. During the same attack, a farmer lamented that 100 acres of his bean field had been 'completely cleared' by the hoppers. Joel's account is not hyperbolic but factual.[1]

---

[1] S. Kraft, 'Africa Girds for New War on Locusts', *Los Angeles Times* (Oct. 13, 1986), pp. 1, 12, lends comment to Joel by describing contemporary locust ravages in Senegal and other African States. A handful of excerpts speak for themselves. On *proliferation*, 'One female grasshopper that lays eggs in June . . . may have 18 million living descendants by October'. On *density*, 'the concentrations were as high as 1000 per square yard'; 'swarming mobs . . . ride high on the wind, sometimes blocking out the sun'. On *devastation*, 'last year, (one farmer) planted three successive crops of millet . . . But the grasshoppers ate every one.'

45

8. The whole nation, which is to suffer unspeakable anguish, is addressed (in the feminine singular) without being named. The Hebrews knew two terrible examples of mourning: (1) the grief of a betrothed woman whose intended husband (*bridegroom of her youth, i.e.* one to whom she is legally pledged, probably at an early age, but not yet married; on *youth,* see Ho. 2:15) dies before they can enjoy sexual intercourse and who sorrows because her husband's name has been cut off before he can produce an heir; (2) mourning for an only son with whom the family name has died (*cf.* Am. 8:10). Girding with sackcloth (usually woven of black goat hair) is a sign of mourning (Is. 3:24; Am. 8:10). (For the description of the nation as a virgin, *cf.* Je. 14:17; La. 1:15; Am. 5:2.)

9–10. Here we find the reasons for the awful anguish described in verse 8. The first and more painful cause is that the fellowship with God expressed in *cereal* and *drink offerings* has to cease. These offerings, rather than animal sacrifices, are mentioned because they would be more directly affected by the locusts. The *cereal offering* (*minḥâ*; Am. 5:22, 25) prescribed in Leviticus 2, is comprised of fine flour, oil and salt. Frankincense is poured upon it. Part is burnt on the altar; the rest is eaten by the priests. The cereal and drink (a libation of wine) offerings were to accompany the continual burnt offerings which were celebrated every morning and evening (Ex. 29:38ff.; Nu. 28:1ff.). These sacrifices seem to have been conditions of God's meeting with his people (Ex. 29:42–43). The importance of these continual offerings for the postexilic community may be seen in Nehemiah 10:33, where the governor and his colleagues pledge themselves to perpetuate these rites. Similarly, among the tragedies brought upon the people by the 'Little Horn' and the 'King of the North' is the cessation of the continual burnt offering (Dn. 8:11; 11:31). Keil aptly sums up the situation: 'Now Israel could not suffer any greater calamity than the suspension of the daily sacrifice; for this was a practical suspension of the covenant relation – a sign that God had rejected His people' (Keil, 1, p. 184).

The *priests,* shorn of their daily duties (*cf.* Ezk. 44:15–31), are singled out as special victims: they *mourn* (*cf.* Ho. 4:3; 10:5; Am. 1:2; 8:8; 9:5) rather than rejoice before Yahweh (*cf.* Dt. 16:11; 26:11). Here and in 2:17 the priests are called *ministers of the Lord* (*cf.* Is.61:6; Je. 33:21), while in 1:13 they are named 'ministers of the altar'. 'Minister' means special attendant or helper.

Verse 10[1] gives the reason for the cessation of the cereal and drink offerings: (LXX adds *hoti* 'because' to make this clear) the fields are devastated (Heb. *šdd*; *cf.* Ho. 10:2, 14) and stripped of their crops. Here we see Joel the poet at his best. He employs several devices to make his message more graphic: personification (the fields, ground and crops are treated as persons), alliteration and assonance (*šuddad̠, śād̠eh*; *'āb̠eʾlâ, ʾad̠āmâ*), and a terse, telegraphic style. George Adam Smith's description is apt (II, p. 405): 'Joel loads his clauses with the most leaden letters he can find and drops them in quick succession, repeating the same heavy word again and again, as if he would stun the careless people into some sense of the bare, brutal weight of the calamity. . . .' The three staple crops of Palestine – grain, new wine and olive oil (used for lamps, medicine, hygiene, as well as food) – are also the three main ingredients in the cereal and drink offerings.[2] The personification of these crops by the prophet is seen especially in the phrase the *wine fails* (*hôb̠îš tîrôš*) which could be translated 'the new wine shows shame or disappoints.' This verb, a favourite of Joel's, occurs also in 1:11, 12 (twice), 17.[3] *Languishes* ('*umlal*) is used of withering trees or crops in 1:12; (*cf.* Is. 16:8; 24:7, which contains a personification similar to Joel's; Ho. 4:3; Na. 1:4).

11–12. The mention of the important crops in verse 10 leads the prophet to address those who produce the crops: the *tillers of the soil* (those who plough or peasant farmers, who work the land but do not own it; *cf.* 2 Ch. 26:10; Is. 61:5; Am. 5:16) are to be ashamed, *i.e.* to show open signs of disappointment because their most basic crops from which they baked their daily bread – *wheat* (*cf.* Gn. 30:14, Ru. 2:23) and *barley* (*cf.* Ru. 1:22; 2:17, 23; 3:2, 15, 17; Ho. 3:2) – have been ravaged before they could harvest them.

Vinedressers (for *wail*, see 1:5) appears to be used here in a

---

[1] For a structural analysis that connects v. 10 with vv. 11–12 rather than v. 9, see E. D. Mallon, 'A Stylistic Analysis of Joel 1:10–12', *CBQ*, 45, 1983, pp. 537–548.

[2] These three prime products of the land are frequently viewed in the Old Testament as God's blessing which may be given or withheld. See Dt. 7:13; 11:14; 28:51; Ho. 2:8.

[3] The AV translation 'dried up' implies the root *yāb̠ēš*. But Joel uses *yāb̠ēš* in *Qal* not *Hiphil*, 1:12, 20. *Hôb̠îš* is derived from *bôš* 'to be ashamed', as v. 11 indicates.

wider context to include orchard-keepers, because verse 12 indicates that a wide range of fruits comes under their care. Here, along with the most important fruits – grapes and figs (*cf.* v. 7) – are mentioned pomegranates (abundant in Palestine and highly esteemed, Nu. 13:23; 22:5; Dt. 8:8), date palms (now relatively rare but more common in biblical days, especially near Jericho which was the city of palm trees; Dt. 34:3; Jdg. 1:16; 3:13; 2 Ch. 28:15), apple trees (one of the choice fruit-producers, Song 2:3). The singular nouns are to be understood as collectives. *All the trees of the field* are said to *wither* (Heb. *yābēš*) in order to show that the preceding list was representative not exhaustive and to balance the summary clause – *the harvest of the field has perished* (v. 11). The passage climaxes in an emphatic (Heb. *kî*) – 'surely' (NIV), 'yes' (NAB) – summation of the impact of all this on the whole populace (*sons of men*; *cf.* Ps. 12:1, 8): *gladness* (Heb. *śāśôn*; *cf.* Est. 8:16–17; Is. 51:3, 11), normally produced by the fruits of the harvest and expressed in the great annual feasts of First-fruits (Dt. 26:1–12), Pentecost (Dt. 16:9–12) and Tabernacles (Dt. 16:13–15), has been smitten with the same shame (Heb. *bôš*) that chagrined the wine of verse 10.

13–14. The prophet turns finally to the priests and calls them to join in this national lament (*gird on sackcloth, i.e.* tie strips of it around the loins; *cf.* v. 8; Is. 32:11) because they, too, are directly and painfully affected. The command to *pass the night in sackcloth* (2 Sa. 12:16; 1 Ki. 21:27) in the temple (*go in*) indicates the extremity of the situation. No token penitence will do. The cessation of the daily sacrifices, whose ingredients have been *withheld* (Heb. *mn*'; *cf.* Am. 4:7, 9), is as great a calamity as the loss of loved ones and evokes the same attitude of grief. *Ministers of my God* seems to show that the prophet, not God, has been speaking throughout this section.

But priestly mourning is not enough. It must lead to true repentance on the part of all the people. The idea of repentance has been anticipated in verse 13 with the mention of sackcloth, which may be the garb of contrition as well as grief (*cf.* Ne 9:1; Jon. 3:5–6). The purpose of the *fast*, which the priests are commanded to call, is to propitiate God's favour (*cf.* Jdg. 20:26; 1 Sa. 7:6). Though no specific sins are indicted by the prophet, it is clear that he regards the locust invasion as a visitation of God's judgment on the sins of the people. Joel's prophecy is forged in the heat of disaster. Even as he speaks, the hand of God is heavy upon the land. Solution, not cause, is the pressing problem.

The imperative *sanctify* (Heb. *qdš* in the intensive stem; *cf.* 2:15–16; 3:9) brings out the holy nature of this fast, which probably lasts a day (Jdg. 20:26; 1 Sa. 14:24) and requires intense dedication of all who take part. *Solemn assembly* is used here and in 2:15 in a general sense to refer first to a stoppage of all hard work (Nu. 29:35) and then to a religious gathering (*cf.* Lv. 23:36; Is. 1:13; Am. 5:21; *cf.* Driver, p. 186). *Elders* is probably used here in a technical sense, 'rulers' or 'officials' in contrast to verse 2 where the same word is translated *aged men*. As the disaster was total, affecting the whole population in the whole range of its life, so the repentance must be universal, embracing not only those in responsible positions but *all the inhabitants of the land* (*cf.* v. 2). The repetition of the two audiences (*old people* and *inhabitants*) serves to bracket verses 2–14, the call to lament (complaint) and verses 15–20, the complaint itself. *Cry to the Lord* loudly and importunately (Heb. *z'q*; Ho. 7:14; 8:2) for mercy, forgiveness and deliverance. Yahweh is thus seen as the source of the judgment and the hope of deliverance. 'Hence, especially the final strophe is theocentric' (Prinsloo, p. 27).

iii. Its relation to the day of the Lord (1:15–20). The connection between verse 14 and verse 15 is not completely clear. Does verse 15 give the substance of the penitential cry of the preceding verse, or is it a separate statement by the prophet? It may be both (Allen, p. 59). Apparently verses 15–20 contain both a communal and an individual complaint. Verse 16 uses *our* twice, and in verse 19 the prophet seems to speak on his own behalf, *unto thee, O Lord, I cry*. So it seems that a group is speaking in verse 16 and an individual in verse 19. The difficulty comes in trying to determine when the cry of the group ceases and the lament of the individual begins. Perhaps verse 17 is the point of transition, inasmuch as verse 16 with its mention of *the house of our God* seems more intimately related to the preceding context, while verses 17–18 may provide elements of the picture of drought and famine painted in the last two verses of the chapter.

Inasmuch as verses 15–16 contain a group complaint, it seems fitting to interpret them as being a summary of the cry of repentance mentioned in verse 14.[1] In other words, the prophet here not only entreats the people to repent but gives them the substance of their prayer of penitence (*cf.* Ho. 14:1–3). They are to recognize in this disaster something far more serious than even a locust-plague: the judicial arm of God intervening in righteous wrath. In the acknowledgment that the Day of the Lord is near there is an implicit confession of the sins which have brought on the Day. Joel appears to lean on the interpretation of Amos (see on 5:18–20; *cf.* Ze. 1:14–18) who set straight the thinking of his contemporaries when he showed that the day is darkness not light, a time of hazard not security. (Contrast this doom-laden message to Judah with the announcements of judgment on the nations found in Is. 13:6 and Ezk. 30:2–3.)

15. *Alas* (the lament-cry is repeated three times in the LXX and the Vulg.) *for the day* occurs in almost the same form in Ezk. 30:2; *for the day of the Lord is near* is found verbatim in Joel 3:14; Obadiah 15; Zephaniah 1:7; Isaiah 13:6. This last verse also contains the clause 'as destruction from the Almighty it will come'. Although there may be direct literary dependence here, it seems more likely that the prophet uses phrases which were current in prophetic circles. Whatever be the final verdict on the etymology of *šadday*, 'the Almighty', it is evident that the Hebrews connected the name with the idea of power and destruction, as the word-play indicates: *kᵉšōḏ* (*cf.* 1:10 for the verb *šdd*; see Ho. 7:13; 9:6; 10:14; 12:1 for *šōḏ miššadday*).[2] Driver (pp. 81–81) tries to render the force of this into English by 'as overpowering from the Overpowerer', and Smith (II, p. 413) suggests 'as vehemence from the Vehement'.

16. The lament continues in a rhetorical question, weighted to catch Yahweh's attention, as the people deplore the lack (lit. *cut off*) of *food* for temple sacrifices. When the daily sacrifices are called to a halt there can be no *joy and gladness* (*cf.* 1:12) in the house of God. The phrase *before our eyes* is in an emphatic position in the Hebrew text and shows graphically the seriousness and suddenness of the emergency.

17–18. The sad note is expanded with a description of

[1] This interpretation has the support of G. A. Smith, I. Engnell (in Kapelrud, p. 4, n. 5), and AV punctuation, *inter alios*. Keil rejects this view (p. 186).
[2] For various theories (mountain God; many breasted goddess; One who is sufficient; Destroyer; demon spirit; Omnipotent) of the origin of *šadday*, see KB, p. 950, and the conclusion stated there: 'No explanation is satisfactory.'

unproductive ground, empty barns and famished flocks. The first line of verse 17 is probably the most difficult in the book of Joel because three of the four words occur only here in the Old Testament. That it has to do with ruined grain can probably be deduced from the parallel lines in verse 17b–d. The verb (Heb. *'bš*) may be translated 'have shrivelled' or 'dried up', on the basis of its Arabic cognate. The subject (Heb. *p^erudôt*) is probably an unusual word for seed, given that its root may mean 'divide' or 'scatter' (although KB reads 'dried figs'). The final word (Heb. *meḡr^ep̄ōt̄êhem*) is even more problematic, being read either as 'clods' (RSV; NIV; NAB; Wolff, p. 19; Bič, p. 33; Keller, p. 117) or as 'shovels' (Allen, p. 56; KB, p. 494). My reading would be: 'The seeds have shrivelled under their shovels.' The Greek and Latin versions are of little help because they represent a text quite different from the Masoretic. The English versions have maintained *clods* because it suits the context better, although philologically 'shovels' is a far more defensible translation,[1] though we cannot be sure whether the shovels were used to spread water in irrigation or probe the soil to check on germination of the seeds. Despite these difficulties the major thought is clear: no crops can be raised under the present circumstances.

Neither *storehouses* (lit. treasuries; *cf.* Ho. 13:15) used for wine, oil and grain (1 Ch. 27:27–28; Ne. 13:13) nor *granaries* (*mamm^eḡurôt* may be a misspelling of *m^eḡūrôt*; *cf.* Hg. 2:18) remain; left derelict, their frail structures collapse (lit. they are 'made desolate' [Heb. *šmm*] and 'torn down' [Heb. *hrs*]; *cf.* Je. 31:40), for the entire crop of grain has failed (*cf.* v. 10 for *hôbîš* = 'put to shame').

This drastic grain shortage has dire effects on the domestic animals (v. 18). By personifying the beasts the poet adds vividness to his picture and demonstrates the Hebrew conviction that the whole creation enjoyed personal vitality as a gift of Yahweh. The *beasts* (*b^ehēmâ* is a collective noun here) who *groan* comprise both the *herds of cattle* (cows, oxen) and the

---

[1]The suggested emendations for this line are legion. Kapelrud (p. 65) conjectures that *taḥat* 'under' should be pointed *tēḥat* from *ḥātat* and renders the line: 'Shrunk are the grains, disheartened are their irrigation spades.' Though this reading does not alter the consonantal text and avoids the troublesome *clods*, the imperfect tense of the verb seems somewhat out of place among the series of perfects.

51

flocks of sheep).[1] Although the verb *groan* (*ne'enḥâ*) is not used elsewhere of the sound made by animals it need not be emended here because the whole passage redounds with personification. *Are dismayed* ('succumb'; Wolff, p. 20) presupposes the root *šāmam* (*cf.* v. 17b; it is used of famished people in La. 4:5) rather than Masoretic *ne'šāmû* (Heb. root *'šm*; *cf.* Ho. 4:15; 13:1) which is difficult to handle here (its only passive [*Niphal*] use in the Old Testament). If it is the correct reading, *ne'šāmû* must mean 'suffer punishment' or 'are held guilty'. Its subject, *even the flocks of sheep*, alludes to the fact that, though sheep require less food than cattle and will put up with inferior pasture, even they go hungry.

19–20. In the traditional language of Hebrew prayer (*cf.* Pss. 28:1; 30:8; 86:3; Allen, p. 63), the prophet enters his personal plea before the Lord, exemplifying the complaints to which he has called his people and anticipating their cry, 'Alas for the Day' (v. 15a). The locust damage is compounded by a scorching *fire* which ravages pasture lands and trees (on *fire* as a means of divine judgment, *cf.* Ho. 8:14; Am. 1:4, 7, 10, 14; 2:2, 5; also Pss. 50:3; 97:3). Because it affects the *water brooks* (v. 20), this fire is probably not a poetic allusion to the plague but to a drought which accompanies it. Many observers have noted that locust invasions are worse in unusually hot summers (Bewer, p. 89). The fire, then, must be either the intense heat of the sun producing a drought, or an actual fire kindled among the parched herbage. The former possibility seems more likely in view of the entire context which has stressed the complete devastation of all verdure, with the result that there would be little herbage left to burn (*cf.* Am. 7:4, for judgment by drought). *Pastures of the wilderness* (v. 20) are unfenced and uncultivated, but not necessarily barren, lands. 'Steppe', 'prairie' or, in America, 'range' would be accurate descriptions. The *trees of the field*, stripped of their bark coats (v. 9) by the locusts, are scorched by the flaming heat of the drought.

In verse 20 the *wild beasts* (lit. 'beasts of the field'; *cf.* 2:22; Ps. 8:7), deprived of water and pasture, join in the lament and *cry* (*ta'ᵃrôḡ*) with intense longing to Yahweh. This verse should be compared with Psalm 42:1 where the hart pants (*ta'ᵃrōḡ*) for

---

[1]The lxx reads 'what shall we put in them', which is accepted by some commentators, *e.g.* G. A. Smith and Bewer. But S. R. Driver points out that this would be a very weak addition to 'for the grain has failed' in v. 17.

streams of water. In Joel, having been denied the streams of water, the animals pant unto God. More than any other example of Joel's skill in personification, this picture captures both the extremities of the suffering and the extent of the divine sovereignty that has caused and can ease it. Beyond that, it may be a cogent argument: if wild animals call upon Yahweh's help, how much more should his people who have been summoned to fasting and prayer.

b. The imminent Day of the Lord (2:1–17)

The description of the plague continues but with a dramatic change: in vivid poetic imagery the prophet compares the locusts to an invading army. This attack is so awful in its scope that it must in some way be connected with the Day of the Lord (vv. 1, 11), already announced (1:15). The locust army is the van, and the full revelation of God's wrath will follow in its train. The locusts are *real*, not images. But the reality itself is so overwhelming as to carry overtones of an even larger reality – God's exercise of universal judgment.[1]

i. The army of destruction (2:1–11). The whole scene turns military and more than military as its cosmic implications begin to be grasped at verses 10–11. Blowing (Heb. *ta'*; Ho. 5:8) the *shofar*, or ram's horn (v. 1), was a signal by which a sentinel – here Yahweh himself – on the wall warned of enemy invasions (Ho. 8:1; Je. 4:5; 6:1) and other calamities (*e.g.* Am. 3:6), including the Day of Yahweh (Zp. 1:16). *My holy mountain* (the prophet is speaking for Yahweh), *Zion*, is the site mentioned because of its elevation, because it housed the priests whose duty it was to sound alarms (Nu. 10:5ff.), and because its inhabitants may wrongly have thought it to be

[1] At this juncture in the text, commentators have a major choice to make. They can read 2:1–11 as an account of a military invasion of which the locusts in ch. 1 are precursors (*cf.* Wolff, pp. 41–43) or they can read it as a more dramatic, semi-apocalyptical account of the locust invasion which itself is a harbinger of the Day (*cf.* Allen, pp. 64–65). The approach in the present Commentary is to follow the latter course. A third option would be to read the entire work as a cluster of figurative descriptions of military incursion; to do so, however, seems to find a fantastic visionary cast in the work for which the author has not given us adequate preparation. For his third option, see G. S. Ogden, 'Joel 4 and Prophetic Responses to National Laments', *JSOT*, 26, 1983, pp. 97–106.

inviolable, permanently protected by the presence of the temple (Je. 7). Frightened by the alarm (Am. 3:6), the inhabitants (*cf.* 1:2, 14) *tremble* (Heb. *rgz*; lit. 'quake'; *cf.* 2:10; Am 8:8) before events so awesome and ominous that they can be described only as *the day of the Lord* (*cf.* on Am. 5:18–20), *is coming* (Heb. *qārôḇ*, an infinitive absolute that highlights the sheer action not the time or the subject).

The division between verses 1 and 2 should probably be disregarded (Syriac; Wolff, p. 37), so that the end of verse 1 and the beginning of verse 2 together would read: *For there is near a day of darkness* (Heb. *ḥōšeḵ*; *cf.* Gn. 15:12; 2 Sa. 22:12; Ps. 18:11) *and of gloom* (Heb. *ʾăpēlâ*; *cf.* Dt. 28:29; Zp. 1:15), *of clouds* (Heb. *ʿānān*, singular but collective; Ex. 16:10; Dt. 1:33; Ze. 1:15) and *thick darkness* (Heb. *ʿărāpel*; Ex. 20:21; Ze. 1:15), all terms that signify the divine presence in the midst of his people, obscuring all light so that their focus of attention will be on him.[1] The phrase 'like dawn' (NIV; Heb. *šaḥar*; RSV *like blackness*, *šāḥōr*, an unneeded emendation) alludes to the brightness of sunlight reflected from the locusts' wings. As dawn struggles with darkness, so shafts of light break through the thick insect-cloud and create an awesome shimmer on the mountains around Jerusalem. Again the insects are compared to a people (*cf.* 1:16), and the unprecedented, unrepeatable nature of calamity is stressed (*cf.* 1:2–3) in even more hyperbolic terms.

3. *Before them* is a catch phrase that introduces each new facet in Joel's description of devastation in 2:3–11 (*cf.* vv. 3, 6, 10). In a powerful picture of contrast, the bountifully verdant areas are turned to *desolate* (*šᵉmāmâ*; *cf.* 1:17; 2:20; 3:19; Ho. 2:12; Am. 7:9; 9:14) *wilderness* (1:19–20). *The garden of Eden* symbolizes abundance of verdure as in Ezekiel 36:35, which gives a picture opposite to that of this verse. (Compare the 'garden of the Lord' in Gn. 13:10; Is. 51:3 and 'the trees of Eden' in Ezk. 31:9, 16, 18.) The final clause is made emphatic by *gam* 'nothing *at all* escapes (Heb. *pᵉlēṭâ* speaks of surviving a battle; 2 Sa. 15:14; 2 Ch. 20:24) them.'

4–5. The locusts are compared with horses in appearance

---

[1] R. P. Carroll, 'Eschatological Delay in the Prophetic Tradition?', *ZAW*, 94, 1982, pp. 54–55, treats *kî qārôḇ*, 'for there is near', as a gloss added by a later hand to explain that the Day of Yahweh had not come in Joel's time. There are no adequate reasons to support such a suggestion, which is scarcely provable or unprovable, as Carroll notes.

(*cf.* Rev. 9:7), swiftness and military use (*cf.* Ho. 14:3; Am. 6:12). The Italian *cavalletta* and the German *Heupferd*, both meaning locust, reflect the resemblance (*cf.* Jb. 39:20 for a picture of a horse leaping like a locust). The parallelism suggests *war horses* (NIV, 'cavalry') as the correct translation (*pārāš* may denote either the animal or the rider). The noise of the insect swarm gorging itself on the mountain tops, as terrifying as their appearance, sounds like the *rumbling of chariots* (*cf.* Rev. 9:9) and the *crackling of a flame* lapping at stubble. (See Driver, pp. 50–51, for first-hand reports concerning the sound of locust attacks. Recently a friend raised in the Sudan compared the noise of locust wings to that of a jet engine.) The two-fold sound of the whirring wings and the crunching jaws strikes terror into the hearts of onlookers, as though they saw a *powerful* (again *'āṣûm; cf.* 1:6; 2:2, 11) *army* (Heb. *'am* in the sense of garrison or contingent of troops, *cf.* Is. 36:11) arrayed for battle and bounding over the mountains as it advances against them.

6. The description focuses on the effect upon the victims, especially the residents of Jerusalem, and thus is somewhat parallel to 1:8–10. *Peoples, i.e.* whole communities or clusters of people (although an international sweep to the *peoples* or 'nations' [NIV] is possible; Edom, Ammon, Moab may all have been hit by the invasion) writhe as in travail (*ḥyl; cf.* Is. 13:8, another glimpse of the Day of Yahweh) *before them* or 'because of them' (*mippānāyw* is virtually causal in force). The next clause (Heb. *qibbᵉṣû pā'rûr; cf.* Na. 2:11) is difficult to translate, because we must choose between ideas of blushing/flushing/glowing and growing pale/blanching. The former understanding (Allen, p. 65; Keller, p. 121; Wolff, p. 38; KB, p. 750) seems to connect the troublesome and rare *pā'rûr* with *pārûr*, 'pot' (Nu. 11:8; Jdg. 6:19; 1 Sa. 2:14), and then derive a meaning 'glow' from the picture of a heated pot. The latter approach (RSV; NEB; NIV; NAB; Bič, p. 47) follows a suggestion by Driver, Keil and others to render the phrase 'gather in beauty' (deriving *pā'rûr* from *p'r, cf. tip'ārâ,* 'beauty', Is. 3:18; 28:5) *i.e.* withdraw colour and freshness, therefore grow pale.

7–9. The insects advance relentlessly and systematically. No obstacle or adversary can halt their fierce charge. Not content with the produce of the field and orchards (2:3), they attack the cities of the land. The final clause in verse 7 presents a textual problem. The verb *ye'abbᵉ ṭûn* would ordinarily mean 'they take a pledge from' (*cf.* Dt. 24:10), a reading which makes no sense here where the line seems a clear parallel to 'each on his way they march' (v. 7c). Better than the sprinkling of possible emendations '*bt*, to wind or weave [*cf.* Mi. 7:3] or '*wt*, 'to bend, make crooked' [*Piel, cf.* Ec. 7:13] is the suggestion that the Masoretic '*bt* be derived from an Arabic root meaning 'spoil what is sound' or 'disturb what is intact'.[1] The resultant translations are 'no confusion in the ranks' (NEB) or 'without overlapping their tracks' (Allen, p. 65). Nothing diverts them from their relentless assault (*cf.* v 8b; Pr. 30:27.)[2]

The last sentence of verse 8 is difficult to translate. The verb 'fall' may be read literally: some of the locusts perish but the mass moves on, unstoppable. Or it may be paraphrased to mean 'break through' (RSV), 'press headlong' (Allen, p. 66), 'plunge' (NEB; NIV). Even less certain is the meaning of the key noun (Heb. *šelaḥ*), which may be read either as a weapon (RSV; NIV; Wolff, p. 38), *e.g.* javelin or other missile (2 Ch. 23:10; 32:5; Ne. 4:11, 17), or as a watercourse or aqueduct (NEB; Allen, p. 66; *cf.* Ne. 3:15). The latter reading seems better since javelins seem unlikely implements to withstand locusts, and the entire context speaks of penetration and infiltration of the cities. Using the water conduits, *e.g.* the Siloam tunnel (Is. 8:6), would be an appropriately dramatic and effective means of entry. Verse 9, in a series of short, staccato sentences depicts the advance of the insects on the cities. The nouns in this verse – city, walls, houses, windows – are placed before the verbs to emphasize the fact that no edifice provides adequate refuge. Systematically the locusts loot houses, gaining thief-like access through the open, lattice-work windows (*cf.* Ex. 10:6). Speed (Heb. *rûṣ* 'run'; vv. 4, 7, 9), agility (Heb. '*lh* 'climb up'; vv. 7, 9), and order (vv. 7–8) are the basic components of their military success.

10–11. Here the picture of the locust-plague merges with the description of the Day of the Lord (*cf.* 1:5; 2:1–2). The quaking earth (*cf.* Am. 1:1; 2:13; 8:8; 9:1) and trembling

---

[1] G. R. Driver, 'Studies in the Vocabulary of the Old Testament VI', *JTS*, 34, 1933, p. 378; KB, p. 674, read 'change, abandon (course)'.
[2] C. F. Whitley, ' '*bt* in Joel 2:7', *Biblica*, 65, 1984, pp. 101–102, following a suggestion by A. Guillaume, arrives at the similar meaning 'deviate' by connecting Heb. '*bt* with an Arabic root *ḥbt*, 'fall', 'strike', with derived meanings like 'going upon what is not the middle or main part of the road'.

heavens, the darkened sun and moon and lightless stars (*cf.* 3:15), are evidence that the Lord himself is coming with his locust army to execute judgment. The language used is reminiscent of other Old Testament descriptions of vengeful theophanies (*cf.* Is. 13:10, 13; Je. 10:10; Na. 1:5–6). The darkened heavens speak of mourning as in Isaiah 1:3. These signs are not merely poetic pictures of the effects of the plague but are the awful, momentous signs which accompany the Day of the Lord (*cf.* 2:30–31 for an even more terrifying picture). Again (*cf.* 1:15), Joel leans heavily upon Amos' account of the Day of the Lord as a Day of calamity and darkness, not peace and light (Am. 5:18–20).

Yahweh's *voice, i.e.* thunder as in Psalm 18:13, adds terror to the scene in verse 11. Because the locusts are performing God's judgment, they are called *his* great army and his *host* (*maḥᵃnēh*, 'camp', may also mean those who encamp, *i.e.* army or host) as they execute his word. This last clause recalls Psalm 148:8 where the elements of nature are said to be fulfilling God's command. The parallelism suggests that it is the locust army – not Yahweh – that is *powerful* as it fulfils God's word (*cf.* NIV against RSV). The concluding sentence of this verse seems to sum up the thought of the entire section, as it asks a question which can be answered only in the negative: so *great* and *terrible* (*i.e.* fear-inducing) is this Day (*cf.* 2:31; Mal. 4:5) and the God who is at work in it (*cf.* Dt. 7:21; 10:2) that no-one will be able to *endure* it (*i.e.* cope with it successfully or victoriously; *cf.* Ho. 12:4; Je. 10:10; Mal. 3:2).

ii. The hope of deliverance (2:12–17). Though judgment is present, it is not too late to repent. The gracious invitation comes from the Lord himself (Joel's only use of the oracle formula; *cf.* on Ho. 2:13; Am. 3:15) and bears the stamp of his authority. The same Lord who thunders before his destroying army (2:11) offers the hope of deliverance. The repentance is called a turning, or returning to God (*cf.* the meaning of *šûb* at Ho. 3:5; 6:1; 14:1–2). This turning is not a token gesture or an act of empty ritual; it must be whole-hearted, *i.e.* with the full weight of moral conviction. Outward manifestations there will be – fasting, weeping, mourning (defection from God is akin to death). But they must be symbols of a broken heart, a will fully yielded to God's demands (*cf.* on 'heart' at Ho. 4:11).

13. The command *rend your hearts and not your garments* is the Hebrew way of saying that inward contrition is more important than an outward show of grief, which by itself could be an act devoid of sincerity or integrity. The rending of garments is often a sign of overwhelming misfortune (Gn. 37:29, 34; 1 Ki. 21:27; 2 Ki. 19:1; Est. 4:1). As the seat of moral and spiritual decision, it is the *heart* that must be dealt with. There evil ideas were hatched and brought to birth. *Rend your hearts* means 'change your whole attitude', with a result akin to the broken, contrite heart of Psalm 51:17 or the circumcised heart of Deuteronomy 10:16 and Jeremiah 4:4. The precise nature of the change is underscored by the prophet who repeats and expands Yahweh's command: in 'return to Yahweh *your* God' (*cf.* the covenant overtones in Je. 7:23; Ho. 5:4). Note the exclusive relationship. But this return and this relationship are possible only because of the very character of God, marked as it is by grace. The description of grace follows a formula found frequently in the Old Testament (Ex. 24:6; Pss. 86:15; 103:8; Jon. 4:2). It was probably used regularly in worship both in praise and petition. God's compassion, his reluctance to judge and his willingness to change his course of action are all tied to his 'great kindness', *i.e.* his firm commitment (*ḥesed*) to the covenant (*cf.* Ho. 2:19; 4:1; 6:4).

Where God *repents* it is usually in response to human repentance (Je. 18:5–12; Jon. 3:10), but in Exodus 32:12–14 God's repentance is sparked by the reminder of the covenant and in Amos 7:3, 6 (see comments on pp. 207ff.) by an appeal to God's pity for his people. God's openness to change his course of action and particularly to withhold disastrous judgment (here called 'evil'; *cf.* Am. 3:6) has in this passage and in Jonah 4:2 virtually become one of his attributes. Nowhere does Joel specify the people's sins. In the heat of the emergency, care not diagnosis is his concern.

14. The oracle of divine invitation (v. 12) is amplified by the prophet (vv. 13b–14). This ready shift from first to third person is indication of the prophet's conviction that he was God's messenger, speaking in his name. *Who knows* is a humble way of holding out hope. This is no time for presumption, but it is a time for anticipation, held in check by awe of God's sovereignty (*cf.* 2 Sa. 12:22; Jon. 3:9; a similar idea, though expressed by another Hebrew construction ['*ûlay*, 'perhaps'] is found in 2 Ki. 19:4; Am. 5:15). In Jonah the hope is negative: averting judgment. Here it is positive: receiving blessing in the form of a fresh fertility which allows the temple offerings to be resumed. *Cereal* and *drink offering* indicate that the ravages of the locusts are repaired (Joel 1:9, 13). The people's turning to God (2:12) will be matched by his turning to them. His course has been set on judgment; now he will turn to them in grace and leave in his tracks the tangible *blessing* of his providence – the produce which will express the restored relationship as the daily sacrifices are renewed. The lesson in this verse must not be missed: the material provisions God gives his people are as much for his service as for their comfort.

15–16. Heartened by this word of hope, the prophet sounds the orders by which the leaders, probably the priests, will convene the congregation. The call to assemble for the fast and to prepare for the siege are both sounded on the *šôpār* (*cf.* 2:1; Nu. 10:1–3). Because the judgment had become more vexing and the possibility of rescue more promising, the summons to convene is more urgent and detailed than in 1:14. *Sanctify the congregation* (v. 16) means 'hold a sacred religious meeting' on the terms specified by law and tradition. In the theocracy, church and state were not held separate. Political, economic and social problems were treated as religious issues, as the whole context suggests. *Elders*, as in 1:2, refers to age more than leadership, as the contrast with children and nursing babies suggests. The comprehensiveness of the call underscores the urgency of the need and the corporate nature of the guilt. Everyone had to be there, even the *bridegroom*, who was exempt from certain duties to see to it that his bride conceived a child to carry on his name (Dt. 20:7; 24:5); and the unweaned babies, who in corporate personality shared the people's guilt without directly contributing to it (*cf.* the judgment on Achan's family for his sin, Jos. 7:25; Ex. 34:6–7; Je. 31:29–30). Furthermore, the presence of the children would add power to the petition for mercy, as God's attitude toward the youngsters of Nineveh attests (Jon. 4:11). *Room* and *chamber* are virtual synonyms for a nuptial tent within which the newly married couple were to consummate their marriage. The tent in which Absalom met David's concubines may be an illustration of this (2 Sa. 16:22).[1]

17. The instructions to the priests continue (for *ministers*,

---

[1]See W. R. Smith, *Kinship and Marriage in Early Arabia* (1903), pp. 167–170, 291.

see 1:13). The *vestibule*, an area 20 cubits by 10 cubits, was on the east end of the temple (1 Ki. 6:3). The *altar* is the great altar of burnt offering in front of the temple (1 Ki. 8:64; 2 Ch. 8:12). Ezekiel refers to this area (which is near the entrance to the holy place in the inner court) in his description of the twenty-five who turned their backs on the temple to worship the sun (Ezk. 8:16). The priests undoubtedly were to face the temple with the congregation gathered behind them in the court.

Weep is reminiscent of an episode of national weeping early in Israel's history (Jdg. 2:4). God, whose grace has taken the entire initiative in restoration, now supplies the text for their prayer, which is in the form of a communal complaint similar to those in Psalms 44; 79; 80; 89 as well as Lamentations 3:40ff.; 5:1–22. The prayer and praise of Israel tended to take fixed literary form depending on their use in the religious life of the people. The prayer for deliverance in the first person plural and the appeal to the dignity of God's name are characteristic of communal complaints, which were used in times of national calamity like invasion, famine or plague. Joel's picture of the priests and congregation thronging the temple courtyard and pleading with God gives us an invaluable guide to the role of certain psalms in Israel's common life.

The tone of the petition (*spare* in pity and compassion; *cf.* Ne. 13:22; Je. 13:14; Jon. 4:10–11) is clear: the lot and destiny of the chosen *people* (*cf.* on Ho. 1:9; for *your heritage, i.e.* Yahweh's property on whom he staked the future of his programme, see 1 Ki. 8:53; Mi. 7:18), reflect directly on the glory and majesty of their God. In a religious context where each nation honoured its own god and looked to it for welfare, any reversal of the nation's fortunes had to be interpreted as evidence of the national god's impotence. Yahweh's refusal to intervene on behalf of his people would be seriously misinterpreted by Israel's neighbours (Ex. 32:12; Nu. 14:13–16; Dt. 9:28) and probably branded as failure. The very taunt these people would use to deride Israel is cited: 'Where is their God?' (*cf.* Pss. 42:10; 79:10; Mi. 7:10). Their shame becomes Yahweh's shame. The parallel passages from Psalms (44:13; 79:4; 89:41) illustrate both the continuity and variety of expression in the prayers of communal complaint (*cf.* also Ezk. 22:4; 36:30). *Byword* (Heb. *māšāl*; *cf.* Ps. 44:14; 69:11) describes a proverb-like saying or question that is hurled at any enemy as a taunt (*cf.* Is. 14:4). God's failure to rescue Israel would be thrown in their faces by their foes with the same regularity and intensity with which Saul's ill-fated attempts at prophesying were thrown at would-be prophets (1 Sa. 10:12).[1]

With this impassioned plea the first half of the book, with its terrible scourge, comes to a close. Not with the threat of judgment but with an offer of hope. The whole section has moved to a climax in prayer, prayer based not only on the terror of the plague but on the glory of God's name. No higher appeal, no grander motivation, can there be.

III. THE COMING VICTORY (2:18 – 3:21)

a. Restoration of the plague-damage (2:18–27)

Verse 18 is the turning point of the book. From 1:2 to 2:11 the locust invasion with all its frightening intimations of the Day of the Lord has been the theme. The offer of grace in 2:12–17 marks a transition from judgment to restoration. Verse 18, the prophet's narrative introduction to Yahweh's salvation speech in verses 19ff., begins the picture of this restoration with its ramifications both local and cosmic, both immediate and future. Between verses 17 and 18, we should presume that the invitation and commands of verses 12–17 have been accepted and obeyed.

18. If we can recreate the scene, the people young and old have thronged the temple vestibule (v. 17) and the priests have passionately pleaded with God to remove the ravagers from the land for his own name's sake. In response to this penitence and weeping, Yahweh has inspired a prophet, Joel himself, to utter a promise of salvation in Yahweh's own words (for such divine oracles in the Psalms, see 12:5; 60:6–8; a similar scene is found in Ho. 14:1–8). God has begun to act on behalf of *his land* and *his people*. Both are mentioned at the outset of restoration, because both were imperilled by the plague and both were terms of covenant commitment. The jealousy of God, to which the people had appealed in their prayer (v. 17), provides part of the motivation for the restoration. Jealousy (Heb. *qnʾ*), a petty or bitter attribute in our

---

[1]On the range of meanings for *māšāl*, see D. A. Hubbard, 'Proverbs', *ISBE*, rev., III, pp. 1012–1015.

language, describes God's ardent concern, his zeal, for his own glory. Compromise with his uniqueness rouses his wrath, while response to his uniqueness in worship and obedience stirs his love. Where people doubt his power or transfer his honour to another, God's jealousy shows itself (Dt. 4:24; 32:21; Is. 42:8; Zp. 3:8). Nations who have derided and exploited God's land and people may prompt his jealousy, which shows itself in judgment on his enemies and mercy toward those who honour him (Is. 9:7; 37:32; Ezk. 36:5–6). This basic principle is outlined succinctly in Ex. 20:5–6, a key text for understanding God's jealousy. In the present passage God's jealousy is his zeal to care for his land (*cf.* Zc. 1:14) and people 'with all the ardour and the will to possess which mark a jealous person' (Kapelrud, p. 89). For an illustration of the meaning of *pity* (*ḥml*), see the story of Pharaoh's daughter looking at the tears of the baby Moses newly rescued from the river (Ex. 2:6). Because jealousy is a consuming love, it can go hand in hand with pity.

19. Here are quoted the Lord's words in response to his people's complaint. Divine speech dominates the second half of the book as forcefully as descriptions of the plague did the first half. The restoration of the plague-damage is promised in an oracle that runs through to verse 27 and that step by step reverses the damage described in 1:4 – 2:11. *Behold* is used to arrest attention, to assure a careful hearing, and also, perhaps, to signal the 'answer' to a plea (*cf.* Is. 58:9; 65:1; Wolff, p. 58). The present participle, *I am sending*, suggests an immediate fulfilment of the promise. *Grain, wine* and *oil* are specified both as the staple crops and as the assurance that all the damage described in 1:10 will be reversed. *Satisfied* (Heb. *śbʿ* is also used in contexts of judgment; *cf.* Ho. 4:10; 13:6) speaks of restoration in abundant measure (*cf.* vv. 24, 26). Evidently the argument used in the people's prayer (v. 17) has found its mark, because both here and in verse 27 assurance is given that their *reproach* (Heb. *ḥerpâ*; *cf.* Ho. 12:14) and shame before the nations will be done away with.

20. Her produce restored, Judah's next need is to rid her land of the gnawing devastators. Though locust hordes are more apt to invade Palestine from south or east, as Jerome noted long ago, the locusts here may be called *northerner* for several reasons. First, it is possible that on this occasion the winds were from the north and brought the locusts from the

Syrian desert to the northeast. Second, *northerner* may have come to mean destructive enemy, under the influence of Jeremiah's descriptions of terrors of invasion from the north (Je. 1:13–15; 4:6), a reference to Babylonian (or possibly Scythian) armies. The military analogy has already been drawn in detail in 2:1–11 and is picked up again in 2:25 where the locusts are called 'my great army'. Third, despite strong arguments to the contrary (*e.g.* Wolff, pp. 62–63), the context seems to make clear that it is the locusts that are meant by *northerner*: the verses immediately before and after deal directly with the restoration of plague-damage. It is possible, though not so likely, that *northerner* has apocalyptic overtones, from the use of the term *north* as the home of the mountain of the gods (Is. 14:13) and as the site from which Gog is to invade Israel (Ezk. 38:6, 15; 39:2). The context strongly suggests that the apocalyptic elements should be played down and that the *northerner* be interpreted as a dramatic way of labelling the locusts as an hostile and marauding enemy bent on doing their worst.[1]

For he has done great things underscores both the wholesale destruction and the wanton arrogance with which it was accomplished. God's stern judgment is called for and, as ever, it is fully suited to the crime. A *parched* (Heb. *ṣiyyâ*; *cf.* Ho. 2:3) *and desolate* (*šᵉmāmâ*; *cf.* 2:3; 3:19) *land* would not have foliage to sustain them, nor would the two seas toward which they will be driven. As they had rendered Judah uninhabitable, they would now experience the terrors of a hostile environment. *Front* (lit. 'face') and *rear* should be seen as military terms: 'vanguard' and 'rearguard' (JB). *Eastern sea* is probably the Dead Sea (*cf.* Dt. 11:24). The Hebrews literally were 'oriented' in their use of the compass points. They faced the east and called it 'front'. West was behind them as the word *'aḥᵃrôn* indicates. North was often called 'left' and south 'right', a term which persists in the name *Yemen*. It was as though they lived their lives facing the east from which their forebears had ventured at the call of the Lord. Certainly the sea behind them was no welcome friend.

The judgment, then, comes in the form of a rout of the locust invaders, as though God were to drive a wedge (Heb.

---

[1] Kapelrud, pp. 93–108, has a thorough discussion of *northerner*, including the unsuccessful attempts of scholars to emend or delete the passage.

ndh frequently describes God's dispersion of his own people; Dt. 30:1; Je 8:3; 16:15; 23:8) through the ranks and bulldoze their centre into the desert and their flanks to the seas on east and west. The picture is completed by the mention of the *stench* (*cf.* Am. 4:10 for the stench of a destroyed army garrison). Locusts drowned at sea and washed ashore are infamous for the foul odour which their putrid carcasses discharge (Driver, p. 60). The total devastation wreaked by the ravaging insect army is matched by the total destruction they deserved. If the picture of judgment seems at times to shade from historical to apocalyptic, it is because the invasion itself was a harbinger of the Day of the Lord (*cf.* 2:1–11). The fact that the enemy is called *northerner* and that the scene of his judgment sweeps from sea to sea adds this apocalyptic note (*cf.* Zc. 14:8, where the living waters that flow from Jerusalem in the messianic age reached the eastern and western seas). Moreover, the locusts seem to be held accountable for their acts, even though they unwittingly accomplished God's purposes, in a fashion akin to God's treatment of invading armies, whether Assyrian (Is. 10:5–19) or Babylonian (Hab. 2:6–19).

21. Like a leader in temple-worship, Joel addresses three prominent entities which have suffered extensively in the plague: the land (v. 21), the animals (v. 22), the inhabitants of Jerusalem (v. 23). The intent of these verses is to convey full assurance to those who have petitioned Yahweh for respite (*cf.* Ps. 118:5, 23; Is. 41:14–16; Wolff, p. 58). The *land* which earlier mourned (1:10) is now commanded by the prophet to exchange its fear for rejoicing (*cf.* 1:16; *cf.* Ho. 9:1 for commands opposite to these). *Fear not* is a familiar ingredient in salvation promises (Is. 10:24; 41:10, 14; Lk. 2:10). The reason given – 'for the Lord has done great things' (*cf.* Ps. 126:2–3) – is identical to the reason for the harsh judgment on the locusts (v. 20). The insects' great deeds of arrogant malevolence are more than matched by God's great deeds of compassionate deliverance. The literary form used here and in verses 22 and 23 recalls the pattern found in some of the psalms of thanksgiving (*e.g.* Pss. 117; 135): (1) they begin with a command or exhortation; (2) they follow with a vocative of the persons or things addressed; (3) they introduce the reason for the command with the word *for* (*kî*); (4) the reason is stated as an act or an attribute of God. Once again Joel's thorough familiarity with the liturgical patterns of Israel shows itself.

22. Next the domesticated animals (such as cattle, oxen, sheep) are called to lay aside their fears. The picture of full fertility reverses the damage described in several passages in chapter one: the suffering of the animals (1:18, 20); devastation of the fields (1:10), fig trees and grape vines (1:12), trees (1:19), and pastures of the wilderness (1:19–20). *Are green* echoes Genesis 1:11 (the only other Old Testament use of *dš'* as a verb) and hence suggests the vitality of a new creation. *Their full yield* is literally 'their strength' (Heb. *ḥayil* was translated 'army' at 2:11). Yahweh empowers the trees to fight back, and their produce overpowers the destruction of the locust army. The personification of land and beast is both a graphic way of expressing the impact of disaster and deliverance and a solemn reminder of the close-knit character of all creation. Simple distinctions between animate and inanimate or between animal, vegetable and mineral were not always made by the Hebrews, who viewed all of reality as the gift of God, charged with his power and sustained by his presence.

23. Joy and gladness, cut off in 1:16, again become the mood of God's chosen people, here called 'children of Zion', *i.e.* those whose life centres in the temple and all that it entails (*cf.* Ps. 149:2). The reason for their rejoicing is abundance of rain. *Has given* is perfect tense to show how certain God's promise is. *Early rain* or 'autumn rain' (JB) usually falls between the latter part of October and the beginning of December; it is especially welcome as it breaks the summer drought. The word used (*môreh*; note that Wolff, p. 55, following LXX, Vulg., Syr., reads *maʰḵāl* 'food') occurs with the meaning 'autumn rain' only in this passage and Psalm 84:7. The more usual form is *yôreh* (Dt. 11:14; Je. 5:24). *Liṣḏāqâ* (lit. 'for righteousness'), the word coupled to *môreh*, has been interpreted in several different ways: (1) 'moderately' (AV), *i.e.* in 'just measure'; (2) 'for your vindication' (RSV), *i.e.* God's saving intervention on behalf of the people to whom he has pledged himself; (3) 'since he is just' (JB), referring to God's justice which he demonstrates by defeating his enemies and defending his people; (4) 'the teacher of righteousness', reading *môreh* as 'teacher' (*cf.* Jb. 36:22; Pr. 5:13; Is. 30:20). The fourth possibility, adopted by the Vulgate (*doctorem justitiae*) and the Targum, is quite attractive, especially since the discovery of the Qumran scrolls that feature a teacher of righteousness. Nevertheless, the context virtually forces us to rule out this possibility. It seems highly unlikely that a brief reference to a Messiah-like figure would be injected without either preparation or follow-up. The entire passage from verses 18 to 27 centres on the destruction of the insects and the restoration of the crops. Of the other options, (2) seems preferable, because it best captures the note of deliverance and victory in the context (Keller, p. 138; Kapelrud, p. 116; *cf.* Allen, p. 86: 'for he will give you the autumn rain in token of covenant harmony'). *Latter rain* (*malqôš*) falls in the spring, usually in March and April, and helps to ensure a good harvest by preventing the grain from drying up. *As before* ('as at the beginning') presupposes that the original preposition was *k* (with LXX; Vulg; RSV; JB; Wolff, p. 55; Allen, p. 86) not *b* (MT; AV). The point is not that the spring rain will come on time ('*in* the beginning' or '*in* the first month') but that the whole cycle of rain, autumn and spring, will be restored to its former beneficence and regularity (*cf.* v. 25).

24. The damage described in 1:10 is here undone. For *threshing floors* and *vats*, see Hosea 9:1–2. God's vindication is lavish in its abundance. Storage places emptied by the plague are full to overflowing (Heb. *šwq*, *cf.* Ps. 65:9; in Joel 3:13, the overfull vat is a figure of readiness for judgment).

25. God's oracle of deliverance, addressed directly to the people (*to you*), continues with his promises uttered in the first person, in contrast to verses 21 to 24 which were exhortations in the second person and referred to the Lord in the third person, as is customary in psalms of corporate thanksgiving. *Restore* (Heb. *šlm* in intensive stem; *cf.* Ho. 14:2) is literally 'pay back' ('make up for'; JB), a legal term for compensation of damages (*cf.* Ex. 22:3–5). *Years* is probably to be understood as 'yield or produce of the years' (Gesenius-Buhl; Kapelrud, p. 119) to account for the expression 'years that the locust has eaten'. The plural seems to imply that the locust invasions were spread over more than one year. Since the passage makes sense as it stands (*cf.* LXX; Vulg.), it seems unnecessary to emend *haššānîm* ('years') to *mišneh* ('double') as in Jeremiah 16:18 (Delcor, p. 163). The context suggests full repair but not in double measure. Again the prophet clearly links the picture of restoration with the scene of damage by using all the names for the insects that he described in 1:4. In doing so he makes clear that, despite the apocalyptic overtones of much of chapter 2, it is the literal locust plague which always forms the background. *My great army* recalls the warlike devastation pictured in the first verses of chapter two, culminating in verse 11 where the destroying host is clearly seen to bear the Lord's insignia. God leaves no doubt as to his responsibility for sending judgment, and in so doing issues a tacit warning that his grace in restoration must not be presumed upon. Amos underscores both God's participation in judgment and also the lessons to be learned from it if greater calamity is to be avoided (3:6; 4:6–12).

26. Because the restoration of food to the hungry (*cf.* 1:7–12, 16–20), is based on God's grace, the people's only response can be *praise* (Heb. *hll*, lit. 'sing psalms of praise', the appropriate counterpart to the previous pleas of complaint; *cf.* 1:14; 2:12–17). *Wondrously* (*pl'* in causative stem; *cf.* Is. 29:14 and the connections with God's covenant love and its provision of rescue in Ps. 31:21) describes the miraculous nature of the restoration both in speed and scope. Since God's *name* or reputation was in danger of being slandered by Judah's enemies (2:17), it is his *name* that must be praised for deliverance. With that name fully vindicated, his people can put behind them any fear of losing face ('be put to shame') before their foes (Heb. *bwš*, 'be ashamed', played a prominent part in the description of the plague; *cf.* 1:10–12, 17). Some scholars, *e.g.* Bewer and Delcor, have omitted 'and my people shall never again be put to shame' as a gloss appropriated from verse 27 where it properly belongs. But the idea is so prominent throughout the passage beginning at verse 12 that the repetition is wholly in keeping with the context. Good crops, brimming vats, full stomachs are not ends in themselves but are signs that God, who had seemed to abandon the people to the misery of their disaster and the mocking of their enemies, has now intervened on their behalf.

27. In climax to this section (2:18–27) and preparation for the next (2:28 – 3:21), Yahweh both calls on the people to recognize his presence in their midst (the recognition formula, *you shall know that* . . .; *cf.* Ezk. 2:5; 5:13; 6:7, 10, 13–14, *etc.*) and introduces himself to them in exclusive terms (the self-introduction formula, *I am Yahweh, your God; cf.* Is. 45:5–6, 18, 22; 46:9; Ho. 12:9; 13:4; note the *there is none else* claim to absolute sovereignty).

The uniqueness of God and his presence among his people – these are the solid joys and lasting treasures which only

Zion's children share (*cf.* Ho. 11:9; Zp. 3:15, 17). The linking of *your God* with *my people* rings with covenantal overtones of a fully restored relationship (*cf.* Ho. 2:23; Am. 9:14–15). To *know* these things means to live in terms of them, to let the truth of them grip and govern life (*cf.* Ezk. 39:22, 28). God's clear demonstration of his unrivalled lordship will forever lay the ghost of any embarrassment to which his people might be put. On this note of ringing hope the first part of God's promise of rescue comes to a close.

b. Outpouring of the Spirit (2:28–32; Heb., 3:1–5)

The divine oracle of salvation, begun in 2:19, continues as Yahweh lifts the sights of the people beyond their recovery from the plague to days of even greater blessing. In the Hebrew text these verses form chapter three.

28–29 (3:1–2). *Afterward* does not necessarily point to end times but serves rather to establish the chronological sequence between the two stages of blessing. (*In those days*, v. 29, points to the *afterward* of v. 28 but also gives these verses an eschatological touch; *cf.* 3:1; Je. 3:16, 18.) The difference between the two stages is not that the first is material and the second spiritual but that the first is the restoration of old damage and the second is the inauguration of a new era in God's dealings with his people. The distinction between material and spiritual blessings makes little sense in a context where the material blessings are themselves signs of spiritual renewal and evidence that true repentance has taken place. Life and land were bound together in such a tight bundle that whatever affected one touched the other, whether in bane or blessing (*cf.* Is. 32:9–20).

The lavish measure and extensive scope of the second stage are spotlighted in a number of ways. First, *pour out*, which can also mean 'spill' (Gn. 9:6; Ex. 4:9), suggests that God is not being niggardly (*cf.* Ezk. 39:29; Zc. 13:10). Second, the fact that *my spirit*,[1] *i.e.* God's own power and vitality, is the channel of the blessing conveys added forcefulness. The same spirit that moved at creation to bring order from chaos (Gn. 1:2),

---

[1] I use *spirit* rather than *Spirit* throughout this section to avoid giving the impression that the full trinitarian understanding of the Godhead was known prior to the revelation in Jesus the Son and the sending of the Spirit at Pentecost.

that empowered Samson to kill a lion with his bare hands (Jdg. 14:6), and that endowed Bezalel with 'skill and perception and knowledge for every kind of craft' (Ex. 35:31, JB) was to be at work among God's people. Joel makes his own contribution to the picture of the ministry of the spirit in the new age that the great prophets foresaw: The spirit's legacy may be (1) righteousness and justice (Is. 32:15–20); (2) fecundity and devotion (Is. 44:3–5); (3) rest and refreshment (Is. 63:10–11); (4) obedience (Ezk. 36:22–28). In Joel the emphasis is on fellowship with God and communication of his word and ways, as the references to prophecy and vision suggest.

Third, *upon all flesh* shows that the entire people of Israel will participate. That *Israel*, not the whole world, is in view is indicated in the pronouns '*your* sons and *your* daughters', *etc*. Whereas the gift of God's spirit had previously been restricted to chosen leaders like Gideon (Jdg. 6:34), the early kings, Saul and David (1 Sa. 10:6; 16:13), and the prophet Micah (Mi. 3:8), now all God's people will become prophets, and Moses' wish will be fulfilled: 'Would that all the Lord's people were prophets, that the Lord would put his spirit upon them' (Nu. 11:29). *All flesh* is defined as comprehensively as possible: sons and daughters, old people (*cf.* 1:2, 14; 2:16) and young men (lit. 'choice men'; *cf.* Dt. 32:25; Je. 31:13), servants and hand-maids. No exclusion will be made on the basis of gender, age or social station (*cf.* Paul's glorious expansion of this openness in Gal. 3:28).[1] The contrasts in categories are virtual *merisms* to include all ages and stations in a fashion that parallels the summons to repentance (2:16). The gift of the spirit is a blow for justice and community as well as a display of power. It readies the people for a new era of oneness, when superficial distinctions are set aside and even outcasts become core members of God's new fellowship (Ezk. 39:29). The connection between flesh and spirit in these verses recalls the sharp contrast drawn between flesh and spirit by Isaiah: 'The Egyptians

---

[1]Hanson (pp. 313–314) hears in Joel's inclusiveness 'the egalitarian impulse characteristic of early Yahwism' and sees it coupled 'with the emphasis on the free movement of the spirit' typical of the great Yahwistic prophets. All of this Hanson finds as an expression of Joel's 'antiestablishment, eschatological spirit' which sought to counter the pompous institutionalism that gripped the Jerusalem priesthood under the Zadokites in the 4th century BC, where Hanson dates the book. This is a reminder of the intimate connections between a proposed setting for the book and the way it is read.

are human beings and not God; and their horses are flesh, and not spirit' (Is. 31:3). 'All flesh is grass' when left on its own (Is. 40:6) It takes the outpoured spirit to make the needed difference.[1]

Fourth, God's grace shows itself in a spate of prophetic activity. Though ecstatic experience like falling, writhing, dancing, babbling, chanting is not foreign to the Old Testament prophets, especially in the early periods (*cf.* Balaam in Nu. 24:1–4; Saul in 1 Sa. 10:6–10; 19:23–24), there is no need to overstress the ecstatic character of prophecy here as Kapelrud, among others, has done. The experience of Amos, for instance, shows that prophecy and vision can occur in a setting devoid of more exuberant forms of ecstasy (for *vision, cf.* Am. 1:1; for *prophecy*, Am. 7:12–15). The emphasis here must surely be on a deeper knowledge of God, a richer form of the relationship which 2:27 promises (*cf.* Je. 31:33–34). The abuse by false prophets of these modes of revelation, especially the *dream* (*cf.* Je. 23:25; 27:9; 29:8) does not prohibit their use in the new age when God's spirit has full-play. The New Testament, even before Pentecost, gives ample evidence of this (*e.g.* Mt. 1:20; 2:12). The basic difference between *dream* (Heb. *ḥᵃlôm; cf.* Gn. 20:3, 6; Nu. 12:6; Dn. 2:1–3) and *vision* (Heb. *ḥizzāyôn; cf.* 2 Sa. 7:17; Is. 22:1, 5) is that the dreamer is usually asleep, while the visionary is awake during the reception of the revelation. We should note that it is not the various means of revelation that should be underscored. The variety is probably mentioned for the sake of enriching the poetic parallelism. It is the true knowledge of God (v. 27) and the power to share that knowledge that the prophet intended to stress (*cf.* Nu. 12:6–8).

Fifth, the envelope structure of verses 28–29, where the promise of the spirit both begins and closes the passage, serves to emphasize these generous promises as well as to add symmetry and balance. Yahweh's initiative in sending his own spirit is the central theme, more than the specific work-

---

[1]Wolff (p. 66) and Watts (pp. 38–39) cite these words about the divine spirit from a Qumran hymn (1QH 7.6–7): 'I thank you, Lord, for you have supported me with your strength, you have sprinkled your holy spirit upon me, that I might not stagger. You have strengthened me before the battles of wickedness.' A powerful word, yet defensive in its thrust compared to the wide-open outreach of the spirit's ministry as Joel and Peter (Acts 2:17–21) see it.

ings of the spirit.

30–31 (3:3, 4). We should understand 2:30 – 3:2 as poetry (*cf.* NIV; NAB; NEB; Wolff, p. 56; Allen, pp. 97, 105–106) not as prose (RSV). The blessings of the spirit are accompanied by *portents* (Heb. *môpēt*), powerful signs, omens sure to be fulfilled, clear-cut indicators that God is at work. Their cosmic scope (*heavens . . . earth*) highlights their extraordinary character. The specific mention of *blood, and fire and columns* (or 'mushrooms'; Wolff, p. 56, connects the word with *tāmār*, 'date palm' and reads it 'tree-shaped' or 'mushroom-cloud' like that of an erupting volcano) *of smoke* serves several purposes: (1) it reminds us of the deeds of God in the Exodus, where Egypt's judgment meant Israel's liberation (Ex. 7:17, where the Nile is turned to blood; Ex. 9:24, where hail and fire smite the land; Ex. 19:18, where Sinai is shrouded in smoke from the fire of the Lord's presence; *cf.* Pss. 78:43; 105:5, 27; 135:9 for *portents* in descriptions of Exodus miracles); (2) it conveys the sights and smells of battle, as the Lord wages war against his enemies, leaving bloody troops, burnt cities and smoking rubble in his wake (*cf.* Is. 34:5–10; Ezk. 32:6–7; 38:22, where the destruction of Edom, Egypt and Gog are described in terms of blood and fire); (3) it pictures God's judgment as a world-wide sacrifice to his holiness, as the nations which played loose with his glory became a burnt offering whose blood, fire and smoke are grim testimony to their tragic mistake (*cf.* Is. 34:6, where the Lord carries a sword sated with blood and makes a sacrifice in Bozrah; *cf.* also Is. 34:10, where Edom's smoke shall go up forever; *cf.* also Jdg. 20:40, where Gibeah is put to the torch like a whole burnt offering). The darkened *sun* and the blood-coloured *moon* are reminiscent of the effects of the locust clouds described in 2:10. But the context here clearly points to the end times (*afterward* in 2:28, *in those days*, in 2:29, and *in those days and at that time* in 3:1). Prophetic passages like this one from Joel and Isaiah 13:10 have made a distinct contribution to the language with which Christ's second coming is described in texts like Mark 13:24 and Revelation 6:12, but it is probably better to view them not as pictures of Messiah's advent but as dramatic descriptions of battle with smoke so thick it obscures the very lights of heaven. For the phrase, *great and terrible day*, see at 2:11.

32 (3:5). As the Lord provided means of rescue for his people in the locust plague, so he gives pledge of deliverance

(Heb. *mlṭ*; *cf.* Am. 2:14–15; 9:1 for negative threats using this word) in that final catastrophe. He promised, 'my people shall never be shamed' (2:17), and here he gives the means for keeping that promise: *call upon the name of the Lord*. No vague theism is acceptable. Exclusive commitment to *Yahweh*, God of Israel, is what is meant. In public and personal worship, his name and his alone is the one on which they are to call (*cf.* Gen. 12:8 for Abraham's example; 1 Kgs. 18:24 for Elijah's; also Pss. 50:15; 91:15). As the hymnwriter put it, 'Venture on him, venture wholly; let no other trust intrude' (Joseph Hart, 1712–1768, *Come Ye Sinners Poor and Needy*). *Mount Zion* and *Jerusalem*, implicitly featured in Joel's treatment of the temple (1:13–16; 2:17) and of Judah's capital (2:1, 7–9, 15–16), are thrust into full prominence here as the site of God's presence, the centre of his power, the seat of his covenant, the place where his glory has been seen in brightest form in the Old Testament revelation (Pss. 99; 110; 122; 125; 126; 128; 134; 146; 147). *Those who escape* (Heb. *pelêṭâ* stands for the group escaping as well as the act of escape and recalls 2:3 where all escape was barred) stands in parallel to *the survivors* (Heb. *śārîd*, one saved from catastrophe; Dt. 2:34; 3:3), the two terms combining to reinforce the idea of divine rescue. Some editors (*e.g.* JB; NEB) have emended the words *in Jerusalem* to connect them with 'the remnant', so the two lines would be roughly parallel, 'on mount Zion there will be some who have escaped ... and in Jerusalem some survivors ...' (JB). This change is possible but not necessary. For one thing, the passage has prose-like as well as poetic qualities and therefore should not be amended to make it stylistically more balanced than it really is.

As the Lord has said bases this promise on God's prior affirmation, usually identified with Obadiah 17, although both Obadiah and Joel may have drawn from a well-known divine oracle that was preserved in Judah's oral tradition. The promise of rescue ends as it began with *call*. This time it is God who does the calling. The two uses forcefully express the connection between God's election of his people in love and grace and their response to him in worship and obedience: those who call on the name of the Lord are those who in the deepest sense have been called (*i.e.* virtually 'appointed' or 'elected'; Is. 51:2) by him. In his picture of the Day of Yahweh, Joel takes us past the darkness which shrouded the pages of

Amos (5:18–20) and Zephaniah (1:14–18) to a time of glorious light. With Obadiah (vv. 15–21) he sees a Day beyond the Day, a Day when Israel's transgressions have been judged (as by the locust plague), and Yahweh stands ready to preserve and restore his people, while he pursues the task of judging the nations (Joel 3:1–21).

When Peter quoted this passage (2:28–32) at Pentecost, he used not only the portions about the outpouring of God's spirit but also those that describe the wonders in heaven and earth (Acts 2:17–21). Peter sketches the sweep of the 'those days' which Joel saw coming and finds their fulfilment in the outpouring of the Spirit which constituted the church and demonstrated its unique qualities as God's people. Pentecost triggers a series of powerful events which begin with the birth of the church, expand in its world-wide mission, where 'all flesh', *i.e.* all Israel, is given a larger meaning, *viz.* all believers who become part of the new Israel, whether Jew or Gentile (Rom 1:16; 10:12; Gal. 3:6–9; 6:16; Eph. 2:11–22), and move on step by step to God's final judgment of his enemies and his vindication of those who truly trust him. The pivotal clause of Joel 2:32, 'all who call upon the name of the Lord shall be delivered', not only serves as a key text for Peter's invitation to the diaspora Jews at Pentecost (Acts 2:21) but also anchors Paul's argument about the centrality of faith, not law, in the reception of salvation (Rom 10:13). Not only the text itself but its original significance is apposite to Paul's argument: 'the original Hebrew means ... that the Israelite ... professes allegiance to Yahweh, and so for Paul, the words mean "to profess oneself a Christian"' (*cf.* Acts 9:14, 21; 22:16; 1 Cor. 1:2; 2 Tim. 2:22).[1]

c. Threshing of the nations in judgment (3:1–14; Heb., 4:1–14)

The ominous intimations of judgment on the nations, presaged in the portents (2:30–31), are expounded in detail through most of chapter 3, and the bright hints of hope for God's people (2:32) become open affirmations in the last few verses (3:16–21). Like a photographer, Joel has used a wide-angle lens for the overall picture in 2:30–32. Then he zooms

[1]M. Black, *Romans*, NCB (Marshall, Morgan, and Scott, 1973), p. 139.

in for a close look at the Day of the Lord, with its mixture of judgment and grace, in chapter three.

1–3. There can be no ultimate rescue of God's people without a day of reckoning for their enemies who have contributed so generously to their suffering. Oracles of Israel's salvation frequently ring with the note of judgment on her neighbours (*cf.* Am. 1 – 2; Ob.; Na.; Hab. 2 – 3). The Lord speaks first about the *time* of the judgment. *In those days and at that time* connects the events with the future period mentioned in 2:28–29 (*cf.* Je. 33:15; 50:4, 20 for the double phrase). In that coming season or opportune period (*time* in the Old Testament frequently carries these meanings), the Lord will not only pour out his spirit on Israel (2:28–29) and rescue her in the midst of cosmic signs and wonders (2:30–32), he will also *restore* her *fortunes* (a better translation than 'bring again the captivity', AV; *cf.* Jb. 42:10; Ho. 6:11; Zp. 3:20). The restoration to wholeness transposes all of human history into a higher key. It is, perhaps, not going too far to connect it with Peter's 'time of universal restoration ... of which God spoke by his holy prophets' (Acts 3:21, NEB). Here as throughout this chapter the focus is on *Judah and Jerusalem.* The Northern Kingdom seems nowhere to be in view, though the entire nation is called Israel (3:2, 16).

The *recipients of judgment* are *all the nations,* though the context seems to limit the sweep of this phrase both by listing the specific crimes and by mentioning certain places (Tyre, Sidon, Philistia in 3:4; Egypt and Edom in 3:19). The focus then is on Judah's neighbours who harassed them periodically throughout their history; without their punishment Judah's salvation is not complete. The cosmic language (*cf.* also the mention of the nations as 'Gentiles' or 'heathen' in 3:9, 12) gives the picture a universal application as well.

The *place of judgment* cannot be identified. *Valley of Jehoshaphat* is best understood not in connection with Judah's king of that name or any specific site in Judah but in terms of its etymology, 'Yahweh has judged.' The parallel 'valley of decision' (3:14) seems to confirm this. The emphasis is on the legal character of the judgment not on the geographical site. The verbs are instructive: *gather* (Heb. *qbṣ* in intensive stem) is often used in contexts of divine judgment (*e.g.* Is. 66:18; Ho. 8:10; 9:6; Mi. 4:12); *bring down* (Heb. *yrd* in causative stem) may mean to 'prostrate', 'topple' or 'humiliate' (*e.g.* Ps. 56:7;

Is. 10:13; Am. 3:11). The Lord himself will both bring an indictment as prosecutor and render a decision as judge.

Several prophets mention *valleys* (suitable terrain both for great throngs and for military conflict, one form the judgment takes; *cf*. vv. 9–12) where judgment is to be held, but with no unanimity of description: valley of the son of Hinnom (Je. 7:31ff., 19:7); valley of vision (Is. 22:10); valley of the travellers (Ezk. 39:11); the valley formed by the cleaving of the Mount of Olives (Zc. 14:4–5).

The *basis* on which Yahweh will *enter into judgment* (Heb. *špṭ* in reflexive stem; *cf*. Is. 66:16; Je. 2:35; Ezk. 17:20) with them is their ruthless treatment of my *land* (Heb. *ḥlq* in intensive stem means *divide* and parcel out, as though they, not Yahweh, had full right of ownership; *cf*. Jos. 13:7; Pṣ. 22:19; Is. 52:12) and the people of Judah, to whom, with his jealousy ablaze (*cf*. 2:18), he shows his special relationship – '*my* people'; *my* heritage'; '*my* land'. His legal rights to ownership had been violated by the scattering (Heb. *pzr*, used of Israel's scattering and isolation in Est. 3:8; Je. 50:17); of the people and the occupation of the land (for *heritage* and *people* in parallel, *cf*. 2:17; Pss. 28:9; 78:62, 71; 94:5; 106:40; Is. 47:6; Mi. 7:14).

He argues his case even more cogently when he describes the slave trade which used his people as pawns. Scarcely anything rankles God more than inhumanity. People are treated like property to be had by the casting of *lots* (*cf*. Ob. 11; Na. 3:10). At prices ridiculously low, persons are bartered like goods (*cf*. Am. 2:6; 8:6) for a moment of pleasure – an evening with a *harlot* (Heb. *zônâ*; *cf*. Ho. 4:14) or a skin of *wine* (Am. 4:1). Though the victims in this passage are Judah's children, the same principle of inhumanity, of depersonalization, is scathingly denounced in Amos 1 – 2 where foreign nations are the ones humiliated and in Deuteronomy 21:14 which bans the sale of captured troops.

4–6. The prophet turns his attention to *Tyre* (*cf*. Ne. 13:16; Is. 23:8; Je 47:4; Ezk. 27:32; 28:1, 11), *Sidon* (*cf*. Gn. 10:15, 19; Jos. 11:8; Jdg. 18:28; Isa. 23:4; Je. 47:4; Ezk. 28:21–23) and the *regions of Philistia* (Jos. 13:2) with its five great cities (Gaza, Ashdod, Ashkelon, Gath, Ekron), perhaps because of the mention of slave trade, which centred in those Mediterranean ports. Philistia and Phoenicia were traditional enemies of the Israelites. At times there were uneasy alliances with the Phoenicians (*e.g.* in Solomon's day, 1 Ki. 7:13–14; 9:10–14),

75

but Amos and other prophets show how deep and long standing the hostility was (Am. 1:6, 9; Is. 9:11; 14:28–32; Je. 47:4;
Zp. 2:1–5). The conduct of these Gentile city states was so
harsh and cruel that Yahweh asks them if they are trying to
settle a grudge to pay him back for some prior misdeed. The
language is sarcastic, but the meaning is clear: if it is retribution (Heb. *gml* means to 'deal fully with' [BDB] or 'bring a
transaction to its conclusion' [*e.g.* 'wean' in Ho. 1:8]; with *šwb*
or *šlm* the noun *gᵉmûl* means to 'pay back in full'; *cf.* 2 Ch.
32:25; Ps. 28:4; Je. 51:6; Ob. 15) they are after, they need to
beware, because they are dealing with a master of retribution
(*cf.* on *šlm* at 2:25, where the use is positive). 'What have you to
do with me?' in this context (3:4) means something like 'What
have I done to you that you dare treat me this way?' (*cf.* Ho.
14:8).

The indictment is based on two main crimes: looting of
treasures (probably from the palace and temple of Jerusalem;
on *silver* and *gold*, see Ho. 2:8; on *rich treasures*, lit. 'my good
precious things', see Ho. 9:6, 16) and the selling of slaves to
the Greeks. Haggai looks to a time when God will shake all
nations and fill his house with their treasure (Hg. 2:7). Here
the opposite had taken place. On Tyre's involvement in slave
raiding, see Amos 1:9. For *Greeks* (3:6) a more accurate rendering would probably be 'Ionians' (Heb. *yᵉwânîm*), the residents and colonists on both sides of the Aegean Sea. Contact
between these Ionians and the Assyrian empire as early as the
eighth century BC is well documented, while Ezekiel describes
the commerce between Tyre and the Ionians in terms which
comment on our passage: 'They exchanged the persons of
men and vessels of bronze for your merchandise' (Ezk. 27:13).

7–8. The indictment of sin is followed, as usual in oracles
like these, by an announcement of punishment. The punishment includes rescuing (Heb. *'wr* in causative stem means to
'stir up', 'arouse to activity'; frequently it describes Yahweh's
special intervention, Is. 13:17; 41:2, 25; 45:13) the Jewish
slaves and exacting appropriate retribution (the language is
virtually identical to v. 4c) from their sellers by enslaving their
sons and daughters. The mention of the *Sabeans* sharpens the
punishment. Not only are they from the same country as the
Queen of Sheba (1 Ki. 10:1–13), *a nation far off* in South
Arabia where their desert life would be most uncongenial to
people raised on the coast, but their penchant for caravan

trading meant that slaves sold to them could ultimately be dispersed almost anywhere from the Indian Ocean to the East Coast of Africa. The retribution is exact: the Hebrews, who had no love for the sea, were sold to sea-peoples; the people of Phoenicia and Philistia, seasoned sea-goers, will be sold to the Sabeans, desert dwellers. The irony is barbed: the Jews, not the Philistines or Phoenicians, are now the trading agents. The oracle of salvation, which seems more prose than poetry (RSV; NIV; Moffatt) concludes with a formula of divine certification to endorse its authority: 'for the Lord has spoken' (*cf.* Is. 1:2; 22:25; 25:8). The incursions of Artaxerxes III Ochus led to Sidon's enslavement (343 BC), while Alexander sealed the fate of Tyre and Gaza (332 BC).

9–10. These verses begin a poetic section that continues to the end of the book. From verse 9 through to verse 14, we hear a call to execute the judgment prophesied in verses 1–8. A spokesperson, probably the Lord himself, summons (imperative *Proclaim*, lit. 'call', 'cry out'; *cf.* Is. 40:6; Am. 3:9) unnamed messengers (angelic heralds?) to utter a call to battle *among the nations* (*cf.* Je. 46:3–6, 9–10). The *nations* (*cf.* vv. 11–12), on our interpretation of a post-exilic setting, are probably the lands named earlier in the chapter – Tyre, Sidon, Philistia (v. 4) – as well as Edom and Egypt (v. 19). If Joel was speaking against a seventh-century background (*cf.* Koch, pp. 158–159), then Assyria, though not named, would be included. The strong eschatological thrust of the passage warns against attempts to define *nations* too specifically. Total justice for the nations and total security for Israel is Yahweh's intent.

Prepare is literally 'sanctify' (*cf.* on 1:14; 2:15), a reminder that *war* for the ancients was a religious enterprise, prepared for with prayer and sacrifice (*cf.* 1 Sa. 7:8–9; Je. 6:4; 22:7; 51:27–28). The warriors (*cf.* 2:7) are called to duty (the verbs are *stir up, draw near, come up*; *cf.* Jdg. 20:28; 21:5, 8); each connotes military preparation for battle and their countries are summoned to total mobilization. In this battle-call the Lord deliberately reverses the wording of the familiar millennial passages where weapons of war are forged into tools (Heb. *'ēt,* usually rendered 'ploughshare', may well mean 'hoe'; *cf.* 1 Sa. 13:20–21; Allen, p. 326) for agriculture (v. 10; *cf.* Is. 51:4; Mi. 4:3). Since David's day, iron had been plentiful enough in the Middle East for all but the poorest farmers to possess iron tools.

The mobilization is so total, and the reversal of normal patterns so complete, that even people who lack the nerve or physique for battle (*the weak*) volunteer as warriors (*cf.* Moab's boast in Je. 48:14). The line is deliberately humorous, since the root of *warrior* (*gbr*; *cf.* Ho. 10:13) means to be 'strong' or 'mighty'.

11–12. The divine messengers carry out their mission commanding the *nations* (Heb. *gôyîm*, *i.e.* non-Jewish nations, Gentiles) to battle. *There* is the valley of Jehoshaphat (3:2, 12). The last line of verse 11 seems to be a signal from the messengers that the troops of the nations are being readied for battle and that the Lord should now muster (Heb. *nḥt* 'descend' is used of acts of aggression; Pss. 18:35; 38:3; Je. 21:13) his own forces to meet the enemy. He who rallied locusts to do his bidding (2:11) will not lack *warriors* (2:7) to fill his ranks and match the warriors of his foes (3:9–10). The Lord responds (v. 12) by repeating the invitation to battle (*cf.* v. 9) and declaring the real purpose of the encounter: judgment. The nations may be marshalling their troops for war, but the sovereign God is not threatened. He knows who is in full charge, and he plans to *sit* in judgment (for sitting as the posture of judges, *cf.* Ex.18:14; Ps. 61:7; Mal. 3:3) on the enemies.

13. The figure changes again. Yahweh is neither warrior, nor judge; he is a farmer (probably a grape-grower; *sickle* may be read 'vintager's knife'; Wolff, p. 80) shouting instructions for *harvest* (*cf.* 1:11, where the shout depicted the impossibility of harvest) probably to his heavenly hosts (*cf.* the relationship between battle and farming established in v. 10). The command to *tread* the grapes in the full *wine press*, whose vats are already overflowing, deliberately mimics the picture of prosperity in 2:24. The final line explains the metaphor. The *wickedness* (Heb. *rā'â*, 'evil'; on this use, *cf.* Ho. 7:1–3; 9:15; 10:15) of the nations is so *great* that they are as *ripe* (Heb. *bšl*, usually 'boil', by extension comes to mean 'ripen', *i.e.* ready to be used; *cf.* Gn. 40:10) for judgment as grapes would be for harvest at the peak of their seasons. *Harvest* as a metaphor for judgment is found in both Testaments (*cf.* Is. 17:4–6; 63:1–6; Ho. 6:11a; Mt. 13:36–43; and especially Rev. 14:14–20, a passage that draws heavily upon this scene in Joel). For the idea that sin may reach a level when judgment becomes unavoidable, *cf.* the line in Genesis 15:16: 'for the iniquity of the Amorites is not yet complete'.

14. The repetition of *multitudes* gives the expression a superlative ring: the largest possible gathering of multitudes. The word (Heb. *hᵃmônîm*) also catches the idea of tumults in confusion, the uproar that would sound forth from a huge crowd in the grips of anxiety. More than once, as Joel does here in what seems to be his awe-filled account of the packed valley, prophets use it as description of the enemies summoned to judgment (*cf.* Ezk. 39:11; Is. 17:12; 29:5ff, and especially 13:1–11, which has a great similarity to Joel 3:9–14 in conscripting the nations to do battle with God). *The day of the Lord* takes us back to 2:31 where God's massive intervention in grace and judgment was pictured, an intervention of which the locust plague was a preliminary expression (see above at 1:15; 2:1, 11). The decision which gives the valley its name is, of course, the Lord's decision. The nations have already decided against him. It is his turn to do the deciding. 'Valley of decision' and 'valley of Jehoshaphat' (3:2, 12) mean, therefore, essentially the same thing: the place where Yahweh will carry out his devastating judgment (*cf.* 1 Ki. 20:40; Is. 10:22–23, where *ḥrṣ*, 'decide', has a clearly destructive meaning).

d. Rescuing of Judah (3:15–21; Heb., 4:15–21)

The division here is arbitary. It is impossible to tell whether verse 15 should be coupled with verse 14 as a comment on the Day of the Lord (*cf.* RSV) or with verse 16 as a prologue to God's words of rescue (*cf.* JB; Allen, p. 116; NEB makes the basic break at v. 17 where the divine speech begins). The transition from the judgment of the nations to the rescue of Judah is deliberately subtle and ambiguous because they are both parts of Yahweh's programme of ultimate rescue and restoration as verses 16 and 19–21 make clear.

15–17. The darkened skies (*cf.* 2:10 where the locusts are the cause and 2:31 where the darkening forebodes the coming Day of deliverance) again point to the staggering intensity and the cosmic scope of the divine activity. The whole creation – including the dependable sources of light, time and orientation – boggles at it. Their eclipse means that the judgment scene, so thoroughly prepared for in 3:1–14, is no longer in the limelight. The *fact* of judgment is crucial to the prophet's theme; the *details* are not. In verse 16 the emphasis shifts from visible to audible evidence of Yahweh's intervention. The lion-like roar from Zion is the note with which Amos' prophecy begins (Am. 1:2). The voice which spoke the universe into existence at creation has the power to rattle it (as his locusts did the land in 2:10) in judgment and restoration. The context suggests that the divine Lion is roaring words of assurance to his own (*cf.* Ho. 11:10–11) more than threats of disaster to the outsiders.

Neither the darkened skies nor the quaking universe are menaces to God's people. Yahweh himself will provide them with fort-like protection (for *refuge* see Pss. 14:6; 46:2; 61:4; 62:8–9; 71:7; 73:28; 91:2, 9; 94:22; 142:6; for *stronghold*, Pss. 27:1; 31:5; 37:39; 52:9; for both together, see Is. 25:4). This promise in verse 16c–d clearly marks the transition to the final oracle of salvation. The purpose of the whole event is summarized in the *recognition/self-introduction* formula (v. 17; *cf.* 2:27) which is so widely employed in Ezekiel (*cf.* 12:15–16, 20; 13:4).[1]

Zimmerli's summation is apt: 'The purpose of all this encounter of Yahweh with his people can be none other than the self-disclosure of the Lord of Israel to his people, and beyond this to the wider world of nations.'[2] In both 3:17 and 2:27 the self-revelation is followed by an assurance of God's full presence and protection: Jerusalem's holiness (*i.e.* complete freedom from corruption or intrusion) is guaranteed by God who will not again allow the pollution of foreign conquerors (v. 17c–d).

The picture of protection and prosperity in the salvation promise with which Joel concludes is centred in Judah's sacred capital, the earthly dwelling of Yahweh (*cf.* Zc. 14:20–21 for a more detailed picture of Jerusalem's ultimate holiness). The geographical-covenantal significance of Jerusalem/Zion at the end of the book complements its central role throughout Joel. The powerful assurance that Yahweh dwells in Zion (vv. 17, 19; *cf.* on 2:32) is the ultimate answer to the calls to complaint issued when no offerings were available in the temple (1:8–10, 13); it ratifies God's response to the calls to 'sanctify a fast' (1:14; 2:15); it proves that Yahweh did become 'jealous for his

---

[1]For discussion of this formula and the view that it combines an element of legal proof – 'that you may know', as in Gn. 42:34 – with a formula of self-introduction – 'I am Yahweh', as in Ex. 20:2 – see W. Zimmerli, *Ezekiel*, Hermeneia (E.T., Philadelphia: Fortress Press, 1979), I, pp. 36–40.

[2]*Ibid.*, p. 37.

land' (2:18). Anguish for Zion marks the beginnings of Joel's message; assurance to Zion marks the ending. For a people to whom the land has been given as a gift in Joshua's day, to whom Jerusalem and its temple had been bequeathed under David and Solomon, from whom all of this had been snatched in the judgment of Exile, there could be no stronger promise that all would be well than for the prophet to describe the Lord and his people dwelling in peace in Jerusalem.

18–21. The song of future restoration proceeds to its climax with a poetic description of a fertility that thoroughly reverses the locusts' devastation (v. 18), a prophetic announcement of judgment against ancient enemies, Egypt and Edom (v. 19), a promise of continuity for Judah and Jerusalem (v. 20), and a repetition of the crowning assurance that Yahweh, zealous to give the guilty nations their due, is dwelling in Zion (v. 21).

The poem on prosperity, introduced by the eschatological formula *in that day* (*cf.* Ho. 2:16, 18, 21; Am. 8:9, 13; 9:11) which links this speech to the preceding one, echoes motifs found elsewhere in the prophets: (1) mountains dripping with *wine* are part of Amos' view of future salvation (9:13), though Joel adds *milk*, probably as a recollection of the ancient account of Canaan as a 'land flowing with milk and honey' (*e.g.* Ex. 3:8; Lv. 20:24; Nu. 13:27; Dt. 6:3; Jos. 5:6); (2) streams and fountains that water the land resemble the prophecies of Ezekiel 47; Zechariah 14:8. But Joel is doing more than declaring an end to Palestine's constant battle against drought and infertility. He is also announcing that the specific damage inflicted by the locusts has been undone and abundantly so: the lavish supply of wine replaces what was cut off when the vines withered (1:5, 9, 12); the flow of milk means that herds of cattle are no longer perplexed for want of pasture (1:18); the spate of water replenishes the dried-up brooks (1:20).

The presence of the Lord is the only explanation of this bounty. His commitment to the sustenance and refreshment of his people and their land, once his judgment has done its work, is symbolized in the *fountain* that issues from his house (*cf.* Ps. 46:4–5; Zc. 14:8). Jerusalem's age-long struggle for water, well known from the Siloam inscription which chronicles Hekekiah's efforts to dig a tunnel to assure an adequate supply especially in times of siege (*cf.* on 2:8), was past.[1] *Shittim* (v. 18) means acacias (the wood of which had been essential in the fashioning of the tabernacle with its ark and altars, Ex. 25:10, 23–24; 26:15; 27:1; 30:1) and, if it is to be given a literal location, probably describes the *Wadi-en-Nar* which leads from the Valley of Kidron to the Dead Sea. Acacias still grow there. Ezekiel vividly describes the freshening impact of this eschatological stream on the Salt Sea (Ezk. 47:8–9). And these Old Testament pictures that connect closely physical and spiritual blessings carry over to the New Testament vision of the Holy City, whose perpetual fertility is watered by a river that flows from the throne of God (Rev. 22:1–2).

Joel includes a political note in his picture of paradise (v. 19a). Two ancient enemies are earmarked for desolation in contrast to the enduring prosperity of Judah and Jerusalem (v. 20). Essential to the message of salvation for Israel is the certitude that God has avenged the *innocent blood* which *Edom* and *Egypt* have *shed* in *Judah*, which must be the grammatical antecedent to '*their* land'. Involved here is not only the relief of pressure from the south, which the desolation of these enemies guarantees, but even more the revelation of God's righteousness in settling all accounts (3:4, 7–8) and demonstrating his saving power on behalf of his covenant people (2:32; 3:7).

Specific documentation of the crimes of Edom and Egypt may not be needed. Both nations were ancient enemies of Judah: *Egypt*, in addition to its reputation as the 'house of bondage' (Ex. 13:3), had periodically raided or invaded Judah's borders and wrought mayhem on God's people – under Sheshonq I (*c.* 925 BC; 1 Ki. 14:25–26; 2 Ch. 12:2–12) and under Osorkon I and his Ethiopian general Zerah (*c.* 897 BC; 2 Ch. 14:9–15; 16:8); *Edom* sought to bar the Israelites from the king's highway, a main route of travel between Egypt and Asia, after the Exodus (Nu. 20:14–21; 21:4; Jdg. 11:17–18), fought with Saul (1 Sa. 14:47), was conquered by David (2 Sa. 8:13–14), and raided Judah in Jehoshaphat's day in concert with Ammonites and Moabites (2 Ch. 20:1).

If specific acts of violence are in view, one can point to Josiah's death at the hands of the Egyptian pharaoh, Necho, at

---

[1]For the text of the Siloam Inscription, see *DOTT*, pp. 209–211.

Megiddo (*c.* 609 BC; 2 Ki. 23:28–30) and to Edom's cruel joy and vicious opportunism when Judah, denied any Egyptian help, finally fell to the Babylonian forces of Nebuchadrezzar (Ps. 137:7; Je. 49:7–22; Ob. 10–14). The *desolation* (Heb. *š*ᵉ*māmâ*; *cf.* 2:3, 20) which Joel threatens is a favourite term in Ezekiel where it is also applied to *Egypt* (29:10, 12; 32:15) – a distinct irony since the Nile kept Egypt so regularly fertile that the patriarchs used it for refuge in Canaan's time of famine – and *Edom* (35:3–4, 7, 9, 14–15). By *innocent blood* (a legal term to describe undeserved capital punishment; *cf.* Dt. 19:10, 13; 21:8–9; 27:25; Je. 2:34; 7:16; 22:3, 17) the prophet does not imply Judah's sinlessness but rather the outrageous and uncalled for loss of life which foreign invasion entailed.

After the promise of the perpetuity (Heb. *tēšēb* should be translated 'will remain' [*cf.* Ps. 121:1; Mi. 5:3] not *be inhabited* as RSV; NIV) of Judah and Jerusalem (v. 20), a reminder that Yahweh has lost none of his ancient power to preserve his dwelling place and to redeem his people from their enemies as well as their sins, the salvation oracle returns to its interest in judgment on the neighbour nations which began in 3:2 (Heb. 4:2). Unfortunately, the Hebrew text of verse 21a is not as clear as most of Joel and has prompted a number of divergent interpretations. The tie to verse 19 is made plain by the catch-word *blood* which in both verses refers to violence against Judah. The reading which leaves the text entirely intact and requires no emendation is that of H. Steiner (followed by Allen, p. 117): 'And shall I leave their bloodshed unpunished? I will not, as surely as Yahweh has his home in Zion.' The question and answer formula with the same verb (though in the *Niphal* [passive] stem rather than the *Piel* [intensive] as in Joel) occurs in Jeremiah 25:29: 'And shall you go unpunished? You shall not go unpunished . . .'.

The closing line, *the Lord dwells* (Heb. *šōkēn*, 'is continuously dwelling', *cf.* God's presence in the Exodus and wilderness; Ex. 25:8; 29:45; Nu. 5:3; 35:34; *cf.* John's description of Christ's incarnation as 'tabernacling', Jn. 1:14) *in Zion* (*cf.* v. 17; Is. 8:18) serves several purposes: (1) it guarantees the promised revenge on Judah's enemies; Yahweh's presence is the pledge that all such wrongs will be righted; (2) it underscores the sanctity of Jerusalem and its future freedom from all hostile foreign intrusion, reiterating and reinforcing the promise of verse 17; (3) it sums up the picture of restoration begun in 2:18 when 'the Lord became jealous for his land'; the locust plague was interpreted as divine absence: 'Why should they say among the peoples, "Where is their God?"' (2:17).

The ultimate characteristic of Yahweh's Day is not his warfare with his enemies in the valley of decision, nor his refreshment of his people in the valley of acacias, dominant though these elements be. It is his renewed, restored and permanent presence with them. Ezekiel saw that and renamed the Holy City, 'The Lord is there' (Ezk. 48:35). John knew that and revelled in the fact that 'the Word became flesh and dwelt among us' (Jn. 1:14). John knew that even more fully when the voice from the throne announced, 'Behold, the dwelling of God is with humankind. He will dwell with them, and they shall be his people' (Rev. 21:3).

AMOS

INTRODUCTION

I. THE PROPHECY OF AMOS[1]

The words of Amos burst upon the landscape of the Northern Kingdom, Israel, with all the terror and surprise of a lion's roar. Though their main targets were the palaces of Samaria and the shrines at Bethel and Gilgal, the prophet's words were to resound throughout Israel's entire landscape leaving no part nor person unscathed.

Abuse of power in the social realm and compromise with paganism in the religious were the two besetting sins which Amos denounced. At particular fault were the powerful, the landed, the wealthy and the influential, in short, the leadership, who had not only seduced the underprivileged from obedient worship of Yahweh but had conscripted their lands, confiscated their goods, violated their women and cheated them in business along the way. The lion-like roar was a divine No, shouted through the prophet at every basic component of Israel's political, social, economic and religious life.

And the No carried overtones of finality.[2] The divine Judge was to rap the gavel with a bang that would collapse both altar and palace. At stake were the survival of the ruling dynasty, the political perpetuity of the Northern Kingdom, the occupation of the land and the very lives of its citizens. Even more, at stake was the continuation of the covenant with its beginnings in the patriarchal periods, its powerful love demonstrated in the Exodus, its specific structure revealed to Moses, its renewal in the days of Joshua's conquest and its royal setting in David's time. In five brief visions and a handful of

[1]In addition to the introductory essays found in all the basic commentaries, and to the chapters in the major Old Testament introductions, three surveys of the scholarly debate on Amos have proved particularly helpful: A. S. van der Woude, pp. 34–43; R. Martin-Achard; A. G. Auld.
[2]*Cf.* R. Smend, 'Das Nein des Amos', *EvTh*, 23, 1963, pp. 404-423.

short oracles, Amos saw and heard the *end* (*cf.* 8:2) of all of this and had no choice but to declare it (3:8; 7:15).

The denunciations of sin – whether of the neighbour nations or of Israel – and the announcements of judgment – whether by fire, earthquake or foreign army – triggered a barrage of prophetic activity which shaped and interpreted the life of Israel and Judah for four hundred years. By their message of awful, damning judgment when covenant-privileges were presumed upon, these prophets, with Amos at their van, prepared the way for the New Testament announcement of a Saviour in whose blood a New Covenant would be written. The fact that Amos and the prophets who followed – prophets like Hosea, Isaiah, Micah, Zephaniah, Habakkuk, Jeremiah, Ezekiel, Joel and Malachi – found hope *beyond* the judgment or, better, hope *through* the judgment, has added immeasurably to our understanding of forgiveness through the cross of Christ, itself history's greatest instance of divine judgment.

In Amos' view of God's actions, sovereign judgment and majestic compassion are both found, though not always in equal amounts. But the grandeur of his grasp of Yahweh's greatness frames the backdrop for biblical discipleship in every era, not least our own. Our covenant privileges must be enjoyed with humility, since Yahweh cares for and commands the destinies of all peoples, even our enemies. Our sense of security must ever be anchored in our God alone, since our days of prosperity are his blessing and our times of austerity may be his discipline. Our worship must motivate and inform our acts of righteousness and justice towards all humanity, especially the poor, afflicted and oppressed. Our piety must have as one essential aim (and one vital test of validity) the emulation of the concerns of the One whom we adore, the One who has shown himself to be ultimate righteousness and justice, final truth and grace, in Jesus Christ.

II. THE PLACE IN THE CANON

Why was Amos placed third (second in the LXX, whose order is Hosea, Amos, Micah, Joel) in The Book of the Twelve, as Jewish tradition has named what we call less felicitiously the Minor Prophets? The answer to that question is settled, in large measure at least, when we have tried to discern why

Hosea is first and Joel second (see pp. 22–23). Hosea's greater length and its major themes of religious apostasy with the Baals and of Yahweh's covenant faithfulness combined to provide significant and necessary background to the prophetic books that followed. Hosea's constant references to Assyria make clear the identity of the invading army that lurks nameless in the wings of Amos' drama. Joel, who thrived probably two and a half or three centuries after Amos, is placed before him in the Canon, not only because of similarity of theme and language, but more particularly because his book with its movement from disaster to rescue distills the themes both of individual prophetic works and of the collection as a whole.

If the insights which account for the positions of Hosea and Joel are sound, what book could come next but Amos? Its length, age and comprehensiveness warrant its place towards the beginning of the Twelve. So does its influence on other prophets like Micah, Zephaniah, Zechariah and Joel. Its emphasis on the social horrors spawned by corrupt worship serves as a complement to Hosea's preoccupation with religious and political apostasy. Either work without the other would give an underdrawn picture of Yahweh's demands and Israel's defection from them. Together they recount the life and history of the Northern Kingdom through its final four momentous decades, issue warnings to Judah about a similar fate, and picture the manifold aspects of Yahweh's sovereignty in a way that has struck terror and planted hope in the hearts of God's people for countless generations.

III. THE DATE OF THE BOOK

All markers in the book itself point to a date towards the end of the reign of Jeroboam II, who occupied the throne at Samaria as co-regent with his father, Jehoash, and as sole ruler for forty-one years (793–753 BC; 2 Ki. 14:23–29). The relative brevity of Amos' ministry seems clear: (1) in contrast to the title in Hosea 1:1 which lists a succession of Judean kings from Uzziah (792–740 BC) to Hezekiah (715–696 BC), thus suggesting an extended period of prophesying, Amos' title-verse (1:1) names only Uzziah and Jeroboam; (2) the title pin-points Amos' preaching to a period of not more than two years (and possibly a much shorter time) in connection with a memorable earthquake (*cf.* Zc. 14:5); (3) the conflict with Amaziah (7:10–17) suggests that Amos' ministry may have been cut short by the combined opposition of Israel's king and Bethel's high-priest; (4) the ominous shadow of a mighty invader (3:11; 5:3, 27; 6:7–14; 7:9, 17; 9:4) points to an Assyria ready to free herself of responsibilities nearer home and to resume the annual westward marches which had wreaked havoc in Israel during the half-century before Jeroboam came to power; Tiglath-pileser III (*c.* 745–727 BC) was the agent through whom Amos' (and Hosea's) grim prophecies of military disaster began to be fulfilled; (5) a solar eclipse, duly recorded in Assyrian annals, took place in 763 BC and may help to account for Amos' descriptions of cosmic terror in 4:13; 5:8; 8:9.

For Amos' ministry, then, a date between 760 and 755 BC seems to have gained almost unanimous support among scholars. And it accords well with what is said about the military expansiveness and what is implied about economic prosperity in 2 Kings 14:23–29 (*cf.* Am. 6:1–6). The actual date of the book as we now have it is a more complex matter, dependent on a reconstruction of the process of composition (see below on Unity and Composition). It is enough here to say that the approach of this Commentary will find a close correlation between the prophet's date and the production of the book, so that the background posited for Amos' ministry may also serve as the background of the text.

IV. THE SETTING OF THE BOOK

Personal background

Discovering the personal background of Amos is as complicated as projecting the date of his ministry is simple. What kind of man was Amos? What was his vocation, when he was not serving as a prophet? What spiritual and cultural influences shaped his outlook, language and content? These questions are soaked in controversy. The passages that contain bits of information about the prophet have been sifted by dozens of scholars for every hint of information, and the language of the text has been combed by a crew of equal size and thoroughness for any further clues. And many decades of this sleuthing have left us miles from any real consensus.

Our Amos (Heb. '*āmôs* in contrast to '*āmôṣ*, Isaiah's father) is referred to by name in the Bible only at Amos 1:1; 7:8, 10–12, 14; 8:2. No member of his family is mentioned, let alone named. That Judah was his home seems clear from the identification of his region as Tekoa, since arguments for a connection between Amos and a Galilean Tekoa (about 12 kilometres NW of Capernaum) are largely inferential.[1] The only Tekoa the Old Testament knows is about 10 kilometres south of Bethlehem and 16 south of Jerusalem. Its site, Khirbet Taqu'a, is in the highlands of Judah at an elevation of perhaps 850 metres, and its physical prominence led Rehoboam to see that it was adequately fortified (2 Ch. 11:6; *cf.* 2 Sa. 13:37 – 14:24; 23:26 for its role in the intrigues of David's life). Though Tekoa is not mentioned in Amos 7:12–14, the most natural reading of Amaziah's command to Amos to 'flee away to the land of Judah, and eat bread there' is that it is an order to return home where Amos belonged.

The sole mention of Tekoa in Amos (1:1) has as its chief purpose to highlight his agricultural background (*among the shepherds* or sheep-raisers) not to feature his home town.[2] Therefore, in seeking what influenced Amos, we are surely on solid ground if we keep in mind his agricultural vocations (1:1; 7:14). We are on shakier ground if we emphasize the fact that 'he haunted heights, and lived in the face of very wide horizons', as though the geographical context itself contributed largely to Amos' view of Yahweh's majesty and sovereignty.[3]

That Amos' vocation has to do with agriculture can scarcely be doubted, though his precise tasks can be suggested only with a degree of tentativeness (see discussions at 1:1 and

---

[1]K. Koch, p. 70, argues from the absence of 'mulberry trees' (see discussion below and at 7:14) in Tekoa of Judah and from the unlikelihood that Amos could proclaim judgment as a spectator whose own life and family would not experience the 'end' he predicted.

[2]On the continued role of Tekoa in Maccabean times and its veneration as a shrine of Amos by Byzantines and Crusaders, see V. R. Gold, 'Tekoa', *IDB*, IV, pp. 528–529. For a summary of discussion on the size and status of Tekoa and for the conclusion that it was a 'famous city' during the prophet's time, a city whose political, cultural and agricultural importance matched the military importance it had earlier enjoyed, see W. Vischer, 'Amos, citoyen de Teqoa', *ETR*, 50, 1975, p. 134.

[3]G. A. Smith, *The Historical Geography of the Holy Land* (London: Hodder and Stoughton, [14]1908), p. 314.

7:14–15). A number of oracles reflect the eye of one who looked at life, as a farmer: the lament for the pastures of the shepherd in 1:2, the descriptions of drought and blight in 4:6–9, the special concerns for vineyard and farmer in the pending judgment (5:16–17), the abhorrence of locusts and fire in 7:1–6, the basket of summer fruit in the report of the fourth vision (8:1–2), the joyful picture of enhanced fertility in 9:13–15, scenes of hunting and encounters with wild animals in 3:3–8 and 5:19.

All of this is not to brand Amos as a 'simple, cultured rustic' (Mays, p. 3). If Tekoa of Judah was his home territory, his work with sycamore fruit called for seasonal travel either to the north in Galilee or to the west on the slopes of Judah's lowland that fringed the regions of Philistia (see on 7:14–15).[1] Beyond that, as P. Craigie has argued (see at 1:1), *shepherds* (*nōqᵉdîm* in 1:1) were more likely to be men of substance and influence, who owned and managed sizeable flocks, rather than simple herdsman. Amos' knowledge of international events (chs. 2–3; 9:7), his acquaintance with patriarchal history, his close observations on life in Samaria (3:9–11, 12; 4:1–3; 6:1–3; 8:4, 8) and Jerusalem (6:1) as well as Bethel (2:8; 3:14; 4:4; 5:5–6, 21–27; 7:10), his polished skills in debate and his familiarity with a host of literary forms (see below) all mark him as a man of uncommon experience, opportunity and sensibility, fully equipped by personal background as well as divine command to carry out his mission.

Call

What event or episode was used to snatch Amos from his agricultural tasks in Tekoa and elsewhere and thrust him into a prophetic ministry? That something dramatic did happen is attested in Amos 7:15. But as to just what happened and how Yahweh 'took' Amos from his sheep and said, 'go, prophesy to my people Israel,' we are left guessing. The *fact* of the call, together with its *direction* to Israel, is what counts. The text is silent on the rest. What Amos does seek to make clear to Amaziah is that he is not now and never has been a *prophet* (Heb. *nābî'*) in the sense that Amaziah understands the word, *i.e.* a professional prophet holding permanent office and

---

[1] Crenshaw, p. 252, speaks of 'migrant work', a term that is probably too lowly for the kinds of activities in which Amos engaged.

attached to a shrine or a guild of prophets. Whatever prophesying he does comes by divine gift not by formal office or even personal inclination (3:8). Amos holds that he cannot not prophesy to Israel since he is under binding command from the Lord himself.

Scholarly attempts to penetrate the silence and gain further word on the nature of Amos' call have not produced satisfactory results. At least since Wellhausen (see Rudolph, p. 248, n. 18), students of Amos have sought some tie between Amos' five visions (chs. 7–9) and his call: 'It seems very likely that the experiencing of these visions was the way in which Amos realized that God was calling him to be a prophet.'[1] Others view the visions as prior and preparatory to the call, an approach that has much to commend it but finds little actual substantiation in the text and is based on attempts to reconstruct the time-sequence of Amos' experiences with Yahweh.[2] Another option is to place them after the time of Amos' call and to find in them a milestone on Amos' journey towards a full understanding of the reality and certainty of divine judgment. Such a tack can be taken without necessarily endorsing the view that the visions account for a transformation in Amos' role from prophet of salvation, functioning in the cult, to prophet of doom, condemning the official worship.[3]

Three comments are evoked by this discussion of Amos' call. First, the call should probably be treated as an event independent of the visions of judgment. These visions lack any specific word of commissioning, any expression of reluctance to prophesy, any word of the assurance of God's presence in the prophetic ministry. If the pattern of call-visions has been set in the descriptions of the commissionings of Moses (Ex. 3 – 4), Isaiah (ch. 6), Jeremiah (ch. 1), Ezekiel (chs. 1–3), then it seems clear that Amos' visions are of another kind. Second, placement in the text itself, in a context so far removed from the beginning of the book, suggests that the visions occurred in the course of, not prior to, the prophet's preaching in the north. This opinion is not altered

---

[1] R. E. Clements, *The Conscience of the Nation: A Study of Early Israelite Prophecy* (Oxford University Press, 1967), p. 28.
[2] Various versions of this approach are found in A. Weiser, *Old Testament*, p. 242; Rudolph, pp. 248–249; Wolff, p. 296; Mays, p. 126.
[3] This latter view has been argued by E. Würthwein, in 'Amos-Studien', *ZAW*, 62, 1949–50, pp. 10–52.

by the observation frequently made (*e.g.* Mays, p. 125; Wolff, p. 295), and with considerable merit, that we should distinguish between the experience of the visions itself and the literary shaping and placing of them in the text at a time subsequent to the experience. Third, the visions occurred most likely over a period of time, since we find a clear break in form and content between the first two (7:1–6) and the rest, and also a distinct difference in form between the first four (7:1–8; 8:1–2) and the fifth (9:1). In sum, all five visions centre on the substance of the message, not in the nature or circumstances of the prophet's call (Koch, pp. 41–43).

Spiritual influences

Even more puzzling than the character of Amos' call is the nature of his cultural and spiritual background. What shaped his language and his concerns? The *cult* – Israel's (or Judah's) formal and official worship with its shrines, priests, offerings, hymns and feast days – is an answer frequently offered: 'he has hardly said a single word which is not in some way influenced by the cult. . . . Amos built his whole appearance as well as his oracles, contents and style, upon a long and solid tradition, mainly preserved in the cult.'[1] Once the scholarly wall of partition, which fenced prophets out of the cult and divided them from their arch-enemies (the priests), had been perforated, the shrines and temples of Palestine were held to be populated by prophets who laboured side by side with priests.

This shift in the understanding of Amos' relationship to the cult that made an insider of one whom earlier students had always reckoned an outsider gained momentum from the work of A. Würthwein, mentioned above. He claimed to see in the movement of the five visions – especially in the change of Amos' role from intercessor to announcer of judgment between visions two and three – a picture of an actual vocational shift from the kind of prophet who blessed the people, partly by pronouncing doom on their enemies (*cf.* Am. 1 – 2) and partly by reminding them of Yahweh's covenant-pledges to be

[1]A. Kapelrud, p. 81. We should note that, with a battery of arguments, Kapelrud seeks to connect Amos to the temple at Jerusalem, where he was introduced to the majesty and the shortcomings of the people's worship (pp. 78–81).

their Lord and Saviour, to the kind of prophet that confronted the people with threats of fatal and final judgment. Würthwein held that both types of prophets had roles in the official cult.[1] It has been H. Graf Reventlow who gave this cultic view its most ardent advocacy. More than his predecessors he formalized Amos' status as a cult office-holder by interpreting the prophet's main literary forms as components of cultic ritual, usually connected with a festival of covenant renewal.

Coming at the question of what influenced Amos from a completely different angle was H. W. Wolff (*Prophet*) who isolated *wisdom* not cult as Amos' intellectual homeland. The wisdom was not from school or court but from the clan in which were preserved and transmitted the values and ideals of ancient Israel: a concern for the right way, for justice and righteousness, for compassion with the poor and needy, for distrust of an extravagant life. And the transmission took place in forms well-documented in other wisdom sources: didactic or rhetorical questions, cries of woe, numerical proverbs, antithetical word-pairs, and admonitions (see below, pp. 102ff., for Amos' use of these literary devices).[2]

Seeking to counter both the cult-prophet and the wisdom approaches was J. Crenshaw's theory of the influence of a festival of covenant renewal, expressions of which were preserved in snatches of hymns and sayings that reflect a *theophanic tradition*, celebrating God's advent in Israel's life and history.[3] Central to Crenshaw's approach was the contention not only that Amos used theophanic language but that he regularly reversed it to turn it back on his hearers and judge them with it.

None of these three representative efforts to suggest a

[1]E. Würthwein, 'Amos-Studien', *ZAW*, 62, 1949–50, pp. 10–52.
[2]Wolff's thesis had been anticipated in part by J. Lindblom, 'Wisdom in the OT Prophets', in *Wisdom in Israel and in the Ancient Near East*, VT Supp., 3, 1955, pp. 192–204, and by S. Terrien, 'Amos and Wisdom', in *Israel's Prophetic Heritage*: Fs. J. Muilenburg (New York: Harper & Row, 1962), pp. 108–115. For more recent summaries of the debate about Amos' use of wisdom see Whybray, pp. 181–199, for a somewhat negative view; *cf.* also D. F. Morgan, *Wisdom in the Old Testament Traditions* (Atlanta: John Knox Press, 1981), pp. 76–82, 144–145, for a more positive assessment.
[3]J. Crenshaw, 'The Influence of the Wise upon Amos', *ZAW*, 79, 1967, pp. 42–51; 'Amos and the Theophanic Tradition', *ZAW*, 80, 1968, pp. 203–215.

single, dominant influence to account for Amos' language and themes has gained anything like a solid scholarly consensus. Each has sparked sufficient negative reaction to cast a shadow on its claims.[1] It is probably enough to say with Rudolph (p. 99) and others, that Amos was a wise and well-informed farmer who drew on the covenant traditions of his ancestors as they were preserved both in the liturgy and sayings of the clan. The use of various literary forms argues only that Amos wanted to convey certain nuances in his message to stir the emotions and catch the consciences of his countrymen. We can not assume that such literary forms are clear proof of any single setting in which to explain his message. 'Prophets must have been exposed to many, even opposing, influences, though nobody would deny that they could have relied more on one than on another.'[2]

V. UNITY AND COMPOSITION OF THE BOOK

Passages under question

How much of the book is the words or writing of Amos is a sharply debated question. Here we can do scarcely more than list some of the passages commonly atrributed to later sources (*cf.* Mays, pp. 12–13) then point to the fuller discussion of each in the Commentary.

A. The title (1:1) seems quite clearly to be an editorial preface identifying the author, his personal background, and the timing of his ministry.

B. The oracles against Tyre (1:9–10), *Edom* (1:11–12), and *Judah* (2:4–5) are often viewed as secondary because they lack

---

[1]R. Smend, *EvTh*, 23, 1963, pp. 404–423, and G. Farr, 'The Language of Amos, Popular or Cultic?' *VT*, 16, 1966, pp. 312–324, along with H. W. Wolff, *Prophet*, tackled Würthwein's and Reventlow's approaches and exposed their weaknesses; in turn H. J. Hermisson, *Studien zur israelitischen Spruchweisheit* (WMANT Neukirchen-Vluyn: Neukirchener Verlag, 1968) and H. H. Schmid, 'Amos. Zur frage nach der "geistigen Heimat" des Propheten', *Wort und Dienst* 10, 1969, pp. 85–103, joined Crenshaw in challenging Wolff's thesis; finally, van der Woude, pp. 37–38, has levelled some telling criticisms at Crenshaw.

[2]Van der Woude, p. 38. On the judicious use of form-criticism, which separates literary form from the function or office of the speaker, *cf.* G. Fohrer, 'Bemerkungen zum neueren Verständnis der Propheten' in *Studien zur alttesta-*

the closing messenger formula 'said Yahweh' and have only abbreviated announcements of judgment, thus departing from the stereotyped forms found in the speeches against Damascus (1:3–5), Gaza (1:6–8), Ammonites (1:13–15) and Moab (2:1–3). The argument from literary form seems to cut two ways: variety may be as strong as evidence for authenticity as similarity is. Again, the historical allusions in the speeches against Tyre and Edom are too vague to serve as proof for the post-exilic date sometimes assigned them.

C. The saying on how prophecy works (3:7) is credited to Deuteronomistic sources (sixth century BC) as is the oracle against Judah in 2:4–5. The form of 3:7 interrupts the pattern of disputation questions in 3:3–8, but, as is argued in the Commentary, serves both to increase the power of the climactic words in 3:8 and to underscore the special tie between the Lord and the true prophets.

D. The hymn-fragments (1:2; 4:13; 5:8–9; 8:8; 9:5–6) are seen as insertions in the text on the basis of their use in Judah's worship. The purpose of their inclusion is variously interpreted; most commonly they are seen as a redactor's reinforcement of Yahweh's right and power to judge.[1] The pivotal role played by the doxologies, which both buttress the messages of judgment and fortify the notes of finality (*cf.* the relationship between the hymn at 4:13 and the dirge of 5:1–2 and similarly between the hymn of 9:5–6 and the cataclysmic announcement of 9:8), suggests a highly artful and intentional placement of the hymnic literature. Moreover, if recent structural studies are accurate, the hymn-stanza at 5:8–9 is imbedded in the text with such precision that it forms the capstone of an arch-like structure in which the components from 5:1–7 and 10–17 balance each other symmetrically.[2] Auld's (p. 58) modest conclusion is certainly the least that can be said on the basis of stylistic evidence: 'If not actually contributed by their

---

mentlichen Prophetie (1949–1965), *BZAW*, 99 (Berlin: Walter de Gruyter, 1967), pp. 18–31.
[1] J. L. Crenshaw, *Hymnic Affirmation of Divine Justice*, SBL Dissertation Series 24 (Missoula, Montana: Scholars Press, 1975), pp. 152–153.
[2] J. de Waard, 'The Chiastic Structure of Amos V 1–17', *VT*, 27, 1977, pp. 170–177; N. J. Tromp, 'Amos V 1–17: Towards a Stylistic and Rhetorical Analysis', *OTS*, 23, 1984, pp. 65–85.

author, they (the hymn fragments) are certainly appropriately placed.'

E. The aphoristic saying in 5:13 is frequently heard as an aside, which advises the prudent to be silent in an evil time like this, because one cannot know what risks there are in protesting against the injustices that one sees and hears (Hammershaimb, p. 84).[1] The alternative interpretation in this Commentary, it should be noted, assumes the practice of Amos to use varieties of sayings found in many walks of life, including the domain of the sages. If the *evil time* is seen as the time of coming judgment, disaster-laden, the proverb can be readily understood in this context as Amos' own conclusion.

F. The salvation promises of 9:11–15 are a bone of major contention and are frequently heard as a post-exilic assurance of continuity once the repeatedly announced judgment had taken place. These verses have been described as 'wholly devoid of moral earnestness' (Ward, p. 88) and, therefore, discordant with Amos' main themes. From the standpoints of cultic usage (*e.g.* Reventlow, pp. 90–110), covenant continuity (*e.g.* von Rad, *OT Theology*, II, p. 138), and acknowledged prophetic practice (Hammershaimb, p. 143), cogent reasons have been given to crediting Amos with parts or all of these concluding verses.

Possibilities of redaction
Representative of the many attempts to trace stages in the history of the book's composition is that of H. W. Wolff, who seeks to identify six steps and to assign appropriate parts of Amos to them (pp. 106–113).

A. Words of Amos are found in chapters 3–6, especially in what Wolff calls 'free-witness' speeches: 3:3–8; 4:4–5; 5:7, 10–11, 18–20; 6:12. These are texts that carry no messenger formula or any other introductory rubric and usually mention Yahweh in the third person only. Other passages, introduced by Amos, feature an oracle of Yahweh: 3:1–2, 9–11, 13–15; 4:1–3; 5:1–3, 12, 16–17; 6:1–7, 13–14. Added to these are

---

[1] *Cf.* also R. Martin-Achard, ITC, pp. 43-44. Both Hammershaimb and Martin-Achard recognize the possibility that Amos himself is the speaker.

sayings of Yahweh alone: 3:12; 5:4–5, 21–24, 27 and possibly 6:8. Wolff (p. 107) concludes that the 'basic stock of chapters 3–6' is words of Amos, who himself may have shaped the collection of speeches he delivered largely in Samaria or as an 'itinerant' travelling to Samaria, Bethel and perhaps Gilgal.

B. Literary formation of the cycles – notably the series of vision-reports in 7:1–8; 8:12; 9:1–4 and possibly the judgments against the nations in 1:3 – 2:16 – may have occurred shortly after Amos was banished from Bethel. These more tightly structured and carefully sequenced sections were appended fore and aft to the oracles of chapters 3–6.

C. 'Old school' of Amos describes Wolff's proposed reconstruction (pp. 108–111) of the activities of a group of Amos' followers who laboured in Judah about the time of Assyria's resumption of her westward marches, *i.e.* about 743 BC. They added to Amos' words and to the cycles of international judgment and reports of visions a significant number of passages, including the following: the mention of the earthquake (1:1), and of Beer-sheba (5:5a); the third-person account of Amos' conflict with Amaziah (7:10–17) and the preceding oracle (7:9) which uses 'Isaac' for Israel; 5:13–15; 6:2; 8:4–7 and 8:9–10, 13–14; 9:7–8a and 9:9–10.

D. Reforms of Josiah (*c.* 621 BC) are thought by Wolff (pp. 111–112) to be reflected in some of the sayings about Bethel's altar and its destruction (3:14; 5:6; *cf.* 2 Ki. 23:17), in the hymn-stanzas (4:13; 5:8–9; 9:5–6), in the liturgy of past judgments (4:6–11), and in the theme hymn of 1:2, with its emphasis on Jerusalem. Thus, in Wolff's view, the message of Amos was somewhat updated in Judah in the seventh century and used to undergird the attempts of Josiah to enforce the Book of the Law (2 Ki. 22), even to the destruction of Bethel's hallowed precincts.

E. Deuteronomistic editing (*c.* 550 BC) is thought by Wolff to have added the oracle against Judah and Jerusalem (2:4–5) in recognition that the Southern Kingdom too had come under divine judgment, and also the speeches against Tyre and Edom (1:9–12) in imitation of Ezekiel's taunts against the two neighbour nations (Tyre, Ezk. 26 – 28; Edom, Ezk.

AMOS

25:12–14), doomed to judgment because of pride, greed and savagery. References to Zion (Am. 6:1) and descriptions of Israel that seem to include Judah as well (3:2; 6:1) are credited to this exilic editing along with the positive descriptions of the Exodus, wilderness wanderings and settlement in 2:10–12 and 5:25–26. Finally, the fixing of Amos' date in the reigns of Jeroboam II and Uzziah (1:1) and the succinct summary of the relationship between divine activity and the prophetic word (3:7) bear the Deuteronomistic fingerprints.[1]

F. Post-exilic promises of salvation (9:11–15) were added to reflect the ways in which Yahweh had preserved his people and was yet to give them days of glory. As a bridge to these oracles of hope this editing inserted the exception clause that distinguishes between exile and annihilation (9:8b). In Wolff's view no previous redaction had brought anything like the salvation promises of 9:11–15 to the text, though the old school of Amos allowed for the 'it may be' clause of grace in 5:15.

Brief comments in response to Wolff's approach to the history of Amos' composition may be in order. First, Wolff himself acknowledges certain difficulties in assigning some of the components of the text to a given stage: distinctions between the words of Amos and the additions of the 'old school' cannot always 'be clearly determined' (p. 107); it is possible that 5:25–26 and 2:1–12 should be assigned to the 'old school' rather than to the Deuteronomistic editing (p. 110); 'it is uncertain' whether the threat of famine for Yahweh's word is Deuteronomistic or 'old school' (p. 113). Second, the varieties of opinions on the development of the book issued by scholars before and after Wolff suggest that caution be our course in adopting any given theory of the book's history.[2] Hammershaimb's verdict (pp. 14–15) may be cited as

[1]Wolff's view of Deuteronomistic editing was based, in part, on W. H. Schmidt, 'Die Deuteronomische Redaktion des Amosbuches. Zu den theologischen Unterschieden zwischen dem Propheten Wort und seinem Sammler', *ZAW*, 77, 1965, pp. 168–193.
[2]This variety is confirmed by a glance at a sampling of Old Testament introductions. G. Fohrer, *Introduction to the Old Testament* (E.T., Nashville, New York: Abingdon Press, 1968), pp. 433–437, and Weiser, *Old Testament*, pp. 243–245, stress the existence of independent collections of oracles and vision reports combined over time by Amos' followers. Kaiser, p. 218, follows Wolff's schema without much comment. Soggin, p. 244, commenting on

a strong counter-opinion to Wolff's approach: 'there is little against accepting that almost all the book goes back to Amos himself. . . . Indeed most of the book could have been written down in small sections by Amos himself (if he could write) or dictated by him to his disciples.'

Third, the basic method of dating portions of books as additions whose history can be identified by means of their content is under question at present. Our tools are inadequate; our methods may put the emphases where they ought not to be; our results will be probable at best. 'At the present state of our knowledge, a precise and detailed reconstruction of the course that the redaction process took cannot but be conjectural in large part.'[1] Fourth, the text as we now have it must be given at least as much attention as we assign to attempts to reconstruct the history of a book. The Commentary will point out numbers of instances where the literary unity of a passage is more prominent than the distinctives of its component parts.[2] What we now have is a closely crafted, artfully stylized composition. We should look more at it, rather than at how it got to be what it is, if only because of the inadequacy of our attempts at reconstruction. Biblical study is not archaeology. We do not have clearly distinguishable strata as we might find them in an undisturbed *tell*. We have finely woven threads of composition to which the people of God through the ages have clung and from which they have received warning, comfort and instruction. The approach of this Commentary will view the text as it is and seek to garner its meaning from that perspective.[3]

Finally, we must understand the inspiration and authority of Scripture in a way that allows for editorial activity as part of

---

9:11–14, seems to vote with those 'who argue for its authenticity' as an oracle of Amos. Coote (p. 8) has reduced the history of composition to three stages, while acknowledging substantial debt to Wolff: (A) eight century, before 722 BC; (B) seventh century, roughly during Josiah's reign; (C) sixth century, toward or at the close of the Babylonian exile.

[1]Van der Woude, p. 42.

[2]Auld's conclusion is pertinent (p. 74): 'We have detected no tension between the "compositions" such as the opening chapters, or 4:6ff. and 5:1–17, or the visions, on the one side and their constituent parts on the other. . . . The wholes and parts complement each other excellently. There may be no need to postulate in these sections the activity of a different "hand".'

[3]On the need to see texts whole, including the entire Bible, see J. F. A. Sawyer, pp. 243–246.

the process. Works like Proverbs and Psalms show obvious marks of a history of being collected. The diverse forms of Jeremiah in MT and LXX indicate some substantial editing as part of what gave them birth. Caution about the history of any one portion of the Old Testament does not mean we must become absolutists in attributing every word of a book to its assigned author. But, we should not become faddists for a single methodology. Our work should leave no valid tool of research unused, but our ultimate confidence is in the text we have been given, not in the tools we have developed.

VI. LITERARY FORMS

To Amos' literary skill this tribute has been paid: 'No prophet surpasses him in the combination of purity, clarity, and versatility that characterize his language' (Mays, p. 6). Since most of the forms and devices that make the book so distinguished have been pointed out in the course of the comments, we need here to provide only a concise inventory of the major types of speeches and other rhetorical techniques and to suggest ways in which the literary style reinforced the immediate power and lasting impact of the message.

Major categories
Some samples of Amos' main forms:

Judgment speeches, almost entirely poetic, are the backbone of the book. They may be introduced by a 'messenger formula', usually include an accusation (or indictment) of sin and an announcement (or threat) of punishment, sometimes employ 'therefore' as a word of transition between accusation and announcement, and may conclude with an oracle or closing messenger formula ('said Yahweh' or 'utterance of Yahweh'). They may take a first-person form with Yahweh as speaker (*e.g.* 1:3 – 3:2; 5:25–27; 6:11–14; 8:2–3, 7–14; 9:7–10) or a 'free-witness' form (to use Wolff's term, p. 91) in which the prophet proclaims judgment without directly quoting Yahweh's words (*e.g.* 4:1–3). Each component of the judgment speech has significance for its message: (1) the *messenger formula* authenticates the oracle as the very word of Yahweh and establishes the prophet's role as the Lord's specifically commissioned legate who neither composed the oracle nor volunteered to deliver it (Am. 3:8; 7:14–15); (2) the combination of *accusation* and *announcement* demonstrates the justice of Yahweh who neither overlooks the transgressions of his people nor punishes them arbitrarily but carefully suits the punishment to the crime; (3) *therefore* underscores this equity and reminds the people that their sins will find them out; (4) the closing formulas both mark the end of a speech and reinforce its divine origin. Part of Amos' importance in biblical life is that he was, as far as can be documented, the first prophet to apply the judgment speech and its messenger formula to the entire nation, not just individuals within the nation (*cf.* 2 Ki. 1).

Vision reports are a second major component of the book (7:1–3, 4–6, 7–9; 8:1–2; 9:1–4). Their role is to make clear to Amos and the people to whom he reported them the fact, need, timing and inescapability of judgment. The graphic autobiographical prose form ('he showed me'; 'I saw') makes the message indelible, while the interpersonal communication described in the vision allows for conversation (including questions) between Yahweh and the prophet as well as divine interpretation of the vision, the latter usually in poetic style. The form and the message combine to authenticate the prophet's divinely appointed role as both seer and proclaimer (Am. 1:1; 7:12).

Biographical narrative describes the important report of the conflict between Amos and Amaziah, chief priest of Bethel (7:10–17). The report itself is in prose, while the oracle quoted within it (v. 11) and Amos' judgment speech which concludes it (vv. 16–17) are in poetry. The combination of biographical and autobiographical materials in Amos 7 – 8 is paralleled by the stories of Hosea's marriage recounted in Hosea 1 (biographical) and 3 (autobiographical). It is hard to know how much weight to place on this divergence of style. The usual formula of attributing the first-person reports to the prophet and the third-person reports to the disciples is attractive, but may be a little pat when applied to prophetic literature which tends to exhibit a considerable degree of flexibility in grammar and style.

Salvation promise is the appropriate name for the prophecies of hope and restoration with which the book closes (9:11–15). The

103

AMOS

eschatological formulas 'in that day' (v. 11) and 'behold, the days are coming' (v. 13), the verbs that point to the future, and the use of traditional language of blessing, *e.g.* 'I will restore the fortunes of my people' (v. 14), combine to distinguish this oracle from any other in the book. Its role can be understood best as hope to be proffered after judgment has run its course. It does not witness to Israel's escape from judgment but to God's constancy in keeping covenant after judgment has worked its havoc.

Other categories
Now we will look at some of his other techniques:

Disputation questions, which are usually rhetorical and coupled in parallelism, punctuate the book at several key points. They draw undebatable lessons from nature (3:3–6, 8) and history (5:25–26; 9:7) or ask absurd questions to call attention to absurd actions (6:12). The arguments from natural observation appear to reflect the techniques often employed in Israel's wisdom literature and have the force of exposing Israel's wicked stupidity by pointing out what they plainly should have understood.

Instructions to a herald are used to dramatize Israel's corruption in 3:9. Commands are issued to summon Ashdod and Egypt, two bastions of paganism, to serve as witnesses to the crimes of God's people.

A legal proof saying, in prose, seems to have been employed in 3:12. Amos' vocation had undoubtedly made him familiar with the laws that required a shepherd to preserve any bits or pieces of sheep slaughtered by a wild beast in order to demonstrate that the sheep's disappearance was not the result of rustling or carelessness.

Admonitions based on the instructions of priests are offered both in parody form (4:4–5) and in full sincerity (5:4–7, 14–15, 23–24). The inference to be drawn is that the official priests had failed in their responsibility to teach the way of life, and Yahweh, through the prophet, had himself to discharge that duty.[1]

[1]See A. V. Hunter, p. 278, for the view that the exhortations did not offer a way of escape through repentance before judgment fell but reinforced the need for judgment by facing the people with what they should have done.

104

Oaths have the effect of giving the judgment threats their ultimate solemnification (4:2; 6:8; 8:7). God resorts to them as the strongest way of promising the certainty of punishment. The third oath in this trio seems to be another instance of irony or sarcasm: Yahweh swears not by himself but by the *pride of Jacob* that had apparently swelled to monumental proportions.

Woes are found twice in the text (5:18; 6:1) and are special promises of trouble that will accrue when unacceptable behaviour has been practised.[1] They add a note of lament, almost funereal, to the text, while suggesting that bad behaviour and wrong beliefs inevitably lead to disaster as the wisdom of the clans had indicated.

Hymn stanzas punctuate the text at several key points, using the Hebrew participles to describe the unique activity of Yahweh in his mastery of the creation (4:13; 5:8–9; 8:9; 9:5–6) and the sovereign power of his judging word (1:2). In each case these snatches of Israel's hymnody have been torn from their liturgical setting and used, in virtually ironic tones, to confront Israel with Yahweh's awesome power to judge and to commandeer any part of the created order to implement that judgment.

Reports of God's past judgment are linked together in a five-part chain (4:6–11), each part clearly divided from the preceding by the indictment *yet you did not return to me* and the oracle formula *says the Lord* (lit. 'uttered of the Lord'). The reports and their negative result serve as a highly patterned form of accusation to which verse 12 is attached as announcement. Together they remind the people that judgment is an act of grace designed to draw the nation back to Yahweh and that such grace spurned becomes the ground for greater judgment (Vollmer, pp. 8–20).

Dirge or *lamentation* is what 5:1 calls 5:2. The doleful language, usually reserved for the bereaved to express the pain of fatal loss, is applied to Israel in a way that throws the dark shroud of doom over any hope of survival.

---

[1]RSV and some commentaries (*e.g.* Wolff, pp. 229–272) assume that *woe* was

Frequent literary devices

Some examples of these are:

Repetition, especially in the sequences of materials that high-light the book (*e.g.* 1:3 – 2:8; 3:3–6, 8; 4:6–11; 5:4–5, 14–15; vision reports, chs. 7–9; hymn stanzas, 4:13; 5:8–9; 8:9; 9:5–6), was frequently and artfully used to aid the memories of the hearers (or readers) and thus to reinforce the impact of the materials so that the climax of each sequence would be spotlighted. If repetition is the first law of pedagogy, Amos was a master of the craft.

Calls to attention seem to substitute for the messenger for-mula in several pivotal speeches. *Hear this word* (3:1; 4:1; 5:1) and *hear this* (8:4) are like introductions to the announcements of a herald and serve to rivet the audience's attention on the importance and authority of what is to be said.

Quotations frequently help to back-light the audiences' points of view (2:12; 4:1; 6:2, 13; 7:11, 16; 8:5–6, 14; 9:10). The effect is to increase the condemnation by citing the words of the accused hearers (including Amos in 7:11) as testimony against them.

Responses to verbal opposition seem to be part of the background of the disputation questions (see above) and other sayings. Some abrupt changes in tone or style may well signal that Amos' public proclamations were interrupted by members of the audience, perhaps priests (see Introduction to Hosea for similar situations), who in turn were answered, usually with bite and barb, by the prophet (*e.g.* 2:11; 3:3–8, following 3:2; 3:12 answering protests after 3:11; 5:25–26 as further argu-ment when the people had rejected the point of 5:21–24).

Punning was a ready tool of the prophets and Amos used it at a notable point in predicting the downfall of the shrines at Bethel and Gilgal (5:5). The message of the fourth vision was based on the pun between *qāyiṣ*, 'basket of summer fruit', and *qēṣ*, 'end' (8:1–2).

originally in the text at 5:7 and 6:3 (or 6:4 rsv). Rudolph (p. 101, n. 1) proposes that *woe* has dropped out of 5:7 and 6:13 (not 6:3). See Commentary for ways to handle text as we have it.

Gestures to reinforce and clarify a point may be the best way to understand the *thus* and *this* of 4:12. Some threatening action like stabbing or throat-cutting may have been symbolized by the prophet's own body language as he spoke for Yahweh.

A study of Amos' rhetoric would be a book in itself. This sampling will suffice to help us know some of the key forms and techniques in the book and the light they cast on its pages. At our distance from Amos we are deprived of some of the chief tools of oral communication: tone of voice, facial expression, body language. The absence of these makes it imperative for us to catch as many clues from the text as we can.

Literary forms and stylistic patterns are like background music in the cinema. They do not tell the whole story; the dialogue and pictures carry the larger burden of communication. But the music helps to alert the emotions to grasp the connotations of the action. It prepares our feelings to catch the varied moods of the film and thus, almost subliminally, aids in the reception of the inner meanings of the story.

To hear a battle cry, a love song, an oath, a lament, a hymn, a proverb, a parable, a complaint, a herald's command, or a messenger's attestation is to begin to flesh out the nuances of the text in ways that a simple reading of the words will not do. It is that concern to hear as much as possible of what the biblical words are saying that has prompted the attention to form and technique in this Commentary.

This is not to say that by a study of literary forms we can reconstruct the intellectual and spiritual background of the prophet. From the forms we can discern something of the *literary intent* of the speeches and their composition into the larger whole of the book. And we can do this without becoming advocates of a specific background for Amos and without reducing him to the shadow-role of compiler of pre-formed material. With all the other great prophets he used what he had acquired from the traditions of his people and their faith and then with startling artistry, under the Spirit's guidance, recombined the literary approaches into an assemblage that can only be called unique, original and compelling.

VII. THE MESSAGE

Major themes

Amos' dominant emphasis is *Yahweh's rejection of Israel's social*

and religious practices. 'The sum total of his visions and oracles
is contained in a single word: "no"' (Crenshaw, p. 247). Amos
pulls out all the literary and theological stops to play this
negative theme at full volume. Israel, notably the political,
economic and religious leaders, are held accountable. They
have said 'no' to Yahweh in every area of their lives. The list of
their crimes would fill an out-sized police-blotter: enslaving
their countrymen for petty debts (2:6; 8:6), perverting justice
for the disadvantaged (2:7–8; 5:10, 12, 15), practising incest
(2:7), exacting harsh taxes (2:8; 3:10; 5:11), throttling the
prophets who would condemn such deeds (2:12; 3:8;
7:12–13), maintaining an extravagant life-style at the expense
of the poor (4:1; 6:1–6), failing to heed the warnings implicit
in their experiences of disaster (4:6–11), engaging in religious
exercises that were both insincere and tainted with paganism
(5:4–5, 21–27; 8:4–5, 13–14), presuming that the Lord's
future held only blessings for them (5:18–20; 9:10), resting
securely in their military prowess and invulnerable defences
(3:11; 6:2–3, 8), peacocking in their covenant privileges while
ignoring God's sovereign care of other nations (3:1–2; 9:7).[1]

Yahweh had no choice but to say 'no' to such conduct. And
its indelible and persistent character led him to say an even
stronger 'no' to Israel's future as a political entity. Almost two
centuries of crime-laden living were enough and more than
enough. A nation that could not be corrected had to be rejected. The judgment announcements and vision-reports
made graphically plain the nature, necessity and thoroughness of that judgment. The *end* (8:1–2; *cf.* 7:8; 9:1–4, 8–10) is
the succinct summary of Israel's fate, as sure and final as the
ringing down of a theatre curtain or the final frames of a
motion picture. More than any of the prophets before him,
Amos sees that Israel is engulfed in 'ruin which can no longer
be dealt with in terms of domestic politics, either through
reform or revolution' (Koch, p. 66). Judgment was the only
effective answer.

Four levels are discernible in that programme of judgment
(*cf.* Koch, pp. 63–65). First, at the *personal, divine* level, Yahweh takes full responsibility for the judgment – 'I will send

---

[1]For further background on the exploitation condemned by the prophets,
including legal oppression, by the plutocracy, see J. Pons, *L'Opression dans
l'Ancien Testament* (Paris: Letouzey et Ané, 1981).

fire' (1:4, *etc.*), 'I will punish' (lit. 'visit'; 3:2, 14), 'I will set my eyes upon them for evil and not for good' (9:4). The crimes are directed towards him and, consequently, the ultimate obligation to punish them is his. Second, at the level of *creation*, the earth is engaged in the judgment task. It rises up against the wicked Israelites (8:8) and shakes under their feet (2:13). Its quaking seems to be what Yahweh used to fulfill the command for the shrine and its altar to be shattered on the heads of the rebellious pilgrims (9:1). Amos' tendency to use theophanic language suggests that the earth does not quake on its own but in manifestations of the divine presence on the march in judgment. Third, at the level of *'moral causality'* (Koch's term, p. 64), judgments take place as the appropriate effects of Israel's wicked behaviour: their violence towards others triggers violence against them (3:11; 5:11); their rejection of the divine word through the prophet (2:12; 7:12–13) will launch a famine of that word throughout the land (8:11–12). The Lord of heaven and earth has so constructed life's patterns that present behaviour, in large measure, determines future outcome, a point that Israel's wisdom teachers made a regular part of their curriculum.[1] Fourth, at the level of *political history*, military intervention (probably by the Assyrians, though Amos does not name them) becomes a major means of judgment, involving invasion of the land (3:11), devastation of Israel's armies (5:3), destruction of the cities and shrines (3:14), decimation of the populace (6:9–10), occupation of the territory (6:14), and exile of the leadership (4:2–3; 5:27). Taken together these four levels form a remarkable tribute to the sovereignty of Yahweh who has means beyond measure with which to enact his righteous will. No wonder he is frequently called 'Lord of hosts' (3:13; 4:13; 5:14–16, 27; 6:8, 14; 9:5).[2]

Correlative to the theme of divine judgment on Israel's social and religious rebellion was Amos' declaration of *Yahweh's sovereignty over every area of life in heaven and on earth.* Whatever else can be said about Amos' background and the ways it influenced his message, 'first and foremost must have been his overwhelming encounter with God' (Gottwald, p.

---

[1] D. A. Hubbard, 'Proverbs, Book of', *ISBE*, rev., III, p. 1019.
[2] See Wolff, pp. 287–288, for the opinion that this form of the divine name was the redactor's way of describing Yahweh's sovereignty.

357). This encounter shaped both his call (of which he has left us no detailed account) and the content of his message, whose major subject is Yahweh. The other possible strands that are woven into his message – the covenant and election traditions of his tribe and family, the international (even cosmic) understanding of life transmitted by the sages, the ancient customs that regulate tribal and village life and perhaps some memory of the connection between *'El 'Elyon* (the supreme God of Jerusalem; Gn. 14:18–22) and Yahweh which freed Amos to think of Yahweh in universal terms[1] – appear to be held together by the awesome impact of Amos' own experience with Yahweh. He had heard and faced the Lion (1:2; 3:8), and his whole ministry was framed by that meeting.

The people's past deliverance from Egypt, gift of the land and establishment of righteous leaders (2:9–11; 3:1–2; 9:7) were the works of Yahweh's hands. So were their future judgment (9:1–4) and restoration (9:11–15). No disaster crushed a city except by his doing (3:6). The history of his people – with its cycle of salvation, judgment and salvation – was his affair.

The special covenant relation with Israel in no way fenced off Yahweh from the activities of the pagan nations. Their migrations were governed by his majesty as had been Israel's Exodus (9:7). Their rulers were no less accountable to him than was Jeroboam II (1:3 – 2:3; 7:9). The welfare of Israel's enemies was Yahweh's passionate concern; their inhumanity was as insufferable to him as was Israel's exploitation of the needy. And their future destiny – the fire of Yahweh's anger – was determined by him, not by their local deities, whose names they invoked and whose shrines they frequented. What is explicitly true of the tiny states of Syro-Palestine who are hailed into court in 1:3 – 2:5 is implied of the powerful nation that stands on call, poised to invade, destroy, occupy and exile the Northern Kingdom. Assyria, proud and powerful and anonymous in Amos, will be a tool in Yahweh's hand, the *sword* that denies escape to even the sturdiest survivors (9:4).

Sovereign over his own people, over the nations, and, indeed over the whole creation was Amos' Lord. Famine, drought, blight, plague and holocaust were all within his

---

[1]We may posit some such background without leaning as heavily on Canaanite precedents as has Kapelrud, pp. 42–47.

power, when lessons of judgment were to be taught (4:6–11). The mountains, wind and daily cycles of light and darkness bow to his authority (4:13). Constellations, eclipses, rainstorms, earthquakes are in his charge (5:8–9; 8:8–9; 9:5–6). Locusts ravage at his bidding and retreat at his signal (7:1–3). His fiery presence can consume both the land and the deep, which are his creations (7:4–6). Brown, barren mountains teem with life-giving fruit when he says the time is right (9:13–15).

This all-embracing picture of sovereignty serves one basic purpose in the text: to bring Israel's fantasies of invulnerability down to size. The misunderstood sense of chosenness had combined in the eighth century with a measure of military advance, territorial enlargement and material prosperity to elevate Israel in their own eyes. Superior to the nations was how they viewed themselves, and special to God. That self-exaltation inevitably clouded their sense of obligation to and dependence on him and threatened to reduce him to their benign, private caretaker. His righteousness was interpreted as a readiness always to do right by them.

Amaziah's attempt to ban Amos from the shrine at Bethel and to stifle his prophetic activity was nothing less than an affront to Yahweh's sovereignty. 'The prostitution of the cult into a sanctuary of the king pushed Yahweh from the centre, and placed an idol at the heart of the nation's worship' (Hanson, p. 157). Spiritually the situation was intolerable. It threatened the very order of the universe that Israel celebrated in their worship.

Then came the prophets, first Amos and next Hosea. They denied 'that Israel's life was divinely guaranteed as permanent. Such an unprecedented relativizing of Israel's life in the face of God's righteousness was itself a decisive advance in the perception of the nature of Yahweh as transcendent' (Nicholson, pp. 208–209). A chief task of Amos, then, was to confront Israel with a realistic picture both of their frailty and failure and of Yahweh's unchanging uniqueness as Saviour, Lord and Judge. So intense was his focus on that uniqueness that he says nothing about the pagan deities like Baal (Wolff, p. 101).[1]

Underlying Amos' notes of sovereignty and judgment is the

---

[1] For a possible exception, see comments on 5:26.

theme of *Yahweh's election of Israel in a covenantal relationship.*
Amos never uses the word 'covenant' (Heb. *bᵉrît*; *cf.* on Ho.
2:20; 6:7; 8:1; 10:4) to describe the bond between Yahweh
and Israel (*bᵉrît* in 1:9 is a treaty between nations'; *cf.* on Ho.
12:1), but the concept of such an alliance seems to serve as
foundation for many of his chief emphases.[1] The evidences of
covenantal motifs are more than ample, despite our inability
to pin-point their source (see The Setting of the Book, above).
In indicting Israel for the oppression of the poor and the
violation of the rights of the under-represented in society,
Amos never cites a specific law nor spends time instructing in
the law. The primary assumption of such indictments is that
Israel knew right from wrong on the basis of the traditions of
their faith, whether transmitted within the cult, the written
law (*e.g.* 'The Book of Covenant,' Ex. 20:21 – 23:19), or the
humanitarian teachings of the clan elders. There was a relationship, a bond, that set the bounds of Israel's behaviour,
branded the transgressions of these bounds as wicked, and
prescribed judgment as the appropriate divine response.
    That bond was intimated in the references to Israel's elec-
tion and Exodus (2:9–11; 3:1–2; 9:7) and in the description of
Israel as 'my people' (7:8, 15; 8:2; 9:10, 14) which is balanced
by the other half of the covenant-formula, 'your God' (9:15;
cf. on Ho. 1:10; 2:23). For Amos the demands of the covenant
were summed up in two words *justice* and *righteousness* (5:7, 24;
6:12), on which he never expounds except in his descriptions
of the wickedness wrought in their absence. The fact that he
neither attempts their definition nor applies them directly to
Yahweh seems to be a clear indication that Israel knew what
they meant and why they were important as expressions of the
Lord's own person.

---

[1]Some of the more recent commentaries have played down the contribution
of the covenant to Amos' message (*cf.* Martin-Achard, pp. 75–77) under the
influence of scholars who have argued for a late development (7th century) of
covenantal motifs in the Old Testament, *e.g.* E. Kutsch, *Verheissung und Gesetz.
Untersuchungen zum sogenannten 'Bund' im Alten Testament*, BZAW, 131 (Berlin
and New York: Walter de Gruyter, 1973); L. Perlitt, *Bundestheologie im Alten
Testament*, WMANT 36 (Neukirchen-Vluyn: Neukirchener Verlag, 1969). The
approach of the present Commentary is that covenant-theology is fundamental
to Amos (and Hosea), even where technical terms may not be present. Support
for this view is found in J. Bright, *Covenant and Promise* (Philadelphia:
Westminster Press, 1976) pp. 83–87; van der Woude, p. 38; Phillips, p. 218;
Nicholson, pp. 206–210; Hanson, pp. 148–158.

Again, Amos seemed to have taken for granted (and to have expected his hearers to do likewise) the intimate connection between true worship and sound conduct. The first two references to the dirth of justice and righteousness occur in contexts that either encourage proper worship (5:4–7) or denounce improper worship (5:21–24). Yet Amos never makes the connection explicitly. We do not hear him say that God's people must emulate the characteristics of the Lord whom they serve if their worship is to be valid and that two of those characteristics are justice and righteousness, especially towards the underprivileged. What can such silence signal but the assumed relationship between privilege and responsibility that is central to the concept of covenant? That signal becomes even clearer when we note the disputation questions with which Amos argued for the indispensability of justice and righteousness in the common life of Israel (6:12). To fail to practise them is to succumb to absurdity, like a cavalry officer who would run horses up the rocky steeps or a farmer who would yoke a brace of oxen to plough furrows in the sea.

'The covenant-theology represented at once an indicative and an imperative: the indicative, Israel's constitution as the people of Yahweh; the imperative, Israel's vocation to be the people of Yahweh' (Nicholson, p. 210). The *indicative* part of the grammar was firmly in place: 'You only have I known of all the families of the earth' (3:2). God's elective love (*known*) had made Israel his people, both in the patriarchal traditions – note Amos' use of Jacob (7:2, 5), Joseph (5:6, 15; 6:6), and Isaac (7:9, 16) – and in the Exodus and conquest (2:9–11; 3:1–2; 9:7). But the *imperative* would not parse: Israel rejected the divine vocation – a far more intimate relationship to Yahweh than the nations enjoyed – and thus shattered the syntax of the covenant oath.

Finally, the assumption of a covenant relationship probably accounts for the brief elements of hope found in the text.[1] The *admonitions* to seek Yahweh and his good ways (5:4–7, 14–15), with the muted expectation that his grace may set aside his judgment, best make sense in their dark context of doom when heard as reminders of Yahweh's commitment to

[1] Some Jewish interpreters find ground for hope in 4:12, reading it as a call to repentance. *Cf* Buber, p. 106; Heschel, pp. 36–38 and especially p. 36, n. 9, where he cites Rashi and Kimhi as support. For a contrary interpretation, see comments.

Israel and his desire for fellowship – a key component to the covenant along with obedience (Nicholson, p. 215) – with his chosen ones. Amos' *pleas* for reversal of judgment are couched in terms of Jacob's smallness, an expression that may well suggest Israel's covenant dependence on Yahweh and helplessness without him (7:2, 5; see Commentary). The *exception clause* that closes 9:8 also may have covenantal intimations. It points to a continuity of the people, a remnant perhaps, even when the political structures of the Northern Kingdom are levelled. The concluding salvation promise (9:11–15) seems to reflect this pivotal role of the covenant. What Hosea saw so clearly and wove into the very fabric of his book, Amos surely could have sensed and uttered, if only to his own followers: after the covenant God had inflicted the necessary curses, the love that had prompted him to elect Israel in the first place would again prevail to continue his work of salvation in history by the reinstitution of Davidic power and righteousness and the restoration of material prosperity (Koch, pp. 69–70).

The evidence surveyed here has pointed to a covenantal relationship between Yahweh and Israel as one of Amos' prime assumptions. We cannot, in my judgment, go beyond this to view Amos as covenant mediator, nor to see his speeches as covenant lawsuits, nor to find in his words relics of covenant renewal ceremonies (van der Woude, pp. 38–39). Moreover, nothing in Amos supports the theories, now being sharply modified if not abandoned, that sought to understand the covenant in the light of ancient Middle Eastern (especially Hittite) treaty patterns.[1] Rather we have tried to see the covenantal bond as a unique expression of Israel's faith framed in the context of the encounter with Yahweh as Lord and Saviour. The elements of love that underlie both Yahweh's election and his wrath at Israel's wicked responses to the election cannot be accounted for on the basis of political analogies alone. They are better explained in the language of the marital and familial love displayed in the life and words of Hosea.[2]

The last 'theme warranting comment here is *Yahweh's*

---

[1]Nicholson, pp. 56–82, traces the rise and fall of this theory.
[2]I have found Nicholson's *God and His People* a helpful resource for tracing covenant backgrounds in the Old Testament. I do not, however, agree with his conclusion that the prophets were innovators in their understanding of the covenant (*cf.* pp. 191–193).

INTRODUCTION

irresistible word.[1] Crucial to our appreciation of the Hebrew prophets is our grasp of what the divine word meant to them. More than anything else it was that reception of the word that marked them off from their friends and neighbours. And their proclamation of that word only increased the distance between them and others. 'The prophet's word is a scream in the night. While the world is at ease and asleep, the prophet feels the blast from heaven' (Heschel, p. 16).

Amos had not only to announce the word with its blast of judgment, but he had also to defend before his angry countrymen his right to declare it. He did so in two key passages, both of which pound home the inevitability of his mission: (1) the chain of disputation questions (3:3–8) builds to its climax with the declaration that, once God has spoken, the prophet's response is a reflex action, as much beyond personal control as the chilling fear prompted by a lion's unexpected roar (3:8); (2) Amos' rebuttal to Amaziah's command to go home centres in the involuntary nature of prophetic ministry – 'the Lord took me . . . and the Lord said to me, "Go, prophesy to my people Israel"' (7:15).

Consequently, Amos' ministry stemmed not so much from the fact that he had grasped the word, as that the word has grasped him – and irresistibly. He knew not only theologically but personally that, once launched, the word of Yahweh would accomplish its purposes unless Yahweh himself called it back. The theme verse (1:2) sounds the warning that no spot in the whole land offers shelter once that word is on the wind. What Yahweh will not call back (*revoke* or 'cause to return') in the oracles against the nations (1:3 – 2:5) is the word which works its wrath. Only he, not the prophet, could nullify the words of devastation in the first two visions (7:1–6). Amos might plead, but the Lord alone could reverse the word with, 'this shall not be'.

Given the nature of the divine word, to try to resist it was both the height of folly, as the disputation questions indicate (3:3–8), and the depth of wickedness, as the threats to Amaziah (7:16–17) and the people (2:12–16; 8:11–12) reveal. The word was irresistible because it was virtually an extension of Yahweh's person. It is more than sound-waves or collections

---

[1]On this whole theme, see H. W. Wolff, *Confrontations with Prophets* (E.T., Philadelphia: Fortress Press, 1983), pp. 9–21.

of syllables. It has to it 'something of an objective reality'.[1] The fact that Hebrew *dābār* means both 'word' and 'thing' bears this out. At considerable pain to the prophet the word was received and transmitted, its effectiveness assured by the God who had decreed it. At considerable pain it was received by the people; even greater pain was their lot when they ignored it.

Contribution to other Old Testament passages[2]
We will look first at Isaiah and then Jeremiah.

Isaiah of Jerusalem appears to have been familiar with texts and themes preserved from the ministry of Amos. Of special note is the relationship between certain woe oracles (Am. 6:1–7; Is. 5:11–13). Beyond that are general themes found in both prophets: condemnations of the cult (Am. 2:7–8; 5:10–12; Is. 1:12–17), of the perversions of justice (Am. 2:7–8; 5:10–12; Is. 1:21–23), of the extravagance of wealthy women (Am. 4:1–3; Is. 3:16–4:1), of the drunken orgies of the nobility (Am. 6:4–7; Is. 28:1–8).[3] In these and other matters Isaiah has both followed the path of Amos' indictments of Samaria and broken fresh ground in addressing the needs of Jerusalem.

Jeremiah, so profoundly influenced by Hosea (see Introduction to Hosea), apparently found the seeds of many of his speeches in Amos, although precise relationships are difficult to trace. The call-visions based on word-play and symbolic object (Am. 7:7–9; 8:1–2; Je. 1:11–15), descriptions of the panic of routed soldiers (Am. 2:15–16; Je. 46:6), the stubbornness of rebel citizens which both prophets decry (Am. 4:6–12; Je. 5:3) are but a sample of suggestions as to how the seventh-century servant of Yahweh in Jerusalem drew on the thought and expressions of his earlier counterpart in the north.[4]

---

[1]A. R. Johnson, *The Cultic Prophet in Ancient Israel* (Cardiff: University of Wales, 1962), p. 37.
[2]The material sketched here is condensed from R. Martin-Achard, pp. 171–175.
[3]For detailed discussions of the possible relationships between the writings of the two prophets, see R. Fey, *Amos und Jesaja. Abhängigkeit und Eigenständigkeit des Jesaja*, WMANT (Neukirchen-Vluyn: Neukirchener Verlag, 1963); pp. 80–85; J. Vermeylen, *Du prophète Isaïe a l'Apocalyptique. Isaie 1–35, miroir d'un demi-millénaire d'experience religieuse en Israël*, tome 2 (Paris: Gabalda, 1978), pp. 519-569.
[4]J. M. Berridge, 'Jeremia und die Prophetie des Amos', *ThZ*, 35, 1979,

Use in the New Testament[1]

Amos' direct impact on the New Testament seems surprisingly small, given his importance in the history of Old Testament prophecy. Some brief verbal affinities may exist between Amos 3:7 and Revelation 10:7; 11:18, between Amos 3:13 (LXX) and Revelation 1:8, and between Amos 9:1 and Revelation 8:3. Also, at least one scholar has suggested some parallels in language and thought between passages in James (*e.g.* 2:6, 12–13; 5:1–6) and the social concerns of Amos.[2] These parallels seem to reflect a common understanding of biblical ethics rather than a direct influence.

There are, however, two passages that are cited directly in the New Testament and also in the Qumran literature: Amos 5:25–27 in Acts 7:42–43; Amos 9:11–12 in Acts 15:16–17.[3] Luke's use of the Amos oracles comes at pivotal places in his arguments (see Commentary for fuller explication): the first passage he used to document the history of Israel's rejection of God and their rejection by him, motifs central to Stephen's defence of his commitment to Christ; the second, found with strong Messianic implications in the Qumran community, is employed in Acts, with James as speaker, to demonstrate that a feature of the Davidic kingdom, restored in Christ, was that Gentiles would seek the Lord and be called by his name.

---

pp. 321–341. For Amos' impact on Joel, see Introduction to Joel above. We may also note similarities between Amos' condemnation of leaders for their abuse of the poor and Micah's similar thrusts. The dark picture of the Day of Yahweh in Zephaniah probably owes something to Amos, while Zechariah's forms of vision reports may be modifications of those found first in Amos. Two passages in the books of Kings have been singled out for comment: first, F. Crüsemann, 'Kritik an Amos im deuteronomistischen Geschichtswerk, Erwägungen zu 2 Könige 14, 27', *Probleme biblischer Theologie*, Fs. G. von Rad (München: 1971), pp. 57-63, has found in 2 Ki. 14:27 a refutation of Amos' message that Ephraim's destruction was final. However, J. Briend, 'Jeroboam II, sauveur d'Israël', *Mélanges bibliques et orientaux en l'honneur de M. Henri Cazelles*, AOAT, 212, 1981, pp. 41–49, has disputed this interpretation. Second, correspondences have been drawn between Amos' conflict with Amaziah (7:10–17) and the experiences of the 'man of God' in 1 Kings 13. *Cf.* O. Eissfeldt, 'Amos und Jona in volkstümlicher Überlieferung', "...*und fragten nach Jesus*", Fs. E. Barnikol (Berlin: 1964), pp.9–13. See S. J. DeVries, *1 Kings*, WBC, 12, 1985, pp. 171–174, for a discussion of Karl Barth's use of this passage and its analogy to Amos and Amaziah.
[1]See Martin-Achard, pp. 180–186.
[2]L. Markert, 'Amosbuch', *TRE*, 2, 1977–1978, p. 484.
[3]The Qumran references are Am. 5:26–27 in CD 7:14–15; Am. 9:11 in CD 7:16 and in 4Qflor 1:12.

Beyond any verbal allusion or direct quotations, Amos brings bright light to our understanding of the New Testament and our practice of discipleship in the church. The very theme of judgment executed by the sovereign Lord alike on Gentile nations and the people of Israel helps us comprehend the meaning of Christ's cross. How gross is the sin of disobedience as Amos excoriates it! How fierce the fires of judgment as Amos depicts them! That sin of ours and that judgment of God's met on Calvary, with forgiveness and reconciliation as the result. The amplitude of that event, from which flowed so great a salvation, is driven home to our hearts and minds as we hear the words of Amos, irresistible in their divine intensity.

But the comfort of release from judgment must express itself in concern for the distressed, oppressed and disadvantaged. If the sons and daughters of the older covenant were held accountable to practise the justice and righteousness of the God whose praises they sang, how much more shall we who have witnessed the fullness of the Deity in fleshly form in Jesus Christ? We know more of his grace and truth, having seen him dwell among us. Such grace and truth constrain us to care as he cared, to share as he shared and love as he loved. A generation sensitive to injustice in a host of forms has adopted Amos' social heart-cry as a credo. He has become *the* prophet of our age. But we shall not understand that heart-cry until we hear it as the cry of our living Lord and let the pathos that moved him to judgment in Amos' day move us to action in ours.[1]

VIII. STRUCTURE

Virtually all commentators agree that the structure of the book of Amos as completed contains the following components:

Introduction 1:1–2
Judgment speeches against the nations 1:3 – 2:16
Judgment speeches against Israel 3:1 – 6:14
Vision reports 7:1 – 9:10
Salvation promises 9:11–15[2]

---

[1]Martin-Achard, pp. 186–271, gives a survey of Amos' impressive contribution to Jewish, patristic (Augustine), pre-Reformation (Savonarola), Reformation, and contemporary teaching and preaching.

[2]Martin-Achard, ITC, p. 2, uses this format almost precisely as the table of contents of his commentary. Running counter to the consensus is A. van der

118

The bulk of discussion, then, centres on the interior relationship of the oracles in 3:1 – 6:14. How do they divide? How
much structural unity do we find in them? These questions
are discussed in the Commentary, where the general
approach has been to find a remarkable inner unity despite
the rich variety of literary forms which enhance these
speeches. This structural unity is being documented increasingly by on-going and detailed research, which appears to
provide a counter-balance to the tendency to find chronological layers in the book's composition (see on Unity above).
Since technical study of structure and inner unity is a fairly
new discipline in biblical scholarship, we can expect fresh
insight into the movement and meaning of the book as further
work is done. Meanwhile the analysis which follows this Introduction will give the reader a workable guide to the structure
as presently understood.[1]

Wal, 'The Structure of Amos', *JSOT*, 26, 1983, pp. 107–113. He divides the
work into only two major sections; chs. 1–6 and 7–9.

[1]Of the many recent works on the structure of Amos we can here note only a
few; by far the most detailed, whose implications are yet to be thoroughly
assessed, is that of K. Koch, *Amos: Untersucht mit den Methoden einer strukturalen
Formgeschichte* (Neukirchen-Vluyn: Verlag Butzon & Burcker Kevelaer, 1976),
3 parts; L. Markert, *Struktur und Bezeichnung des Scheltwortes. Eine gattungskritische
Studie an hand des Amosbuches, BZAW*, 140, 1977; R. F. Melugin, 'The Formation
of Amos: An Analysis of Exegetical Method', *Society of Biblical Literature 1978
Seminar Papers* (Missoula, Montana: Scholars Press), pp. 369–391 – a review of
the approaches of H. W. Wolff and K. Koch, with particular attention to Amos
3 – 4; Y. Gitay, 'A Study of Amos' Art of Speech: A Rhetorical Analysis of
Amos 3:1–15', *CBQ*, 42, 1980, pp. 293–309; Gordis, pp. 217–229; J. de Waard,
'The Chiastic Structure of Amos V, 1–17', *VT*, 27, 1977, pp. 170–177; N. J.
Tromp, 'Amos V 1–17: Towards a Stylistic and Rhetorical Analysis', *OTS*, 23,
1984, pp. 65–85; W. A. Smalley, 'Recursion Patterns and the Sectioning of
Amos', *The Bible Translator* 30, 1979, pp. 118–127; Auld, pp. 50–59

ANALYSIS

I. INTRODUCTION
  a. Title (1:1)
  b. Theme (1:2)

II. SEVEN JUDGMENT SPEECHES AGAINST THE NATIONS (1:3 – 2:5)
  a. Damascus (1:3–5)
  b. Philistine cities (1:6–8)
  c. Tyre (1:9–10)
  d. Edom (1:11–12)
  e. Ammonites (1:13–15)
  f. Moab (2:1–3)
  g. Judah (2:4–5)

III. TRANSITIONAL JUDGMENT SPEECH AGAINST ISRAEL (2:6–16)
  a. Indictment: economic and religious oppression (2:6–8)
  b. Indictment expanded: divine grace in the Exodus (2:9–12)
  c. Announcement of judgment: earthquake (2:13–16)

IV. THREE JUDGMENT SPEECHES AGAINST ISRAEL (3:1 – 5:17)
  a. Judgment speech: abuse of covenant privileges (3:1–15)
    i. Great privilege – great condemnation (3:1–2)
    ii. Divine initiative – prophetic response (3:3–8).
    iii. Ashdod and Egypt – unlikely witnesses (3:9–11)
    iv. Thorough judgment – sarcastic proof (3:12)
    v. Ashdod and Egypt – witness continued (3:13–15)
  b. Judgment speech: rejection of divine warnings (4:1–13)
    i. Judgment speech against Samaria's wealthy women (4:1–3)
    ii. Mock admonitions against the shrines (4:4–5)
    iii. Recital of judgment history: warnings unheeded (4:6–11)

COMMENTARY

I. INTRODUCTION: TITLE AND THEME (1:1–2)

These verses set the stage for all that follows by identifying the prophet, stating his vocation, pin-pointing his home town and the specific time of his prophecy, underscoring the visionary nature of his mission and anticipating its major theme: the threat of judgment that hung over Israel.

a. Title (1:1)

The form of the title features the prophet's name as do the opening verses of Isaiah and Jeremiah, rather than the 'word of Yahweh' as in Hosea, Joel, Jonah, Micah, Zephaniah, Haggai, Zechariah and Malachi. The plural 'words' in the introduction to a speech occurs in Jeremiah 1:1 as well as in the wisdom sayings of Agur and Lemuel (Pr. 30:1; 31:1).

This text anticipates several prominent themes in the book: (1) the five visions of chapters 7–9, which in some ways form the heart of Amos' message, are pointed to in *he saw*, a verb (*ḥzh*) which the Judean prophets alone – with their emphasis on the divine council to which only true prophets had access (Je. 23:18–22) – seemed to have used (Is. 1:1; 2:1; 13:1; Mi. 3:1; Hab. 1:1);[1] (2) Amos' occupation (Heb. *nōqēd*, 'sheepraiser' rather than mere shepherd, 2 Ki. 3:4) reinforces his argument with Amaziah that his profession had been agricultural not prophetic and that the call of God alone could account for his prophetic ministry (7:14–15);[2] (3) *concerning Israel* captures the focus of Amos' mission and explains its

---

[1] D. L. Petersen, *The Roles of Israel's Prophets*, JSOT, supplement 17 (Sheffield: JSOT Press, 1981), p. 86.
[2] P. Craigie, *Ugarit and the Old Testament* (Grand Rapids: Eerdmans, 1983), p. 73, studies the Ugaritic cognate of *nōqēd* and concludes of Amos: 'he probably owned or managed large herds of sheep and engaged in the marketing of their products.'

controversial nature: a citizen of Tekoa (a town of Judah, situated about ten kilometres south of Bethlehem and twenty kilometres south of Jerusalem) was confronting the problems of a kingdom not his own and, thereby, wearing out his welcome (7:12–13); (4) the historical setting in the reigns of Judah's Uzziah (Azariah, 792–40 BC) and Israel's Jeroboam II (793–53 BC) accounts both for the corrupt opulence that Amos denounced (*e.g.* 4:1–3; 6:1–7) and for the threat of Assyrian invasions which were resumed under Tiglath-pileser III in 743 BC (4:3; 5:27; 6:7, 14; 7:17); the threats are purposely vague, although Assyria (which the LXX reads in 3:9, where Heb. has Ashdod) would be the only nation strong enough to account for them;[1] (5) the earthquake (still remembered in Zc. 14:5) was viewed as divine judgment in light of Amos' predictions of it, obliquely in 2:13–16 and directly in 8:8 and 9:1–6.

b. The theme (1:2)

As the actual words of Amos begin, the theme is set for the entire book. The Lord's lion-like roar (*cf.* 3:8) can call for return (Ho. 11:10–11) or threaten judgment (Joel 3:16). The withering effect on the pastures (for *mourn*, see Ho. 4:3) and the *top of Carmel* shows that *judgment* is the message. *Zion* and *Jerusalem* are mentioned as rebukes to the northern shrines whose false worship Amos so roundly renounces. Bethel, Gilgal (4:4; 5:5), Beersheba (5:5; 8:14), Samaria and Dan (8:14) are not the centres of revelation and power. The Davidic capital (*cf.* 9:11) with its divinely ordered temple is. The Lord who lives there is to be reckoned with. His authority stretches from the fertile plain to the most massive mountain (*cf.* 9:3; Song 7:5). Even Amos' fellow shepherds will feel its grasp. It is just possible that *shepherds* also includes the ruling classes (*cf.* Je. 23:1–4; Ezk. 34) whose profligate policies the prophet chastises (4:1–3; 6:1, 4–7; 7:9, 11). The hymn-like cadence of this verse (*cf.* Ps. 50:1–3) is echoed in Jeremiah (25:30) and Joel (3:16), a reminder that Amos and his fellow seers often used familiar hymnody to buttress their messages. Above all, this theme verse assigns ultimate seriousness to Amos' words: the way in which the lordly Lion roars is through the voice of his chosen prophet (3:8).

[1] For historical backgrounds of Amos' book, see 'The Setting of the Book' in Introduction to Hosea.

II. SEVEN JUDGMENT SPEECHES AGAINST THE NATIONS (1:3 – 2:5)[1]

Surprisingly, Amos does not launch into an indictment of Israel's sin as the Introduction has intimated that he will. Instead he targets for judgment a ring of Israel's neighbours from Damascus in the northeast (1:3–5) to Gaza in the southwest (1:6–8), to Tyre in the northwest (1:9–10), to Edom in the far south (1:11–12), to Ammon in the east (1:13–15), to Moab in the southeast (2:1–3), to Judah in the near south (2:4–5).

These seven judgment speeches follow a *stereotyped literary pattern* with only slight variations:

Messenger formula – 'Thus says Yahweh'

General accusation and announcement – 'For three transgressions of . . . and for four, I will not revoke it' (the *punishment*, or even more likely 'my anger')[2]

Specific accusation of sin – introduced by *because* (Heb. *'al* with infinitive construct of verb)

Specific announcement of judgment – introduced by 'and I will send fire ('kindle' or 'set' fire in 1:14) upon . . . and it will consume her fortresses'

Elaboration of specific announcement – spelling out the destruction of the peoples and their rulers (1:5, 8, 15; 2:3; the third, fourth and seventh speeches lack this elaboration)

Closing messenger formula – 'Yahweh has said' (1:5, 15; 2:3) or 'my Lord Yahweh has said' (1:8; again the third, fourth and seventh speeches lack this closing formula)

Some *theological implications* of these oracles need noting:

First, the *messenger formula* (*cf.* Gn. 32:3–4; 2 Ki. 1:4, 6), used by Amos to substantiate a prophet's authority over nations as

---

[1] For a study of the form, text and theology of these speeches, see J. Barton, *Amos' Oracles against the Nations* (Cambridge University Press, 1980).

[2] For a strong argument that the unexplained *it*, which is the literal object of the verb *revoke*, has 'my anger' as its antecedent, see R. P. Knierim, '"I will not cause it to return" in Amos 1 and 2', *Canon and Authority*, ed. by G. W. Coats and B. O. Long (Philadelphia: Fortress Press, 1977), pp. 163–175. M. L. Barré, 'The Meaning of *l' 'sybnw* in Amos 1:3 – 2:6', *JBL*, 105, 1986, pp. 611–631, has

well as individuals, drums home the fact that the words are not his own but the Lord's, who has commissioned him to deliver them; his God-ordained role was central to his message (2:11–12; 3:7–8; 7:14–15); failure to hear the prophets as divine messengers was among the most heinous sins of the people (2:13; 7:16–17; 8:11–12).

Second, the *crimes of the neighbours* are called 'acts of rebellion' (so *transgressions*, Heb. *piš'ê* can be literally read), suggesting that they, like Israel and Judah, are so under the Lord's authority that their wicked deeds are outrages against his rule. Perhaps Amos has chosen to indict these specific neighbours because they were all at one time under the hegemony of David and thus were viewed as part of a greater Israel believed to be especially accountable to the Lord.[1]

Third, the wrongs noted are all *acts of inhumanity*, until we come to the speech against Judah (2:4–5). It seems that the nations are condemned here not for idolatry nor false religions but for offences commonly judged as evil by the prevalent standards of the day: cruelty to civilians in war (1:3, 13), selling of war prisoners into slavery (1:6, 9), violation of treaties (1:9, 11) and mistreatment of a fallen king (2:1). The Lord's concern for human rights and human decency in the conduct of the family of nations is an obvious thrust of this passage; even where war is deemed necessary, it must be waged with restraint.

Fourth, the *judgment* for such aggressions is vulnerability, symbolized in the *fire* that devours walls and fortresses. The very fortifications in which the kings trusted and which made them bold to venture forth and work their mayhem will be levelled, and they will be open to any foe that sallies forth against them, especially their perennial enemy, Assyria. Their vaunted strength will melt like wax before the holy fires of the righteous Judge (*cf.* 7:4; Ho. 8:14; Joel 1:19–20; 2:3).[2]

---

suggested that the *it* refers to the name of each city or nation which is branded guilty and that the verb should be translated 'I will not take it back', *i.e.* into covenant (or treaty) relationship with me as my vassal.

[1] Koch, p. 69. J. Barton, *op. cit.*, p. 60, emphasizes, rather, Yahweh's role as 'avenger of guilt, rather than explicitly the source of the moral norms ... not law giver so much as judge.'

[2] For the use of fire and lightning as agents of divine judgment in the OT and the ancient ME, see M. Weinfeld, in *History, Historiography and Interpretation*, ed. by H. Tadmor and M. Weinfeld (Jerusalem: Magnes Press, 1983), pp. 136–140.

Fifth, the *numerical pattern* – 'for three acts of rebellion …
and for four', is an example of a familiar wisdom device in
which lists of related acts of behaviour (*cf.* Pr. 30:18–19,
21–23, 29–31) or lists of unacceptable social conduct (*cf.* Pr.
6:16–19; Sir. 26:5–6) are introduced by the numerical
sequence formula (x, x+1). The wisdom sayings indicate that
the emphasis is usually on the last item enumerated, *i.e.* the
higher of the two numbers. Amos' use of the formula is
exceptionable, since he omits the first three items in the list
and spotlights what was presumably the fourth, the back-
breaking transgression that triggered the divine judgment.
What the device seems to be saying is that each neighbour has
rebelled enough and more than enough to warrant the Lord's
drastic intervention in its history; therefore, he is entirely
justified in bringing calamity upon them.[1]

Sixth, the *accountability of the nations* seems to be propor-
tionate to the knowledge of God's will granted to them: the
Gentile neighbours were held responsible for standards of
human treatment of one another, not just damage done to
Israel; Judah (2:4–5), on the other hand, was judged in terms
of its response to Yahweh's law, since it had the advantage of
that special revelation.

The *author's intent* in these speeches is to show Israel how
heinous their rebellion was and how dire the judgment they
could expect, when Yahweh unleashed his anger. All of this is
accomplished with a strong note of *surprise.* Judgment
speeches against the foreign nations (*cf.* Is. 13 – 23; Je. 46 –
51; Ezk. 25 – 32; Joel 3; Ob.; Na.) were often considered
salvation speeches to Israel. The defeat of enemies that frequently harassed God's people was 'good tidings' (Na. 1:15).
Part of the misinterpretation of the 'day of the Lord'
(5:18–20) was to hold that it marked the downfall of the
nations and the exaltation of Israel as the chosen people. It
would have been no strange thing for Israel to hear a harsh
denunciation of the pagan conduct of the surrounding
peoples. What made Amos' approach surprising was that the
list of criminal activities did not stop at Israel's borders but
included – indeed, featured – them as well.

[1]For a sketch of the uses of this device in Scripture, Ugaritic literature, and
Ahiqar, see H. W. Wolff, p. 34–44. *Completeness* in sinning would be the force if
the three and four are to be added, as has been suggested by J. Limburg,
'Sevenfold Structures in the Book of Amos', *JBL*, 106, 1987, pp. 217–222.

Sovereignty along with surprise is part of the purpose of this text. Israel's horizons needed expanding. They should have viewed themselves as belonging exclusively to God; instead, they viewed God as belonging exclusively to them. More than once Amos had to shake them from complacency by stirring statements that showed God at work on a larger canvas than Israel had imagined, a canvas that included, for instance, Ethiopians, Philistines and Syrians (9:7). By enlarging the scale of God's sovereign activities, Amos was showing Israel the might and majesty of the One with whom they had to deal.

More than anything else, the judgment speeches highlight Israel's terrifying *accountability*. They are a kind of *a fortiori* argument: if the lesser breeds without the law are to receive harsh recompense for their failure to abide by the accepted norms of international law, how much more culpable is God's people, to whom have been granted the blessings of covenant and law? The catalogue of oracles in 1:3 – 2:5 serve, then, as a preface to the poignant yet damning announcement in 3:2:

> 'You only have I known
> of all the families of the earth;
> therefore I will punish you
> for all your iniquities.'

The *historical background* of the indictments is not easy to trace. Most scholarly opinion settles them in the later part of the ninth century, two or three scores of years prior to Amos' time. Since we have more specific information about international events in that period, the comments on each speech will sketch, where appropriate, those circumstances. At the same time we must take note of Wolff's arguments (pp. 149–152), admitted as possible by Herrmann (pp. 233–234), that the savage events recounted by Amos are to be dated much nearer to, or even contemporary with, the prophet's own times.[1] The extreme turbulence of the early decades of the eighth century in Syria and Palestine would surely allow the kinds of events recounted, even though we cannot yet document the specific activities.

---

[1]Mays, pp. 29–40, and Motyer, pp. 37ff., base their comments on 9th-century settings for the crimes of the neighbours. J. Barton, *op. cit.*, p. 35, remains sceptical: 'There is no hope of dating the events with anything approaching certainty.'

a. Damascus (1:3–5)

The sequence begins with the ancient hub of the Aramaean
territory, the foreign city most influential in the politics of the
entire region, and the local power most threatening to Israel's
security and stability. It is not surprising that the violence of
Damascus sought *Gilead* as its target. That territory, east of
Jordan between the northern end of the Dead Sea and the
Yarmuk River, was ripe for Syrian plucking any time Israel's
kings were too weak or preoccupied to defend it. Reuben, Gad
and half of Manasseh were the fortunate tribes that occupied
it (Jos. 18:7) and enjoyed its rich woodlands (Je. 22:6; 50:19;
Zc. 10:10) and fertile grazing land (Song 4:1; 6:5).

Threshing sledges with iron prongs or teeth are probably a
figure of speech implying extreme cruelty and utter
thoroughness in the treatment of those who opposed the
Damascan invasion. Amos may echo here the reports of the
brutality with which the Syrian kings had annihilated the
troops of Jehu's son, Jehoahaz (814–798 BC): 'for the king of
Syria had destroyed them and made them like the dust at
threshing' (2 Ki. 13:8; for other reports of cruel flaying of
prisoners, see Jdg. 8:7, 16).

The announcement of fiery judgment specifies the *house*
(thus personalizing the judgment more than do the other
speeches which use 'wall', 1:7, 10, 14, or merely mention the
name of the land or city, 1:12; 2:2, 5) of *Hazael* and the
strongholds or fortified places (*cf.* 3:9, 11; 6:8, where it is clear
that such edifices were sources of arrogant pride and false
security that had to be brought low if the sovereign Lord were
truly to be honoured; note also Ho. 8:14) of *Ben-hadad.* These
two rulers are most likely to be identified as the Hazael whose
long reign (*c.* 843–796) caused mayhem for Israel's Jehoram
(852–41), Jehu (841–814) and Jehoahaz (*cf.* 1 Ki. 19:15–17; 2
Ki. 8:7–15, 28–29; 9:14–15; 10:32–33; 13:3, 22–23) and Ben-
hadad III, Hazael's son, (*c.* 796–770), whom Jehoahaz
defeated (2 Ki. 13:14–19, 25).[1]

The elaboration of Yahweh's judgment stresses: (1) its penetration into the very heart of the fortress capital, whose *bar*

[1]On these kings see articles in *IBD* and also M. F. Unger, *Israel and the Aramaeans of Damascus* (London, 1957), chs. 5–10. See also A. Malamat, 'The Aramaeans' in *Peoples of Old Testament Times*, ed. by D. J. Wiseman (Oxford University Press, 1973), pp. 134–155.

which held in place the massive gate would cave under his onslaught; (2) its extent, reaching to other places, like the *Valley of Aven* (probably the region around Baalbek northwest of Damascus) and *Beth-eden* (perhaps Bit-Adini, a tiny state on the banks of the Euphrates south of Carchemish); (3) its terror, carrying captives, including rulers (*sceptre*), into exile; (4) its irony, portraying a return of Syrians to the very place from which the Lord, centuries before, had sparked their migration (9:7). Kir has so far defied clear identification, but the link with Elam (Is. 22:6) may suggest a location in southeastern Mesopotamia, east of the Tigris toward the top of the Persian Gulf.

b. Philistine cities (1:6–8)

Four cities of the pentapolis are hailed before the judgment bench: *Gaza*, mightiest, southernmost, *i.e.* closest to Egypt, about five kilometres from the Mediterranean coastline and about fifty-five kilometres due west of Hebron; *Ashdod*, thirty-three kilometres north of Gaza, also about five kilometres inland and on a latitude just south of Jerusalem; *Ashkelon*, about halfway between the first two cities and directly on the coast; *Ekron*, the northernmost city about twenty kilometres inland and less than ten kilometres from Judah's border. Gath is not mentioned. J. L. Mays (p. 33) lists the possible reasons: (1) Gath was often grouped with the cities of Judah (1 Sa. 21:11–16, 27–30; 2 Sa. 15:18ff.; 2 Ch. 11:8–10; 26:6); (2) Gath may, in Amos' day, have been a satellite to Ashdod, her western neighbour; (3) Hazael's raid (2 Ki. 12:18) may have left her in ruins. Other prophets who rail against the Philistines also ignore Gath (Je. 25:20; Zp. 2:4; Zc. 9:6–7) which was utterly destroyed by Sargon of Assyria in 711 BC.

The sequence in which Amos moves from Damascus to Gaza seems to have three reasons behind it: (1) the extremes in geography from northeast to southwest underscore the sweep of God's sovereignty over the nations; (2) the Syrians and Philistines were the two ancient neighbours most tenacious at harrowing the tribes of Israel and hence were sometimes closely linked in prophetic thought: 'the Syrians on the east and the Philistines on the west devour Israel with open mouth' (Is. 9:12; *cf.* Am. 9:7); (3) these first two speeches are the only ones to contain the threat, 'cut off the inhabitants and

him that holds the sceptre' (1:5, 8), and thus are tied together
with these catch-phrases;[1] (4) the political structures of the
two nations were similar, each comprised of a central city and
a network of other royal cities ruled by sceptre-bearers (Koch,
p. 67).

The act of rebellion described is slave-trading, probably a
purely commercial transaction in which the Philistines raided
the neighbour towns of Judah and Israel and sold their
prisoners to Edom. Whether the Edomites used the slaves to
man their ports and mines or sold them to other nations is not
mentioned. Neither does Amos state where the Philistines got
their prisoners. His emphasis seems to be solely on the outrageous inhumanity of the act, which was a perennial problem in
antiquity (Joel 3:4–6) and is still not eradicated in some parts
of the world.

The announcement of judgment in verse 8 is expanded to
show the overwhelming power of Yahweh: he 'causes his hand
to turn' against *Ekron*, an idiom that pictures the city helpless
in his control (Dt. 26:8; Is. 1:25; 5:25). The final clause sums
up the totality of the calamity when the remnant, the last
handful of survivors, suffers a fate even worse than the exile
of the Syrians with which the first speech closed. Here alone in
these speeches, the concluding messenger formula is expanded to include *'adōnāy*, Master, as well as Yahweh's name, and
thus reinforces the note of divine power and authority.

c. Tyre (1:9–10)

This speech shifts our attention northward to the Phoenician
(Lebanese) coast and its rocky island fortress (*cf.* Joel 3:4–6). It
follows the oracle against Philistia because it too involves slave-
trading with Edom. The scope and tragedy are underlined in
the words 'whole communities of captives' (NIV), as though
entire settlements were uprooted and peddled to the
Edomites. Though *delivered up* (RSV; Heb. *hasgîr*) may mean to
extradite a runaway slave (Dt. 23:15, *cf.* Ob. 14), that is surely
not its intent here where cruel treatment and inhumane use of
power are the points. The indictment is amplified by the

---

[1]For a discussion on the reasons for the sequence of speeches in this whole
section, see S. M. Paul, 'Amos 1:3 – 2:3: A Concatenous Literary Pattern', *JBL*,
90, 1971, pp. 397–403.

reference to a broken 'treaty (lit. 'covenant'; *cf.* Ho. 12:1) of brotherhood' (NIV). Tyre's treaty-partner, with whom she played false, is not mentioned – another reminder that specifics of the case are not so important to Amos as the appalling violations of human decency and honour. Even by her own standards, Tyre deserved the prescribed fire of judgment. Ezekiel's 'taunt-song' set Tyre's insular self-confidence and arrogant high-handedness in bold relief (Ezk. 28).

d. Edom (1:11–12)

Edom has played a villainous role in the two previous speeches. He now comes in for his own indictment. The warfare with *his brother* was the key crime. The brother could, of course, be Israel, since Jacob and Esau, Edom's illustrious ancestor, were brothers (Gn. 25:19–26; for Edom's kinship to Israel, see Nu. 20:14; Dt. 2:4; 23:7; Ob. 10, 12). It is also possible that brother means 'treaty-partner' (1 Sa. 20:29) and Hiram of Tyre called Solomon 'my brother' (1 Ki. 9:13).[1] *Pity* or 'compassion' (NASB) could also be translated 'ally' (*cf.* NIV footnote), thus reinforcing the binding, legal nature of the contract that Edom violated. A better alternative may be to read the word (Heb. *raḥªmāyw*) as 'women' (*raḥªmātayim*), literally 'wombs' (Heb. *reḥem*), following the example of Judges 5:30.[2] The verb *cast off* (RSV; Heb. *šiḥēt*) would then mean 'spoil', 'corrupt', or 'destroy', referring to sexual violence or physical harm inflicted on innocent citizens by Edom's soldiers (*cf.* 1:13).

Whatever the specific offence may have been, it was charged with a bestial anger that *tore* incessantly at its victims. The last line of verse 11 is effectively translated by NIV: 'and his fury flamed unchecked', since fury (or 'wrath'; Heb. *'eḇªrātô*) is the subject of the clause not the object (as RSV reads it, following the ancient versions). Seeing 'wrath' and 'anger' as the subjects of the two clauses both suits the parallelism of the poetry and stresses the point that Edom's violent emotions were utterly out of control.

The form of this speech ('wall' is omitted in the fiery judgment of verse 12, and no concluding messenger formula is

---

[1] M. Fishbane, 'The Treaty Backgound of Amos 1:11 and Related Matters', *JBL*, 89, 1970, pp. 314–315.

[2] S. M. Paul, *op. cit.*, *JBL*, 90, 1971, p. 403, where it is noted that *rḥmt* means 'maid servants' or 'girls' in the Moabite Mesha Inscription. R. B. Coate, *JBL*, 90,

attached) and the content, interpreted in terms of Edom's well-documented exploitation of Judah after Jerusalem's fall in 586 BC (Ps. 137:7; Ezk. 33:5–6; Ob. 13–14), have suggested to some that it was incorporated into the text of Amos after Nebuchadrezzar's final conquest of Judah (Wolff, p. 160; Mays, pp. 35–36). Two objections may be put to this suggestion. First, Edom's conflicts with Judah had a long and violent history stretching back to the reigns of David (2 Sa. 8:13–14) and Solomon (1 Ki. 11:14–15) and continuing right up to Amos' time (2 Ki. 14:22). Judah's ruthlessness may well have led to violent retaliation of the type described, even though we have no specific account of it in Scripture. This could especially be the case if the slaves purchased by the Edomites (1:6, 9) were citizens of Judah or Israel who were severely mistreated in the process. Second, we cannot say for certain who the 'brother' was that Edom treated treacherously. Since any 'covenant-partner' might qualify, the text may not have Israel in mind at all; the Old Testament sources, therefore, would have had no cause to remember the episode.

Teman, probably both the city and the region around it, is singled out for Edom's judgment which, to be effective, has to centre on well-populated areas. Its early role in biblical history is marked in Genesis 36:15, 42, and it continues to be viewed as the centre of Edom's vaunted wisdom through the centuries (Jb. 2:11; Je. 49:7; Ob. 8–9). Though Edom's territory stretches about eighty kilometres south of Teman to the head of the Gulf of Aqabah, Teman is the southernmost substantial city in the land. *Bozrah* lies roughly halfway between Teman and the lower end of the Dead Sea. It was the capital of Edom (Gn. 36:33) and one of the most influential and ancient of its cities, being a major oasis on the King's Highway that ran north-south in antiquity to link the Gulf of Aqabah with the Plains of Moab, north of the Dead Sea and to connect with the route to Damascus and the east. Undoubtedly better fortified than Teman, Bozrah will pay the price in the holocaust that will consume its strongholds (*cf.* Je. 49:7–22).

The two Edomite cities are fitting targets for judgment. Through them, surely, ran the slave-trading that brought Edom such infamy. Edom's independent existence stood in

1971, pp. 206–208, on the other hand, interprets *raḥ*^a*māyw* as 'covenant mercy' in light of Ho. 2:19 and sees Edom's pursuit of his brother as repudiation of his own mercy.

dire jeopardy as the prophets scanned the future (Joel 3:19). The only bright tomorrows open to them were dependent on their merger with Judah (Am. 9:12; Ob. 21).

e. Ammonites (1:13–15)

Ammon's crime was directly related to their geographical location. In the periods when Israel was powerful, Ammon's territory was cramped between the Moabites on the south, the Israelites of Gilead on the west, Bashan on the north and the great desert to the east. The narrow confines centred roughly in the uplands of the Jabbok river and made the Ammonites (the only people in this list referred to by the plural 'sons of Ammon', as they are frequently called in the Old Testament) perpetually restless for conquest (Jdg. 10:7ff.; 11:4ff.; 1 Sa. 11:1–11; 14:7–8). We cannot pin-point the specific campaign that drew them into brutality in order to extend their borders but may assume that it was coincident with the southern incursion of Damascus (1:3), the two ambitious states subjecting Gilead to a pincers' movement.

The vicious assaults on women, together with the mention of the 'sword' (7:9, 17; 9:4) as the instrument of terror, may help to account for the sequence of this speech, if the suggestion (see at vv. 11–12) is adopted that Edom was accused of a similar crime. For other Old Testament instances of this wanton destruction of mother and unborn child, see in Hosea 13:16.

Kindle (v. 14) is probably a stylistic variation for 'I will send', as the formula used in Jeremiah 49:27 suggests. *Rabbah* ('the great city') is often called *rabbat̲-b̲ên̲-ʿammôn* (Dt. 3:11; 2 Sa. 12:26; 17:27;) and is to be identified with the modern Amman, capital of Jordan. The elaboration of the announcement rings with the sounds of holy war – 'war cries on the day of battle' (NIV; the word *t̲eʿrûʿâ* describes Israel's shout at the wall of Jericho in Joshua's day; Jos. 6:5, 20; *cf.* Je. 4:19; 49:2). *Tempest* and *whirlwind* also buttress the sense that Yahweh himself is pledged to appear and work the judgment in a theophany (*cf.* 1 Ki. 2:1, 11; Jb. 38:1; 40:6; Ezk. 1:4). The whole scene reeks of grand conflagration: the fire will be fanned by the very winds of God, and the shouts of the invaders will strike panic in the hearts of any Ammonites who seek to escape. This dramatic announcement of divine

136

participation in the judgment seems to highlight the horror of the crime.

Again (as in 1:5, 8; 2:3) the rulers will be earmarked for punishment, this time by exile. Once more, the political accuracy of Amos' account has been noticed: the Ammonite form of government rested on a king and his ministers (here called literally *princes* or 'officials' [NIV]; *cf.* Ho. 7:3, 5, 16; 8:4; Koch, p. 67).

f. Moab (2:1–3)

Moab is indicted next, perhaps because of kinship with Ammon (the notorious origin of both is chronicled in Gn. 19:30–38), the geographical location, just south of Ammon and directly east of the Dead Sea, and also because the catch word *shouting* (1:14; 2:2) tied the oracles together. The act of rebellion, desecration of the bones of Edom's king (lit. 'judge', in keeping with Amos' bent for political accuracy), presupposes some sharp conflict between the 'brother' states. Israel, Judah and Edom once joined in battle against Moab (2 Ki. 3:6–9), and Mesha's inscription, preserved on the so-called Moabite Stone, refers to a southern incursion that Mesha made against Horonaim, apparently an Edomite city situated about twelve kilometres east of the southern tip of the Dead Sea.[1]

The crime itself violated the mores of the ancient world which called for respect for the corpse of a royal enemy (*cf.* 2 Ki. 9:34, where Jehu ordered a decent burial even for Jezebel). Burning a body was an extreme form of criminal punishment (Gn. 38:24; Lv. 20:14; 21:9) designed to purge completely the land of its wickedness. The Vulgate translates the word *lime* (*sîd*) as 'completely to ashes', and the Targum accuses the Moabites of using the chalk of the powdered bones for whitewash. Again, degradation of personhood is Amos' point. Whether the victims were the unborn infants of Gilead's wives or the corpse (or skeleton, if grave-robbing was part of the crime) of Edom's king, human decency called for decorous respect for personhood.

---

[1] For text of Moabite Stone, see E. Ullendorff, *DOTT*, pp. 195–198; for the location of Horonaim (*cf.* Je. 48:3), see Y. Aharoni and M. Avi-Yonah, *The Macmillan Bible Atlas*, rev. ed. (New York: Macmillan, 1977), map no. 131.

The fiery judgment here (v. 2) is particularly appropriate, a case of *lex talionis* where the punishment precisely fits the crime. *Kerioth* may have been singled out for destruction because it housed a shrine for the Moabite deity, Chemosh, as Mesha himself noted in his inscription. Its suggested site is about fifteen kilometres north of the Arnon river and about twelve kilometres east of the Dead Sea. Sound and fury accompany Moab's demise, the whole scene suggesting a surprise attack that called for trumpets to rally troops and commanders to bark their commands (*cf.* Ho. 5:8; 8:1; Joel 2:1; 3:9–10), attackers and defenders swarming together in total confusion. And when the sounds of battle are stilled, Moab's judge and other officials will be dead, a king for a king.

g. Judah (2:4–5)

In the flow of the judgment speeches, Judah's turn has come, Amos' own homeland. This speech marks a sharp transition from the previous six: though the form remains constant, the content of the indictment has changed markedly. It was not international treaty-breaking or outrageously inhumane conduct that was at stake, but failure to keep Yahweh's laws, especially the laws that called for exclusive worship of God without the representation of idols. This crime, like all the others that Amos has denounced, was against Yahweh. But it was a crime that only the covenant people could commit, based as it was on the *law* (Heb. *tôrâ*) and its specific applications (*statutes*; Heb. *ḥuqqāyw; cf.* Dt. 4:5) which they alone had been given.

By *their lies* which *led them astray*, the prophet seems to mean idols or false gods (NIV). The deceptive character of images or foreign gods was a frequent prophetic theme. Jeremiah used the word 'futility' or 'vanity' (Heb. *heḇel* was the theme word of Koheleth, the Preacher in Ecclesiastes, who applied it to all that people falsely depend on; Ec. 1:2) to describe their worthless unreliability (*e.g.* 2:5; 10:15; *cf.* 2 Ki. 17:15). In 10:14, Jeremiah used 'falsehood' (Heb. *šeqer*) to underscore this point. Idolatry was no new thing for Judah. Amos hinted at a *sin-history* of rebellion endemic in the pattern of their ancestors (*fathers*) just as there had been a *salvation-history* by which God in love sought to keep them loyal to the covenant.

By citing the law with its statues, its specific stipulations,

Amos may indirectly have been accusing his fellow citizens of treaty-breaking worse than Tyre's breach of the 'covenant of brotherhood' (1:9). After all Judah had entered into covenant, not with a brother nation, but with the Great King. One purpose of the law was to spell out the terms of that covenant. Judah's treacherous idolatry made him a rebel of the first order.

The announcement of judgment is stereotyped, following precisely the pattern of Edom's fate (1:12), except that the whole land is to be put to the torch not just its chief cities. Amos' theme verse (1:2) hinted of Judah's and Jerusalem's vulnerability: the roaring Lion was present in their midst.

The interpretation given here assumes that all of these speeches were framed by Amos, despite the variations of form. Judah's crime, law-breaking idolatry, has been read by many recent commentators (*e.g.* Coote, Mays, Wolff) to place this oracle in Jeremiah's day when the influence of the newly discovered lawcode of Deuteronomy had made itself felt. To summarize and respond to all the arguments that underlie that reading would divert us from our chief purpose: to understand the text of Amos before us. It is enough to say that the law and statutes collected in Deuteronomy had a lengthy history with which Amos showed himself familiar in the judgment speech against Israel that comes next (2:6ff.).[1] Whatever date scholars may assign to the completion of Deuteronomy, the ban on idolatry stems from antiquity, undoubtedly from Moses himself.

The speech against Judah has accomplished its purposes: (1) it demonstrated clearly that Amos was not viewing divine judgment in chauvinistic terms, as though Yahweh picked on the neighbours and coddled his covenant people; (2) it changed the grounds of the charges from cruel acts of inhumanity to violation of revealed law; (3) it underscored the fact that God's people in these holy wars, these visitations of fire, will not be God's agent, as they often were in past history, but God's victims; even David's land and capital will not escape; (4) it set the stage for the heart of Amos' message, the judgment on

---

[1]For a recent defence of the unity of the seven oracles against the nations and Amos' authorship of each, see Shalom M. Paul, 'A Literary Reinvestigation of the Authenticity of the Oracles Against the Nations of Amos', ed. by Carvez *et al.* in *De la Torah au Messie*, Mélanges H. Cazelles (Paris: 1981), pp. 189–204. See also Hammershaimb, pp. 32–38, 43–46.

Israel, the Northern Kingdom, by indicting the tribe that had most claim to covenant loyalty and divine protection by virtue of the salvation-promise made to David (2 Sa. 7); if Judah cannot gain exemption, what possible chance does Israel have?

These powerful declarations of judgment ring with notes of divine initiative. It is Yahweh personally who sends the fire, cuts off the corrupt leaders, leads the peoples into exile. The degree of innovation that Amos brought to biblical prophecy should not be missed. Judgment speeches prior to his time were usually addressed to individuals (*e.g.* Elijah's confrontation with Ahaziah, 2 Ki. 1:2–4). Amos directed them against whole nations, demonstrating Yahweh's righteous concerns for international politics and human welfare.

And to do this, Amos developed a fresh literary form. Attempts to connect the form and use of these speeches with Egyptian execration texts, in which the enemies of Egypt were depicted on vessels or figurines and then smashed in a ritual of magic, have proven unsatisfactory.[1] So have the efforts to relate Amos' speeches to a rite of cursing of enemies in connection with an autumn covenant-festival (Reventlow, pp. 56–75).

Spurred by the call of Yahweh and the visions of judgment (chs. 7–9), Amos combined the judgment speech, containing indictment of sin and threat of punishment, with notes of theophany and especially with the numerical sequence formula of wisdom literature, to make an irrefutable case against each of the neighbour nations. The three-four pattern assumes a list of known crimes of which the final and scale-tipping one is listed. What Amos indicates by this kind of argument is that punishment is more than merited and that Yahweh is totally just, not whimsical, capricious, or arbitrary, and thoroughly righteous in sending the judgment. Common sense, so runs the inference to be drawn from the wisdom motif, will make that plain to anyone who stops to think about it.

III. TRANSITIONAL JUDGMENT SPEECH AGAINST ISRAEL (2:6–16)

This impressive arsenal of argument is now aimed at Israel.

[1] A. Bentzen, 'The Ritual Background of Amos 1:2 – 2:16', *OTS*, 8, 1950, pp. 85–99.

The numerical formula (v. 6) connects this speech with the earlier ones, but Amos immediately breaks the pattern: (1) the indictment is longer and more detailed (vv. 6b–8); (2) the crimes listed are more specific and reflect a background in Israel's laws; (3) the accusation is sharpened by the recital of God's gracious provision in the Exodus (vv. 9–11); (4) Israel is addressed directly, 'also I brought *you* up out of the land of Egypt' (v. 10) whereas the nations were uniformly spoken of in the third person; (5) the judgment seems to be not fire to consume walls and strongholds nor exile for the king and court but earthquake that renders helpless the entire citizenry, even the fittest of the military (vv. 13–16).

The speech forms a bridge between the brief judgments against the nations and the longer series of oracles directed against Israel, beginning at 3:1. As such, it anticipates and introduces a number of the dominant themes of the book: (1) the mistreatment of the poor (vv. 6–7; *cf.* 4:1; 5:11–12; 8:4–6); (2) the corruption of worship by debauchery and injustice (vv. 7b–8; *cf.* 4:4–5; 5:21–24); (3) the abuse of the special privileges accorded them in the Exodus and conquest of the land (vv. 9–12; *cf.* 3:2; 9:7); (4) the opposition to the God-given ministry of the prophets (vv. 11–12; *cf.* 3:7–8; 7:10–17; 8:11–12); (5) the inescapable judgment by earthquake (vv. 13–16; *cf.* 3:14–15; 8:8; 9:1).

a. Indictment: economic and religious oppression (2:6–8)

Though the sequence of speeches focuses attention on the Northern Kingdom, called by Amos more precisely the *house of Israel* (5:4; 7:10; *cf.* house of Joseph, 5:6, so named because Joseph was father to Ephraim and Manasseh, two of the most powerful northern tribes, Gn. 48:8–22), the unmodified term *Israel* can be a reminder that the whole people of God is accountable to his law and liable to his judgment. Surely nothing that Amos says exempts Judah from such accountability (*cf.* 3:1 and 9:7, where Israel is clearly the whole people, not just the Northern Kingdom).

Four basic crimes seemed to be cited as ground for judgment in this paragraph: selling the poor into slavery (v. 6b), perverting the justice of the oppressed (v. 7a), engaging in illicit sexual intercourse (v. 7b), taking financial advantage of the unfortunate (v. 8). It may be that Amos has deliberately filled out the three-four pattern by listing a quartet of wrongs rather than skipping down to the last items as he did in all the other indictments of the nations.[1]

The common denominator of these rebellious acts is *abuse of power*. First, creditors, whether using bribes, financial adversity, or rigged evidence, sold innocent (or acquitted, as *righteous* means here) or indebted persons for set sums of money (literally '*the* silver'), a crime compounded where the amount of debt owed was as trivial as a pair of sandals (v. 6; *cf.* 2 Ki. 4:1–7 for Elisha's intervention in a case as tragic as Amos envisaged; *cf.* also Am. 8:6, where similar language to 2:6 is used, but with the emphasis on buying not selling). All of this is in violation of the spirit, at least, of the laws governing humane treatment of slaves (Ex. 21:2–11; Je. 34:8–22), violation of which laws made Israel's crime worse than Gaza's (1:6) or Tyre's (1:9), since Israel used her own people as merchandise for commerce.[2] Second, the harsh and insolent used all their corrupt influence in court (v. 7a; *cf.* 5:12) to strip the poor of human dignity by treating them as though they were dirt (*trample*, RSV, NIV, NEB, is probably better than 'pant', NASB, and involves only amending the root *š'p* to *šwp*, a reading reinforced in the LXX) and by denying them rights of justice (*way*, is short for 'way of justice' as in Pr. 17:23; wisdom ties to this verse can be seen in the parallelism of poor, Heb. *dal*, and *oppressed*, Heb. *'ᵃnî* or *'ᵃniwîm* in Is. 10:2 and Pr. 22:22). Third, fathers, taking advantage of filial obedience and the inability of young women to stand up for their rights, asserted patriarchal authority to have intercourse with their daughters-in-law, despite the laws of Israel which clearly forbade such confusion of sexual relations (*cf.* Lv. 18:15; 20:12; Dt. 22:28–29, 23–27). Neither slave nor prostitute seems to be in view (*contra* Martin-Achard, ITC, p. 22) since Amos uses the simple *na'ᵃrâ*, young woman, girl, to describe her. Fourth, the greedy exploited the unfortunate who have had to borrow money or who have extended themselves to pay a fine assessed for some alleged crime (*cf.* Ex.

---

[1] D. L. Christensen, 'The Prosodic Structure of Amos 1–2', *HTR*, 67, 1974, pp. 427–436; Amsler, pp. 180–181; Wolff, p. 168.

[2] For an alternative interpretation that the sale into slavery has to do with a defaulted land transaction in which the exchange of sandals was a symbol of the transfer of land, see J. L. Mays, p. 45.

21:22; Dt. 22:19) either by keeping overnight the cloak that the destitute needs for warmth (Ex. 22:25; *cf.* Dt. 24:12) or by wantonly carousing with the money paid in fine instead of using it for restitution.

These crimes are seen as unspeakable for three reasons: they were perpetrated by the powerful leaders of the land, including the elders whose task was to enforce justice; the forced intercourse was done in violation of God's instructions about holiness and, therefore, treated his *name* (*i.e.* his person, his character) as something profane and not holy (v. 7); and, some of them took place in shrines set apart for divine worship and thus demonstrated how purposeless, even vile, that worship had become (v. 8; *cf.* 5:21–24) when it spawned no appropriate justice.

b. Indictment expanded: divine grace in the Exodus (2:9–12)

As fierce as these indictments are, the prophet is not through yet. He intensifies his brief against Israel by an account of God's complaining reflection on Israel's past history and the lavish grace that made it possible (*cf.* Je. 2:2–7; Ho. 11:1–4). Beginning in verse 10, he addresses the Israelites directly, using the second person plural *you* and *yours*, rather than 'they' and 'them' of the previous verses, thus sharpening the confrontation. Finally (v. 11), he sets the trap for the final accusation (v. 12), by the disputation question with which this paragraph ends: 'Is it not indeed so, O people (literally, 'sons') of Israel?' The question is phrased to accept one answer only, forcing Israel to sign their own judgment papers. The covenant was like a magnifying glass that showed up Israel's every flaw of disobedience and ingratitude.

The destruction of the Amorites (v. 9) is mentioned before the Exodus (v. 10): (1) because it spotlights the gift of the land which the Israelites were so vilely profaning, (2) because it reminds Amos' hearers that one of the purposes of Yahweh's destruction of Palestine's early inhabitants was to protect the covenant people from polluting temptations (*cf.* the story of Achan in Jos. 7), and (3) because the Amorites' reputation for outlandish size and strength (*oaks* and *cedars* are standard images for grandeur; *cf.* Is. 2:12–13) should have made God's interventions all the more precious (Nu. 13:28; Dt. 1:28; 9:2).

Amorite seems to be a non-technical term almost synonymous with Canaanite (*cf.* Jos. 24:8, 11), though it may refer to the natives who were concentrated more in the territory that Judah occupied and which was conquered first, rather than to the population spread throughout the land. Old Akkadian texts use *Amurru* for various bedouin tribes, but late Assyrian and Babylonian records use it to describe the west, *i.e.* Syro-Palestine in general. The thoroughness of the divine extermination was depicted in the imagery of *fruit* and *roots* (*cf.* 2 Ki. 19:30; Is. 37:31). No opportunity for survival was granted; the covenant King not only trimmed the Amorite population, he uprooted it thoroughly and deforested the land to clear it for the occupation of his people. That Israel used it so badly was, thus, to her greater shame.

In one verse (10), the Lord reached back a step in history and summed up the essential messages of Exodus, Numbers and Joshua. Yet he did not pause to ponder the magnitude of these wonders. The Israelites knew them well, recited them in their history (Dt. 26:5–9), rehearsed them when they renewed their covenant (Jos. 24:1–13) and celebrated them in their Psalms (136:10–22). Besides, Amos was going to deal with the Exodus in due time and with full force (3:1–2). He quoted Yahweh as moving quickly past it to get to an essential, and easily overlooked, gift of grace: the provision of *prophets* and *Nazirites* from among their sons (v. 11).

12. Here the accusation reaches its climax. Not only did the Israelites break the covenant law by manhandling their weaker neighbours in the very shrines that should have reminded them of the covenant, not only did they do all this in the very land that God won for them after great struggle, but, to top it all, they compromised and rejected the spiritual leaders whom God had raised up to demonstrate discipline and to provide fresh revelation.

For background on the *Nazirites*, see Samson's story (Jdg. 13:5, 7; 16:17) and the regulations in the law which forbade drinking wine, putting a razor to the hair, or handling a dead body (Nu. 6:1–8; 1 Sa. 1:11, 18; 2:20 may hint that Samuel was a Nazirite). These acts of austerity symbolized special devotion to God and may have been intended to keep alive the special memories of the wilderness years.

The prohibition of prophecy was of special interest to Amos. Later he argued that prophets could not be muzzled

(3:7–8) and that to try to silence them was to court judgment (7:16–17). *Commanded* suggests that the people act as though they, not Yahweh, were in charge, despite the fact that true prophets knew themselves to be messengers under divine command, as Jeremiah learned when he tried to resist God's commission (1:6–7). This attempt to throttle the Nazirite and prophetic ministries is a reminder that salvation-history, the account of God's gracious interventions and provisions, is precisely paralleled by sin-history, the record of Israel's rebellion and thanklessness (*cf.* Vollmer, pp. 20–28 for discussion of this passage).

c. Announcement of judgment: earthquake (2:13–16)

Behold, used in Amos in connection with Yahweh's action alone, heralds the announcement of judgment, which, if the pattern of the preceding oracles had been carried out, would have occurred at verse 7 or 8. Verse 13 is one of the most difficult texts in Amos. The problem is the meaning of the key verb, which occurs twice (Heb. *'wq* is the root). It is translated variously 'crushes' (NIV), 'presses' (RSV), 'weighted down' (NASB, which uses 'totters' in the margin), or 'groans' and 'creaks' (NEB), 'shakes' (Mays), breaks open' (Wolff).

What is clear is that Yahweh's action in judgment is comparable to what a wagon *full of sheaves* does. But what is that precisely? No-one can say for certain; the Hebrew root occurs only here. The best choice is either to assume that the freighted cart has a crushing effect on anything under it, or to hold that the verb pictures the wheels splitting the earth open under its wobbly, pressing load.[1]

If the cart is seen as crushing, the judgment is probably *invasion*, as the fire, slaughter and exile of the earlier announcements prescribe. If as splitting the earth, then we have another mention of the familiar *earthquake* (1:1; 8:8; 9:1–4).

Whatever the means, the judgment is fraught with panic. It is *Yahweh's* coming; he has marked Israel as his enemy and neither strength (v. 14), speed, weaponry (v. 15; for *bow, cf.*

[1] H. Gese, 'Kleine Beiträge zum Verständnis des Amos Buches', *VT*, 12, 1962, pp. 417–438; H. W. Wolff (p. 134) follows this reading, as does Martin-Achard, ITC (p. 24).

Ho. 1:5, 7; 2:18; for *horse* as military beast, *cf.* Ho. 14:3), nor courage (v. 16; *mighty*, are the choicest soldiers, the finest troops; *cf.* 2 Sa. 20:7; 23:8–22) will make a difference (*cf.* Ec. 9:11). For pictures of Yahweh's ability to spark terror in enemy warriors, see Habakkuk 3 and Nahum 3:11–13. The oracle formula appropriately closes this section and clears the way for the fresh forms and themes that follow.

IV. THREE JUDGMENT SPEECHES AGAINST ISRAEL (3:1 – 5:17)

Amos has clearly established that Yahweh lists Israel among his enemies. His next and central task is to amplify the causes and consequences of this decision. This he does in three rather brief, jabbing speeches, each of which begins with a call to attention, *Hear this word* (3:1; 4:1; 5:1), and each of which ends with a tragic announcement of judgment. And in between, each bristles with the power, pathos and cogency of Amos' prophetic spirit. He ranges widely over crucial topics and spares nothing in literary form and artistry to get his points across.

a. Judgment speech: abuse of covenant privileges (3:1–15)[1]

This speech accomplishes three major tasks. First, it introduces Amos' chief theme for the rest of the book: Israel's special covenant privileges, the abuse of which merits special judgment (vv. 1–2). Next, in a series of disputational (rhetorical) questions (vv. 3–8), it both confirms the fact that Yahweh will bring harm to his own people (v. 6) and that Amos the prophet is obliged to announce that harm (v. 8). Finally, it describes the social injustices of Samaria, Israel's capital city (vv. 9–10), and announces judgment by foreign invasion both on the political capital and on the chief religious shrine, Bethel (vv. 11–15).[2]

---

[1]Chapters 3–4 are linked as one judgment speech in the form of a *rîḇ* or lawsuit by Marjorie O'Rourke Boyle, 'The Covenant Lawsuit of the Prophet Amos: III I–IV 13, *VT*, 21, 1971, pp. 338–362. For further discussion on prophetic lawsuits, see Kirsten Nielsen, *Yahweh as Prosecutor and Judge, JSOT* suppl. 9 (Sheffield: JSOT Press, 1978).
[2]Y. Gitay, 'A Study of Amos' Art of Speech: A Rhetorical Analysis of Amos 3:1–15', *CBQ*, 42, 180, pp. 293–309, argues compellingly for the literary unity of this chapter despite its stylistic diversity.

The links should not be missed between chapter 3 and the other parts of the book. They are clues to the careful composition of the final form of Amos' work: (1) the reference to the Exodus (v. 1) echoes and amplifies the divine complaint of grace-rejected of the previous speech (2:10); (2) the lion illustrations (vv. 4, 8, 12) hark back to the theme verse where God's threat of judgment is likened to a lion's roar (1:2); (3) the defence of the prophetic ministry and its involuntary character, governed by the sovereign call of God (v. 8), builds on the tensions described when the people stifled the prophets whom God has raised up for them (2:11–12); (4) *strongholds* punctuates this passage (vv. 9, 10, 11) as it did the first set of judgment speeches (1:4, 7, 10, 12, 14; 2:2, 5), as though God was mocking the arrogance of his people who thought themselves safe from disturbance in the luxurious fortifications of their palaces and no longer trusted God as refuge and strength (Ps. 46:1); (5) the mutinous, covenant-wrenching crimes of Israel (*transgression*, Heb. *pᵉšāʿîm*; 2:6) are mentioned again as the summary-word for all the social mayhem Israel has worked (v. 14).

i. Great privilege – great condemnation (3:1–2).

This judgment speech serves as an introduction to the remainder of the book. As such it is deliberately general: the accusation (v. 2a), *you only have I known* (*cf.* Ho. 2:20; 4:1, 6; 5:3; 6:6), lists no specific crimes and the announcement (v. 2b), *I will punish*, gives no details of judgment. Amos will see to that. His task in this passage is to make one point: Israel's great privilege of election by God and of relationship to him through the covenant, expressed in the intimate and powerful verb *known* (*cf.* Gn. 4:1; Ps. 1:6; Je. 1:5) exposes them to judgment rather than exempting them from it.[1] Indeed, their greater privilege marks them for greater condemnation – a condemnation in the form of curses that accompany the breaking of covenant (*cf.* Dt. 27:15–26; 28:15–68).

Israel, in Amos' view, seems to include Judah as well, since he calls to attention *the whole family* which enjoyed the Exodus deliverance. The closest parallels to this familial language are

---

[1]See H. B. Huffmon, 'The Treaty Background of Hebrew *Yada*', *BASOR*, 181, 1966, pp. 31–37, for the argument that the verb *know* in 3:2 has strong covenant overtones and could be translated, 'You only have I recognized by covenant.'

found in Isaiah 1:2 and Deuteronomy 32:5.

Verse 2 seems to contain a definite surprise. The first line sounds like a compliment, a pledge of exclusive affection, a tender reminder of Israel's special place in God's heart and programme. It is not until *iniquities* are mentioned at the end of the verse that its full meaning can be understood, since *punish* (Heb. *pqd*) means literally 'to visit' whether with weal or woe (*cf.* on Ho. 1:4; 8:13; 9:9).[1] Hence, the entrapment technique with which Amos began the book – calling the roll of the enemy nations and giving the impression that their judgment somehow meant Israel's relief – continues here. By bringing the verse to its climax in *your iniquities*, he has turned the word into a judgment speech with Israel as the victims, and he has brought down on their heads the weight of the curse that comes from not keeping the covenant (*cf.* Dt. 28:15–68).[2]

ii. Divine initiative – prophetic response (3:3–8). So great was Israel's surprise at the proclamation of judgment, so brazen did they deem Amos for proclaiming it, that there must have been some formal protest lodged contesting both the negative promise and Amos' right to deliver it. The opposition to message and messenger expressed in 7:10–17 is implied in 3:3–8, and Amos deals with it skilfully in a chain of disputational questions, each phrased in such a way as to determine the hearers' response.

Each of the first five questions (vv. 3–5) is marked by the customary syllable (h^a) that introduces interrogative sentences in Hebrew. Each argues from an observed result to an assumed cause. The *result* is two people walking together in a desolate part of Judah's countryside; the *cause* must be an appointment. The *result* is a lion's roar; the *cause* must be his capture of prey. So goes the argument, with the questions posed so as to demand the answer, 'No, you cannot have that result without that cause.' The five-fold repetition would evoke from the audience, especially from those familiar with the shepherding or hunting experiences that underlie them,

---

[1]G. André, *Determining the Destiny. PQD in the Old Testament,* CB.OT 16 (Lund: Gleerup, 1980), relates *pqd* to the sentence of a divine judge.

[2]Various interpretations of Amos' use of the election traditions of Israel (*e.g.* those of O. Cullmann, G. von Rad, G. Fohrer and J. Vollmer) are surveyed and assessed by J. J. Collins, 'History and tradition in the prophet Amos', *Irish Theological Quarterly,* 41, 1971, pp. 120–133.

almost a chant of negative responses.

Trap (Heb. *môqēš*, v. 5) is troublesome. It could mean (1) 'net' (Mays); (2) 'striker-bar' or 'trigger' (NEB) like those pictured in Egyptian paintings where the unwary bird steps on a bar which releases two netted frames that spring up and trap it; or (3) 'wooden missile' hurled at the bird like a boomerang (Wolff). The last interpretation seems most probable since it causes the bird to fall. Other uses of *môqēš* seem to suggest that it was not part of the small snaring net (Heb. *paḥ; cf.* Jos. 23:13; Pss. 69:23; 140:5; 141:9; Is. 8:14). The intent of these five questions is not to instruct us in ancient hunting techniques but to set up a series of automatic 'no' answers to Amos' questions, so that when he springs his trap in verses 6b and 8b we, with his audience, fall into it. Amos is the real hunter here. He is after our assent to what God has told him to say and called him to be.

The setting of the questions moves from country to city in verse 6, and the form of the question intensifies (the question particle is now *'im* not *hᵃ*). The illustration is not from a shepherd's encountering of lions or snaring of birds and small animals but from the terror of battle. In verse 6a the *cause*, the battle warning sounded by *trumpet* (*cf.* 2:2; Ho. 5:8; 8:1; Joel 2:1), is named first; then the *result*, 'the people begin to fear' (Heb. imperfect can be so translated). The point follows immediately. Where the *result* is calamity (so *evil*, *rā'â*, should be understood; *cf.* Ps. 23:4), is there any other place to trace the *cause* than to Yahweh's doing? No, of course not, is the only appropriate answer. So Amos has answered his opponents' first protest: disaster will strike Israel, and when it does, the Lord himself will have been responsible.

Verse 7 presents a bit of a puzzle by seeming to interrrupt the flow of questions in order to explain the God-given role of prophets in interpreting such calamities. It serves as a link between the question on divine activity (v. 6) and the climactic one on the inescapable duties of the prophet. As such, its literary purpose may be to postpone the climax and thus to enhance the suspense of the sequence of questions. Further, it may answer a question put to the prophet, how can he certify that what he has said about Yahweh's working (v. 6) is true?[1] Many commentators, however, have found it so disruptive

---

[1] Y. Gitay, *op. cit.*, pp. 304–305.

that they view it as a later addition. It does, nevertheless, succinctly state a common principle of revelation: God's deeds and his interpretation of them by the prophets go hand in hand. For the intimate relationship between Yahweh and the true prophets who stand in his council and hear his plans, see Jeremiah 23:18–22.

Once again, the form of question changes in verse 8, where *who* (Heb. *mî*) comes at the beginning of the second clause of each line. Here the sequence is reversed: the *cause* is stated first (as in v. 6a) and the *result* is phrased to follow inevitably. Again, and most important, the only allowable answer is negative. Can anyone throttle fear in the face of a lion's unexpected roar? Of course not. Can anyone refuse to prophesy after hearing the Lord speak? Of course not.

Amos has won his points not by reciting a special oracle or reviewing a unique vision. He has done so by leading his hearers through a catechism of common-sense questions to his double conclusion that reinforces all that he said in the beginning verses of this chapter: Yahweh will bring disaster on his people (v. 6b), and Amos has no choice but to announce it (v. 8b).

iii. Ashdod and Egypt – unlikely witnesses (3:9–11).

He gets on with that announcing immediately, and in a highly dramatic form. *Proclaim* and *say* are like instructions given to heralds (the Heb. imperatives are plural) who are to declare a message or, in this case, issue an invitation to neighbouring peoples.[1] The recipients of the message are the powerful leaders who occupy the *strongholds* of Ashdod and *Egypt* (v. 9). The MT Ashdod (NIV; NEB; NASB) is preferable to the LXX *Assyria* (RSV) which was probably substituted in order to provide a balance to Egypt (*cf.* note on Ho. 7:11). Amos does not mention Assyria directly in his book but rather seems to let its ominous presence, as the only logical invader who can fulfil all the dire prophecies of judgment, lurk behind the scene as an awesome yet unspoken reality.

The invitation, expressed in *assemble* (lit. 'gather') and 'look at' (NEB; lit. 'see'), appoints the foreign observers as witnesses,

---

[1] For the proposed literary form 'instruction to heralds', see F. Crüsemann, *Studien zur Formgeschichte von Hymnus und Danklied in Israel*, WMANT, 32 (Neukirchen-Vluyn: Neukirchener Verlag, 1969), pp. 50–55.

called to view at first hand the calamitous behaviour of God's people. The site of the gathering, the *mountains of Samaria*, suggests the scope of the wickedness and turns the whole city and its environs into a courtroom where God will make his case against his people. 'Great terror' (following Wolff's translation of *mᵉhûmôt rabbôt* as an abstract plural indicating intensity; *great tumults*, RSV), which is the effect of violent disorder and lawlessness within Samaria, and 'oppressed people' (reading the passive participle as descriptive of the victims rather than the acts of *oppression*) are the objects to be witnessed.

The selection of Ashdod and Egypt to supply the witnesses has several explanations: (1) their southern locations meant that they would be subject to Assyrian attack only after Samaria was judged by invasion and thus could be present through the whole trial, execution as well as indictment; (2) as ancient enemies of Israel, the Philistine and Egyptian presence would be especially aggravating to Samaria's leaders; and (3) above all, their reputations for injustice and brutality would be resented by the Israelites, who would consider themselves in every way morally superior to those whom God had summoned as witnesses. What Amos intends in this startling device of sending heralds to summon representatives of two pagan nations to witness Israel's corruption is two-fold: (1) to spotlight the depths of decadence to which God's people have sunk, in that nations which are the epitome of evil will judge their misconduct; and (2) to show that covenant law is not the only criterion for testing Israel's behaviour but that by any standards of international decency they have become culprits.[1]

All this becomes even more clear in verse 10, where the evidence against Israel is amplified: (1) Israel does not know how to do what is right, *i.e.* what is upright, honest, normally expected conduct (*cf.* Pr. 8:9; 24:26); (2) instead, they hoard as treasures (*store up*), *violence* to persons and looting of property (so *ḥāmās* and *šōd* should be understood; Ezk. 45:9; for *violence* see Jb. 16:17; for destruction as parallel to *robbery*

---

[1]The contrast in form between the judgment speeches of 1:3 – 3:2 and the summons to gather and witness Israel's crimes (3:9, 13) clearly separates the role of Ashdod and Egypt in this passage from that of Israel (3:1) and the 'cows of Bashan' (4:1). The latter are treated as defendants in the lawsuit not witnesses against themselves, *contra* M. Boyle, 'The Covenant Lawsuit', *VT*, 21, 1971, p. 343.

see Ob. 5). Once again, the *strongholds* (*cf.* on 1:4) come into play, this time as bastions where criminal activities are piled up with seeming immunity to punishment.

The *therefore* of the announcement of judgment, solemnized by the messenger formula, signals that all this is to end (v. 11). An invading enemy will cut off all means of escape by surrounding (reading Heb. *y^esôbēb* with most translations and commentators for *ûs^ebîb*, 'and around' which leaves the clause without a verb) the land. The invasion not only leaves Israel defenceless but seems, ironically, to have a purifying effect on the *land*, assuming that what is plundered from the strongholds (v. 11) is the murder and robbery which the Israelites had cached like treasures in them (v. 10).

iv. Thorough judgment – sarcastic proof (3:12). The messenger formula introduces an expansion of the judgment announcement. The form is a comparison between two scraps of a lamb that a shepherd may rescue from a lion's mouth (*cf.* 1:2; 3:4, 8) and the remnants of fancy furniture that those who 'loll' (Mays' apt translation of *dwell*; *cf.* 6:4–6 for a fuller picture of the opulent indolence of the Samaritan elite) in Samaria manage to save. The exact meaning of the last line is almost impossible to recover. The three most common suggestions read it: (1) 'a corner piece of a bed and a scrap of cloth from a couch' (*d^emešeq* for 'cloth' is doubtful); (2) 'splendid beds and couches from Damascus' (Mays; reversing the order of the last two words and repointing one to spell the Syrian capital); or (3) 'at the footboard of the couch and the headboard of the bed' (Wolff). This interpretation entails one major emendation (reading *b^e'āmešet* for *bid^emešeq*) but conforms well to what we know about Assyrian furniture design, where the wealthy slept between ornate footboards and headboards.

More important than the precise picture of the furniture is our understanding of the background of the comparison in Israelite law. The leg bones or 'a piece of an ear' snatched from the lion by the shepherd recall the *proof of attack* that an animal-herder brought to the owner of the beasts in the event that a wild animal had destroyed one of the flock. Such proof or evidence freed the shepherd from the penalty of paying restitution for the destroyed animal (Ex. 22:10–13). Amos' comparison, then, makes the sarcastic point that when

AMOS 3:13–15

invasion strikes (v. 11) Israel's devastation will be so complete that all that will be rescued is proof of death in the form of scraps of furniture, or, on Wolff's reading, only the tattered memory of lazy luxury on fancy beds.

v. Ashdod and Egypt – witness continued (3:13–15). To whom are the commands *hear* and *testify* addressed? The simplest answer is the representatives of Ashdod and Egypt summoned to Samaria in verse 9. They who were called to assemble and observe Samaria's crimes are now to hear (presumably the divine verdict) and give testimony (or evidence; the word here *hā'îdû* is related to the word for evidence or proof, *'ēd*, in Ex. 22:13) as firsthand witnesses both to Israel's *transgressions* (v. 14; *cf.* 2:6) and to the thoroughness of God's judgment. The commands are solemnized by an expansion of the oracle formula to include Yahweh's titles as Lord (*ᵃdōnāy*) and God of hosts, *i.e.* Ruler of all the armies in heaven and earth. The description of Israel as *house of Jacob* (*cf.* 6:8; 7:5; and especially 9:8) may prepare the way for the announcement of *Bethel's* judgment (v. 14; *cf.* Gn. 28:18–22); with the collapse of the political entity that bears Jacob's name comes the eclipse of the sacred spot where he met God and which he named accordingly. The twice used verb *punish* (v. 14; Heb. *pqd*) harks back to the general announcement of 3:2 and is a clue to the unity of the chapter.

The destruction of *Bethel* is described in a way that adds to the picture of complete judgment: not only is Israel's most important religious shrine attacked (*cf.* 7:13), but its symbols of sanctuary, the horns of the altar that projected up from the table-like top and offered special power and protection to anyone who clung to them, were to be cut off.[1] The picture of devastation apparently returns to Samaria (v. 15). Though it is not mentioned, it is the most likely site of the opulent homes whose furniture was inlaid with ivory and which were custom-designed and situated, some to be suitable for winter and others for summer (*cf.* Ahab's two palaces, one for winter in Jezreel, 1 Ki. 21:1; the other at the higher, cooler elevation of Samaria, 1 Ki. 21:18).[2] The phrase frequently translated

[1] See R. de Vaux, *Ancient Israel: Its Life and Institutions* (E.T., Darton, Longman, and Todd, 1961) p. 414, for a description.
[2] S. M. Paul, 'Amos III 15 – Winter and Summer Mansions', *VT*, 28, 1978, pp. 358–359, calls attention to Babylonian texts that distinguish 'winter palace'

153

'great houses' (RSV; NASB; NEB) is probably better rendered 'many houses', in keeping with the context that attacks the excessive luxury of owning more than one house in a society where poor people were regularly being dispossessed of their staple goods (*cf.* 5:11).

b. Judgment speech: rejection of divine warnings (4:1–13)

There can be little doubt about the literary genre of this chapter, although the various elements of the judgment speech are presented with a good deal of artistic variety: (1) the call to attention and first indictment are addressed not to the people (3:1) or house (5:1) of Israel but to a specific group of wealthy women in Samaria (4:1); (2) the first announcement of judgment is introduced not by a messenger formula (*cf.* 3:11; 5:16) but by a divine oath and an eschatological formula (4:2); (3) the second indictment (4:4–5) takes on the tone of sarcasm, mimicking the way in which priest might admonish worshippers to be faithful in their sacrificing; (4) the third indictment (4:6–11) is a five-part homily, rehearsing God's acts of judgment that were intended to prompt repentance but did not, as the persistent accusation 'yet you did not return to me' reminds us; (5) the final announcement of judgment, typically introduced by *therefore* (4:12), contains no specific threat, only the general warning that God intends to confront his people and they had better be ready; (6) this announcement is underscored by a hymn-like poem which celebrates the Creator's irresistible power and then identifies him as Yahweh, God of hosts (4:13); and (7) the speech is accompanied by the bell-like toll of the oracle formula, 'says Yahweh' (lit. 'utterance of Yahweh', or 'delivered by Yahweh'), which rings home the authority of the speech (vv. 3, 5–6, 8–11).

In its movement and themes, this speech both builds on and contrasts with what Amos has said thus far. The *continuity* may be seen in the persistence with which he couples the twin themes of oppressive wealth and abuse of worship: (1) Israel's rebels sleep on the pledge garments of the poor right in the

---

from its summer counterpart and concludes that the rich Israelites were aping the customs of neighbouring royalty in the building of 'separate pleasure palaces in accordance with the climatic conditions of their country'.

shade of their altars and drink the wine of those unjustly fined in the house of their God, probably a cryptic reference to Bethel (1:8); (2) the altars of Bethel and the lavish houses of Samaria alike and together will suffer destruction (3:14–15); and (3) the greedy women of Samaria's palaces and the self-centred frequenters of Bethel's and Gilgal's shrines are equally condemned. The movement to indict both the social and the religious practices of Israel, so wickedly interrelated, seems to gain specificity, intensity and vehemence as the speeches continue.

The *contrast* is seen in the way history is recited as part of God's indictment. The previous accounts of Israel's history featured God's gracious deliverance and provision (2:9–11; 3:1–2) and faulted Israel for failing to appreciate them. The present five-part indictment (4:6–11) recounts God's acts of judgment and blames the people for not penitently learning their intended lesson. Both the continuity and the contrast seem deliberate and contribute to the evidence that the book is a carefully crafted, skilfully composed piece of prophetic art.

i. Judgment speech against Samaria's wealthy women (4:1–3). The call to attention follows the stereotyped pattern of masculine imperatives (3:1; 5:1), even though the group addressed is feminine (see comments on Joel 2:22 for another example). The sarcastic epithet *cows of Bashan* seems to refer both to the luxury that the wealthy women enjoyed and to a certain voluptuousness and sensuality which their extravagant life-style afforded them. Beyond that, some (Koch, p. 46) have heard overtones of fertility worship in the label *cows* as though they saw themselves as consorts of Yahweh whom they worshipped at the shrines under the figure of bull-god (*cf.* the Baalized calves of Hosea).[1] Bashan, the most fertile part of Gilead along the Yarmuk river in Transjordan, was a byword for prosperity in agriculture and animal husbandry (Ps. 22:12). The robustness that the women and their men viewed as beauty and blessing (*cf.* Ps. 73:4–7; Song 7:1–2; 8:10) was evidence of their crimes, according to Amos. Such prosperity was purchased at incredible cost: cruel oppression (*cf.* 3:9) and

---

[1] P. F. Jacobs, '"Cows of Bashan" – A Note on the Interpretation of Amos 4:1', *JBL*, 104, 1985, pp. 109–110, has claimed confirmation for this theory in drawings and inscriptions from Kuntillet 'Ajrud in N. Sinai which may picture Yahweh and a consort, 'both with bovine features'.

relentless harassment of the poor and needy (*cf.* 2:6–7). 'Lords' (*husbands*), leaves open the possibility that some of the women may have been concubines as well as wives. The desire for drink at any cost may be a further comment on 2:8 as well as an anticipation of 6:6.

The surety of their judgment and its intensity are the themes of verses 2–3. The divine oath (*sworn*) gives ultimate seriousness to the threat of judgment. God backs it with the whole weight of his *holiness*, his divine character, his intrinsic excellence that separates him from the way all his creatures behave (*cf.* on Ho. 11:9). For Amos' use of other divine oaths to solemnize announcements of judgment, see 6:8; 8:7. The drama of the threat is enhanced by the eschatological formula, *Behold, the days are coming upon you*, employed here by Amos for the first time (*cf.* 8:11, another announcement of judgment and 9:13, a promise of salvation). *The days* are the time of God's intervention in history and politics to set right all accounts. The formula used here fortifies Amos' emphasis that the future coming of God will contain heavy surprises for Israel (*cf.* 2:6–16; 3:1–2) and sets the stage for the full development of that surprise in his woe oracle on the day of the Lord (5:18–20).

The intensity of the women's judgment is clear, but the exact character of it is not, largely because we do not know precisely either the meanings of the implements of captivity in verse 2 or the location and significance of *Harmon* (or 'Hermon') in verse 3. Most translations interpret the implements as 'hooks' or 'fish-hooks' (RSV; NIV; NASB; Mays, with question marks). NEB calls them 'shields' and 'fish baskets', while Wolff argues for something like 'ropes' and 'harpoons'. The captors pull and prod their corpulent prey like a balky, bovine herd through the many breaks in the city walls, which have been so thoroughly damaged that gates, if still standing, become unnecessary (v. 3).[1] Some help in identifying *Harmon*, which many commentators emend to 'Hermon', suggesting a location in the anti-Lebanon mountain range beyond Damascus (*cf.* 5:27), may have come from D. N. Freedman and F. I.

---

[1] In a thorough review of the possible interpretations of this difficult verse, S. M. Paul, 'Fishing Imagery in Amos 4:2', *JBL*, 97, 1978, pp. 183–190, suggests that *hooks* and *fishhooks* should be read 'baskets' and 'pots'. The picture would then be of fish being packed in such receptacles for transportation (*cf.* Je. 16:16; Hab. 1:14).

Andersen. Building on a suggestion of W. F. Albright they connect Amos' Harmon with Ugaritic *hrnm* and modern Hermel near Kadesh on the Orontes river. They further point out that such a site accords with Amos 5:27 (*cf.* 2 Kings 25:6, which pictures Zedekiah's presentation to Nebuchadrezzar, his captor, at lblah, only a few kilometres from Harmon).[1]

What must not be missed in this fierce address to the ruthless women, whose closest biblical counterpart is Isaiah 3:6 – 4:1, is the fact that they are held personally accountable. Whatever complicity their husbands (or masters) may have had in their crime, here they alone are indicted and their punishment depicted. Nothing in their social system, patriarchal though it may have seemed by other standards, gave them one jot of an excuse when the days of judgment came.

ii. Mock admonitions against the shrines (4:4–5). The sarcastic attack on the shrines at *Bethel* and *Gilgal* seems to be a caricature of a form of priestly instruction (Heb. *tôrâ*), in which commands are given about ritual practices and reasons (usually introduced by 'for' or 'because', Heb. *kî*) are stated as explanation of the practices.[2] The closest parallels to Amos' form are found in Leviticus 7:22–25; 19:58 and Deuteronomy 14:4–8, 21. Amos twists the command with full irony by ordering the people to enter the shrines not to worship (*cf.* Ps. 100:4) but to *transgress, i.e.* to demonstrate their rebellion by the emptiness of their worship, by their failure to back their ritual with acts of righteousness (*cf.* 5:21–24), and by the greed that sought their own pleasure and good.

For the geography and history of *Bethel* and *Gilgal*, see the comments on Hosea 4:15. Amos' criticism of their practice seems not to centre in any violation of ritual regulations.[3] Indeed, he needles them for doing right acts: they sacrifice in

---

[1]Freedman and Andersen, *BASOR*, 198, 1970, p. 41, helpfully suggest the sequence of sound shifts of which Amos' form *hrmn*, instead of Ugar. *hrnm*, is a middle stage.

[2]J. Begrich, 'Die priesterliche Tora', *Werden und Wesen des Alten Testaments*, ed. by P. Volz, F. Stummer, J. Hempel, *BZAW*, 66, 1936, pp. 63–88. *Cf.* also Wolff, pp. 211–212.

[3]Burning the leavened bread (v. 5) was technically an infringement of the regulations of Lv. 2:11; 7:11–14. But such infringement does not seem to be Amos' point. See Vuilleumier, pp. 50–51, for the views that burning the leavened bread was a sign of Israel's breach of covenant and for the reading of *three days* as 'three years' on the basis of Dt. 14:22–29; 26:12 (*cf.* NIV).

the morning, pay tithes of their crops (Dt. 14:22–29; *cf.* Gn. 28:22 for Jacob's tithing at Bethel) on the third day of their pilgrimage, burn their thank-offerings (Lv. 7:12–15; 22:29–30), and announce their free-will offerings (Lv. 7:16–17; 22:18–23); but they do them for the wrong reasons, as the words *proclaim* and *publish* (or 'announce', v. 5) suggest. Their selfish motivation and lack of concern for God's glory and worship are apparent: (1) *your* sacrifices and *your* tithes, God labels them (v. 4); (2) the people make public show of their offerings (*cf.* Jesus' indictment of such practice in Mt. 6:1–18); and (3) above all, they love to do this sacrificing and eating of the sacrifices (*cf.* on Ho. 4:8–10) as a form of family party, without due regard for their sacred purposes or the obligations of justice that went with them.

iii. Recital of judgment-history: warnings unheeded (4:6–11). The form and content of the indictment change dramatically in this series of accusations. Here divine judgment, in its varied forms, is pictured as an expression of grace that should have induced Israel to repent, turn back to God and trust fully in him. The acts of judgment seem to grow increasingly intense beginning with attack on the food supply: famine (v. 6), drought (vv. 7–8), plight and insects (v. 9). They continue by ravaging the inhabitants with plague and military action (v. 10), and finally conclude with the utter destruction of some of the towns, after the fashion of Sodom and Gomorrah (v. 11; *cf.* Ho. 11:8–9).

The account of God's sovereign intervention is direct and without apology. He is the subject of the leading verb in each section, and that subject is reinforced in verses 6–7 with an emphatic pronoun, 'even I myself'. At the same time, Israel's utter intransigence is drummed home by the five-fold repetition of *yet you did not return to me*, that is 'you did not abandon your rebel ways and come back to your covenant commitment and give the loyalty which you have owed me from the beginning.' (*Cf.* Ho. 2:7; 3:5; 6:1–3; 14:1–2; Joel 2:12–13, for the force of *return*, Heb. *šwb*.) Isaiah (9:13) would have caught the gist of this section:

> The people did not turn to him who smote them,
> nor seek the Lord of hosts.

God's use of famine and drought to achieve his purposes is

well documented from the stories of Joseph and Jacob (Gn. 41:57 – 42:5) to the accounts of Elijah and Ahab (1 Ki. 17:1 – 18:1). Amos' powerful figure of speech, *cleanness of teeth*, is clearly interpreted by the more literal *lack of bread* (v. 6), a technique not uncommon in biblical poetry (*e.g. cf.* Song 4:1–7; Ho. 7:3–7,11; where literal descriptions surround and clarify metaphorical ones). The picture of drought (v. 7) is the most detailed of the section and spares no effort to show the hardships that God had dispatched on his people as messengers of grace: (1) absence of spring rain that was absolutely necessary for the barley (May) and wheat (June) crops which provided *bread*, the main staple of the common people's diet (v. 6); (2) random patterns of rainfall that left townspeople and farmers alike confused and frustrated; and (3) disruption of life and conflict over water rights without any slaking of thirst (v. 8). This frightful picture of famine and drought, a reminder of Palestine's fragile ecology before modern irrigation became prevalent, was displayed also by Amos in 8:11–12, where the withdrawal of God's words was likened to a lack of bread and a thirst for water that again sent people wandering in quest of their basic provisions.

Blight and *mildew* (v. 9) are frequently paired in Scripture (Dt. 28:22; 1 Ki. 8:37; 2 Ch. 6:28; Hg. 2:17). *Blight* is the work of the east wind that dries and scorches the grain prematurely so that it turns brown. *Mildew* is the product of parasitic worms which turn pale the tips of green grain.[1] In the problematic second line of the verse, it is probably best to follow the emendation that makes a finite verb (*heḥᵉrabtî*) out of the infinitive construct (*harbôt*), as, following Wellhausen, many of the modern versions (RSV; NEB; JB; Wolff; Mays) have done. The meaning, then, would be 'I struck' or 'smote' (as with a sword), and the style would be parallel to that of verse 10 where the first two lines begin with finite verbs of divine action, both in the perfect tense.

The emphasis in this verse is again on the thoroughness of the destruction. Every basic crop of grains, fruits, vegetables, grapes and olives is wiped out. Grain, wine and oil were Hosea's list of agricultural staples (2:8, 22) to which he sometimes added fig trees (2:12). Amos' mention of *gardens* only

---

[1] Wolff, p. 221, following the careful descriptions of G. Dalman, *Arbeit und Sitte in Palästina*, vol. 2, pp. 333–334; vol. 1/2 (1928) p. 326.

sharpens the picture of disaster. The prophet's agricultural background (7:14) gave him personal credentials to understand the horror of these scourges on the nation's food supply. See comments on Joel 1, for the abilities of *locusts* to bring devastation. The attack on the crops was particularly significant to Amos because it tied in with his first two visions (7:1–3, 4–6) that helped so significantly to set the tone for his mission. Israel's failure to learn from the lesser disasters of the past would force God to trigger the all-out assaults of the visions.

Defeat in battle is the judgment described in verse 10. The familiar trio of wartime scourges – *pestilence* (a by-product of the lack of water, spoiling of food, failure of sanitation that siege conditions produced), *sword*, and captivity (Je. 43:11; Ezk. 5:12) – are employed to underline the severity of the judgment, a severity heightened by the designation of the soldiers as choice or crack troops (Heb. *baḥûrîm*; RSV, *young men*), and by the stomach-turning mention of the *stench* of rotting flesh. *Egypt* gives the passage a telling thrust: the Exodus is reversed; the divine disaster that once saved Israel (Ex. 12:29–30) has lately been turned against him. Even *horses* have not provided escape (*cf.* 2:15; Ho. 14:3); they, too, are taken captive by the enemy.

The overthrow of some of the cities (v. 11) probably refers to military assault, rather than natural disaster, continuing the picture of judgment by political means. The international mayhem described in 1:3 – 2:3 offers adequate background, though we need not try to connect Amos' reference to any specific invasion. Suddenness and thoroughness of the disaster seem to be the force of the allusion to *Sodom* and *Gomorrah* (Gn. 19; *cf.* Dt. 29:23; Is. 13:19; Je. 49:18; 50:40).

These verses bring to a climax the account of the intensity of divine judgment in the comparison between Israel and the cataclysmic end of the Bible's vilest cities. They also remind the hearers that even where judgment was most fierce grace was extended: some of the Israelites, like Lot and his daughters, were *as a brand plucked* from the fire.

In this litany of judgment, Amos has been mindful of the covenant curses that hung over the heads of the people to warn them against disloyalty to the great King (*cf.* Dt. 29:10–28). Solomon's prayer of temple dedication outlines a schema of judgment, repentance and restoration similar to what

Yahweh has hoped for in 4:6–11 (1 Ki. 8:33–40). Amos has given the covenant curse a special twist by interpreting it not as a promise of future judgment but as a lens through which to look at past judgment, a lens that focuses not just on the wrath of a betrayed Sovereign but on the grace of One who yearns for restored fellowship with his wayward people.[1]

iv. Announcement of divine encounter (4:12). The context (vv. 6–11) with its chain of indictments, and the *therefore* with the divine promise of doing something to Israel, give this verse the formal marks of an announcement of judgment. The difficulty is that the *thus* and the *this* that God announces offer no strong hint of what he will do. Nor is the nature of the meeting with God clear, for which Israel is admonished to prepare. The encounter with Yahweh at Sinai may give us a clue to Amos' meaning. There, *prepare* (Ex. 19:11, 15) plainly means Israel's readying themselves to deal with the holiness and majesty of God. And *to meet God* (Ex. 19:17) is to experience a theophany, an awesome display of the divine presence accompanied by thunders, lightnings, thick clouds, trumpet blasts and smoke from a fiery presence (Ex. 19:16–25).

In capsule form Amos' language assumes that sense of overwhelming, even life-threatening, awe. Yet, Amos' words can hardly be an invitation to worship. Against the Sinai background may be placed Ezekiel's words to Gog, 'Be ready and keep ready' (Ezk. 38:7), where the context is preparation for battle. All of the awful terror which God displayed to Israel in covenant grace at Sinai will now be unleashed in judgment against him because of the triple indictment – the ruthless opulence of Samaria's women (4:1–3), the empty, self-centred rituals of Bethel and Gilgal (4:4–5), and the refusal to read the invitation to repentance in the messages of judgment (4:6–11). The *thus* and *this* may assume some

---

[1]See Mays, pp. 79–81, for further discussion of the covenant curses. Mays seems not to accept H. W. Wolff's arguments (pp. 217–218) that these verses should be dated in Josiah's day. As reason, Wolff cites the relationship of Am. 4:6–11 to 1 Ki. 8:33–37 and Lv. 26, as well as the fact that Amos usually bases his arguments from the past on God's blessing (2:9–11; 3:2) not on his judgment. Wolff's first reason assumes post-Amos dates for the materials in Lv. and Ki. His second seems even weaker, premised as it is on the idea that Amos can have only one way of treating Israel's past history.

dramatic symbolic gesture like a blow from a fist, a cutting of the throat, or a wielding of a sword.[1]

v. First hymn of divine sovereignty (4:13). If judgment is the theme of verse 12, then the interpretation of the hymn stanza that follows must be in line with that theme of judgment. Its purpose seems to be to depict graphically the power and glory of the God with whom Israel must ready themselves to do battle. It may at the same time be an implied call to worship, a hint that if Israel were to take with full seriousness the wonderful name of Yahweh, repentance and life might yet be possible. Its role, then, would be to bring the judgment speech of 4:1–13 to a climax with a glorious portrait of the Judge about to appear before them in theophanic splendour and to prepare for the admonitions of 5:1–17 that urge Israel to seek the Lord and the good that he requires (5:4, 6, 14).

The hymn form is characterized both by the Hebrew participles, usually translated as relative (*who*) clauses, that describe the acts or traits of Yahweh (*cf*. Ps. 104:2–4, 31–32) and by the conclusion that declares *his name*. Two other hymn stanzas, probably from the same poem, are employed by Amos (5:8–9; 9:5–6; *cf*. 8:8c, d), both in contexts that describe God's power to judge (*cf*. also Eliphaz's hymn in Jb. 5:9–14).

In verse 13 creation, revelation and judgment are the main activities ascribed to Yahweh. He moulds (*forms*; Heb. *yṣr*; *cf*. Gn. 2:7) the *mountains* like a potter and *creates* (Heb. *br'*; *cf*. Gn. 1:1) the *wind* out of nothing. Yet in fellowship with human personhood and in accommodation to human frailty he reveals *his* (the pronoun most likely refers to God) musing and contemplation (*cf*. 3:7). At the same time his presence bodes terror. The smoke or clouds that shroud his person (see on v. 12) may obscure the sun and darken the *morning* and his steps may shake the high places of the earth, perhaps a cryptic reference to his power to shatter the shrines of Bethel and Gilgal (vv. 4–5; *cf*. comments on Ho. 4:13, for discussion of shrines as 'high places').

The use of the hymnic material suggests that the celebration of Yahweh's power as sovereign Creator was part of Israel's

---

[1] R. Youngblood, *JBL*, 90, 1971, p. 98, by amending the Heb. *liqra't* to *liqrô' 'et* supports the translation suggested by G. W. Ramsey, *JBL*, 89 (1970), pp. 187–191: 'Prepare to call your gods, O Israel.' The irony is obvious and may find some support in Am. 5:26 and 8:14.

worship at the beginning of the prophetic era. Amos seems to be using language to which he feels no need to add commentary. There is probably a touch of irony intended, as Amos takes Israel's familiar hymnody in which the people would have found great joy and comfort (5:23) and turns it back on them as evidence of God's right and power to judge them.[1]

The judgment speech of 4:1–13 begins and ends with descriptive participles. In verse 1 the women are indicted as oppressing, crushing and begging; in verse 13 God is lauded as creating, declaring, making and treading. We cannot be sure that Amos intended such a contrast, but the idea of it is certainly in line with everything he has said about the ultimate and tragic difference between God's ways and those of his people.

c. Judgment speech: perversion of worship and justice (5:1–17)

Amos continues his denunciations of Israel's sins and his predictions of Israel's demise, carrying over some of the *themes* – the attack on the shrines (4:4–5; 5:4–6), the exposé of oppression (4:1; 5:10–12, 15) and the celebration of divine power (4:13; 5:8–9); as well as some of the same *forms* – the admonitions (4:4–5; 5:4–6, 14–15), the hymn (4:13; 5:8–9) and, of course, the combinations of accusation (4:1, 6–11; 5:10–12) and announcement (4:2–3, 12; 5:3, 16–17).

The tone, however, of this third judgment speech separates it from what has come before: (1) Amos laments as well as

---

[1] On the hymn stanzas in Amos, see Watts, pp. 51–67; Vuilleumier, pp. 88–90; J. L. Crenshaw, *The Doxologies of Amos: A Form Critical Study in the History of the Text of Amos* (Nashville: Vanderbilt University, 1964); K. Koch, 'Die Rolle der hymnischen Abschnitte in der Komposition des Amos-Buches', *ZAW*, 86, 1974, pp. 507–537, who finds in the placement and function of the hymns clues to the structure of the book, and C. I. K. Story, 'Amos – Prophet of Praise', *VT*, 30, 1980, pp. 67–80, who contrasts the Creator-Judge emphasis of Amos with the Creator-Redeemer theme of Is. 45:7, 18 (*cf.* 43:7) and argues that each theme is appropriate to the time of the author and that, accordingly, there is no valid reason to deny the hymn-stanzas to Amos. In contrast, F. Foresti, 'Funzione semantica dei brani participiali di Amos: 4:13; 5:8s; 9:5s', *Bib*, 62, 1981, pp. 169–184, holds that the hymnic participle passages of Amos, with their theophanic emphases, stem from a context which redounds with cosmological themes that derive from Job and Second Isaiah and point the way to the notes of divine retribution in the apocalyptic literature.

denounces (5:1–2); (2) his admonitions are urgent, even passionate (5:4–6, 14–15), but not sarcastic (except, perhaps, for the puns on the names Gilgal and Bethel (v. 5); (3) the real, yet remote, possibility of rescue is offered (vv. 6, 15); (4) in all of these ways the prophet's genuine human concern for a people perched on the brink of oblivion comes through, as it will even more powerfully when he intercedes for them in the visions (7:2, 5); and (5) yet he also speaks, in the dirge (5:2) with which the speech begins and in the call to lament (5:16–17) with which it ends, as though Israel were already dead.

Attention has been called to the symmetrical, chiastic pattern in which the passage, despite its brief and diverse components, has been composed:[1]

Lamentation as announcement (vv. 1–3)
  Admonition (vv. 4–6)
    Accusation (v. 7)
      Hymn (v. 8a–e)
        Yahweh his name! (v. 8f)
      Hymn (v. 9)
    Accusation (vv. 10–13)
  Admonition (vv. 14–15)
Lamentation as announcement (vv. 16–17)

The author's intent (the pattern can hardly be accidental) seems to centre on the inevitability of judgment – the *lamentations* at the beginning and end – and the calls to seek the Lord – the *admonitions* – as the only possible way of escape.[2] The speech is anchored in the middle by the mighty reminders of the power of the God whose covenant name is Yahweh, whom Israel is either to seek in repentance or meet in battle (4:12).

i. Announcement in the form of lamentation (5:1–3). The call to attention is addressed by the prophet to the Northern

---

[1] J. DeWaard, 'The Chiastic Structure of Amos 5:1–17', *VT*, 27, 1977, pp. 170–177. The overall chiastic structure is matched by a profusion of specific chiastic patterns in several of the verses (5, 7–12, 14–16; see comments for details).
[2] See A. V. Hunter, *Seek the Lord! A Study of the Meaning and Function of the Exhortations in Amos, Hosea, Micah, and Zephaniah* (Baltimore: St. Mary's Seminary & University, 1982) for the view that the admonitions (exhortations) confirm the judgment and do not offer a possible escape from it.

Kingdom as an entire political entity (*house of Israel*; cf. v. 4). In addressing a lament to a nation, Amos sets a pattern which both Jeremiah (7:29; 9:10) and Ezekiel (19:1 – Israel's princes; 26:18; 27:32 – Tyre; 32:2 – Egypt) followed. The lamentation as a literary form (Heb. *qînâ*) is characterized by short, almost sobbing lines and by dramatic contrasts which picture the tragic reversal – from strong to weak, from high to low, from noble to disgraced – which persons (cf. 2 Sa. 1:19–27) or cities and peoples (cf. Lamentations) experience. Amos' switch from the hymn of power and glory (4:13) to the lament of tragedy beyond remedy is one of the most deliberately jarring transitions in the book.

The introduction (v. 1) is followed by the actual chant (v. 2). The key verbs, 'she has fallen' and 'she has been abandoned' (cf. Jdg. 6:13; 1 Sa. 12:22; Is. 2:6), describe Israel's plight in the briefest, yet most final way. Amos has joined the mourners at the funeral of a once mighty and beloved people. Those verbs of collapse and rejection are matched by the clauses that speak of rising or standing (Heb. *qwm*): Israel has no capacity to get on her feet again and no helper is at hand to pull her up – least of all the covenant God, who, throughout her history, has been her Saviour. Two words add poignancy to the dirge and highlight the depths of Israel's fall: (1) *virgin* (cf. Je. 18:13, 31:4, 21) depicts the vulnerability of Israel (cf. Jdg. 11:38; 2 Sa. 18:18) and the special sadness that accompanies her death, as though she should have had a whole life of love and fruitfulness before her; (2) *land* (or 'soil'; Heb. *'a̅da̅mâ*) connotes death as the result of invasion, when the land of hope and promise becomes the cruel ditch where her abandoned body is splayed.

The *for* in verse 3 marks its connection with the lament: it tells why Amos had to sing the funeral song. Invasion will take place; Israel's armies will go out (cf. 2 Sa. 18:2–4) to battle, conscripted from each city by thousands (1 Sa. 10:19) or hundreds (Jdg. 7:16; 1 Sa. 22:7; 2 Sa. 18:1, 4); each military unit will be literally decimated.[1] The point, underscored by the messenger formula, is not that a remnant will survive but that the judgment which this verse announces will be virtually total, so sweeping that the only proper response is a dirge.

[1]For the bases on which troops were recruited and mobilized, see R. de Vaux, *Ancient Israel: Its Life and Institutions*, pp. 216–18

ii. Admonitions of opportunity (5:4–7). The divine speech continues but in a new form – admonitions marked by imperatives which issue both negative and positive commands. The antithesis is the key: Yahweh is making clear that to *seek* him (*i.e.* to call on him for help and to cling to him in loyalty) is the exact opposite of making a pilgrimage to a shrine like *Bethel* (*cf.* 3:14; 4:4–5), *Gilgal* (4:4–5), or *Beersheba* (a city in southern Judah revered for its contacts with Abraham and Isaac, Gn. 21, 26; Israelites apparently made occasional pilgrimages there, crossing Judah's border to honour their patriarchal roots; *cf.* Am. 8:14). 'If you seek me, then you will survive whatever judgment comes', is the way we can paraphrase the two imperatives of verse 4. (The connection between seeking and living is made explicit in verse 14 with the addition of the word 'that' or 'in order that'; Heb. *lᵉma‘an*.) In contrast, to make the established religion the object of seeking was to court disaster because the shrines themselves, along with the people who frequented them, were slated for judgment (v. 5; *cf.* 3:14).

The judgment is expressed first (v. 5) in puns (*cf.* Is. 10:28–30; Je. 1:11–12; Mi. 1:10–15; and Introduction to Hosea, for other instances of prophetic word-plays): (1) Gilgal's judgment is exile; the two words for exile have *g* and *l* as their root, so that their very look and sound mirror and echo the name of the famous shrine; (2) Bethel's judgment was to be reduced to worthless wickedness, a place so wrapped up in idolatry that it makes no contribution to life at all; the pun substitutes *'āwen*, worthlessness, wickedness, idolatry, for *'ēl*, the divine name (*cf.* Ho. 4:15; 10:5, 8, for evidence that Amos' pun had become a prophecy fulfilled). The chiastic structure of verse 5, beginning and ending with *Bethel* and mentioning *Gilgal* twice in between, is a reminder of Bethel's supremacy in Israel's life and, therefore, Amos' ministry. Bethel is mentioned seven times (3:14; 4:4; 5:5–6; 7:10, 13), Gilgal three (4:4; 5:5).

A more literal picture of the judgment in the form of fire (*cf.* 1:3 *etc.*; 7:4) comes in verse 6, where the *house of Joseph* (*i.e.* the kingdom of Israel, named here for the father of the two chief tribes, Ephraim and Manasseh; *cf.* 5:15) is threatened along with Bethel. The severity of the judgment is stressed in the clause *none to quench it*, which recalls the earlier description of helplessness, 'none to raise her up' (v. 2).

In verse 6, Amos seems to have repeated for emphasis

166

Yahweh's admonitions from verse 5, couching them in the third person, *seek the Lord*, for 'seek me', and then adding the dreadful consequences of not obeying the admonition, introduced by *lest*. (For a parallel in form to admonitions plus *lest*, *cf*. Pr. 22:24–25.) Amos' dire words for Bethel came to pass both in Assyrian invasion (*cf*. Ho. 10:8) and in Josiah's reformation, which listed the destruction of Bethel among its chief accomplishments (2 Ki. 23:15–18).

The links between verse 7 and the rest of this speech are unclear enough to have sparked hot debate. The most common suggestion is to move the verse to a position between verses 9 and 10 (NEB) and to add the word 'woe' or some equivalent to its beginning (JB; Wolff; Mays; Amsler; Delcor, *etc*.). This relocation, however, has no support in Hebrew manuscripts or ancient versions but is based on the presence of woe oracles in 5:18ff. and 6:1ff. With Cripps (p. 183), and RSV, we can read these words as a dramatic way of addressing the house of Israel, to whom the admonitions were pointed (v. 4). It is a strong reminder of how badly they need to seek the Lord and how severely the shrines had misled them. The similarity of syntax between 5:7 and 6:3 has prompted Wolff (p. 272) to treat the latter passage also as a woe oracle, even though again the keyword 'woe' is missing. Does it not seem wiser to treat both passages as addresses to Israel (RSV) and limit the woe-oracles to those texts where the woe is actually stated (5:18; 6:1)?

The coupling of *justice* (Heb. *mišpaṭ*) and *righteousness* (*ṣᵉdāqâ*) is repeated by Amos (5:24; 6:12) as the best summary available to define the covenant responsibilities of God's people. Just because justice (*cf*. Is. 30:18) and righteousness (Mi. 7:9) are essential activities of Yahweh, they must become prime duties of his people, especially of the leaders (*justice*: Mi. 6:8; *righteousness*: Dt. 6:24; both together: Is. 1:21; 5:7; 28:17; Je. 22:16–17; Ps. 72:1–4, 12–14; Pr. 16:8; 21:3; *cf*. 8:20). One purpose of worship is to come to know God so well that who he is and what he does become concrete realities in our persons and behaviour. Where such imitation of divine activity is not present, worship is deemed worthless (Am. 5:21–24; Ho. 6:6).[1]

---

[1]For the relationship between God's character and the conduct of his people, see D. A. Hubbard, 'Ethics: OT Ethics', *ISBE*, rev., II, p. 166.

Justice and righteousness in the Old Testament carry us beyond strict adherence to law, as central as law is (*cf.* Am. 2:4, 6–8). Both terms have to do with covenantal responsibilities and are close to being synonymous, especially when they are paired (*cf.* Gn. 18:19; Pr. 1:3; 2:9). If there are shades of differences to be discerned, *justice* puts some slight emphasis on establishing and preserving order in society by righting wrongs and punishing the wrong-doers, while *righteousness* emphasizes the relationships that covenantal society entails and insists that each partner in the covenant do all that is necessary to keep the covenant working right.[1]

Both words centre in action on behalf of the poor, the underrepresented and the oppressed, as our immediate context in Amos (vv. 10–12, 15) suggests. 'The justice of Yahweh is not of the type of the blindfolded maiden holding a balance in her hand, the justice of Yahweh extends one arm to the wretch stretched out on the ground whilst the other pushes away the one who causes the misfortunes.'[2]

The chiastic structure, which places these nouns of covenant concern at the centre of the pattern and sets the verbs at the beginning and ending, suggests that the emphasis is on the verbs. That technique helps the verse, though it is formally an address, to serve as an accusation in anticipation of the more detailed indictment of verses 10–12. The verbs catch the heart of the crime: the people express their rebellion (1) by *turning* the sweet words and deeds of justice (*cf.* Ps. 119:103) into the bitterest substance nameable – *wormwood* (*Artemisia absinthium*), a familiar plant in the Mediterranean and Middle Eastern worlds, proverbial for a bitterness (Pr. 5:4), comparable only to the taste of poison (Am. 6:12; Dt. 29:18; Je. 23:15; La. 3:19); in Shakespeare's *Romeo and Juliet* (Act I, Scene III), the nurse recalls the hour of Juliet's weaning, 'When it did taste the wormwood on the nipple of my dug, and felt it bitter, pretty fool!'); and (2) by *casting* (even hurling or slamming; *cf.* Is. 28:2) to the ground, as though it were trash, the righteousness that God counts precious.

---

[1]Some of the best discussions of these terms are to be found in the contemporary Old Testament theologies: *e.g.* G. von Rad, I, pp. 322–323, 370ff., 414ff.; E. Jacob, pp. 94–102; W. Zimmerli, pp. 189–192; Th. C. Vriezen, pp. 388–390.
[2]E. Jacob, p. 99.

One central question remains about verses 4–7. Does not the slight hope of life it offers contradict the death-like finality of the judgment which Amos proclaims? How can the same prophet chant a dirge and urge a return to Yahweh in back-to-back passages? H. W. Wolff's understanding of the passage promises some help with the question. First, Wolff surveys three of the most important suggestions put forward by other scholars: (1) A. Weiser has heard in our text the same irony found in 4:4–5 and thus removed any possible contradiction; Wolff rightly stresses the contrasts in tone between 4:4–5 and 5:4–5; (2) F. Hesse finds in the differences between the two oracles (5:1–3 and 5:4–6) an example of the freedom of Yahweh to say one thing at one time and something surprisingly different at another; while Wolff salutes the emphasis on God's freedom, he does not find sufficient help in Hesse's approach to resolve the problem; (3) A. Alt has suggested the possibility of different audiences for the two sections, the judgment of verses 1–3 being addressed to the corrupt leadership (*cf.* 4:1–3) and the admonitions to life of verses 4–6 to the general mass of the people; Wolff, however, points out that the text addresses both passages to the same audience – the house of Israel, the whole kingdom (vv. 1, 4).

Wolff finds in verses 4–6 a conditional promise of survival, *if* the people will seek the word of the Lord as it comes to them through the prophet. Comparing the imperative *seek the Lord* with similar passages (*e.g.* 1 Ki. 22:5 = 2 Ch. 18:4; 2 Ki. 22:13 = 2 Ch. 34:21; Je. 21:2), Wolff notes that the seeking here is not directed to any cultic activity but is a direct inquiry of Yahweh's will through a prophet. The points made in this passage, then, are that Yahweh still has freedom to offer rescue under the very nose of death; yet such survival is possible only to those who truly heed the prophet's word – another instance where Amos combines a note of divine sovereignty with the prophetic role in interpreting that sovereignty (*cf.* 3:7–8).[1]

iii. Second hymn of divine sovereignty (5:8–9). This hymn stanza (*cf.* 4:13; 9:5–6) reinforces the conditional threat

[1]Wolff, pp. 237–239; *cf.* also A. Weiser, pp. 190–192; F. Hesse, 'Amos 5:4–6, 14f.', *ZAW*, 68, 1956, pp. 7–10; A. Alt, 'Die Heimat des Deuteronomiums' in *Kleine Schriften* 2, p. 269.

of judgment, 'fire ... with none to quench it,' of verse 6. Though as to the details of its interpretation there are considerable scholarly differences, its basic purpose seems to be to remind Israel afresh, in the language of its own worship, how formidable is the sovereign Creator with whom it has to reckon.

Most translators settle on *Pleiades* and *Orion* as the names of the two constellations (*cf.* Jb. 9:9; 38:31), though the ancient versions, which are our best clue to the meanings of the two Hebrew words, show considerable variation in rendering the terms both here and in Job. God's sovereignty over the creation is further expressed in his control of the seasons, with their varying ratios of light and darkness, and his regulation of the periods of drought and rain which characterize the weather of Palestine.

A secondary purpose of this stanza may have been to counter the pagan influences of the Canaanites, who credited El and Baal with control of the heavenly luminaries and the earthly weather. Like most ancients (and not a few moderns), the Canaanites revered and feared the planets and constellations (*cf.* 5:26) and attributed to them uncanny power over human history and destiny. All this false belief and superstition is shattered by the awesome announcement: *the Lord is his name*, a clause which, appropriately, is central to the chiastic structure of this passage (see above) and, indeed, to the whole book.[1]

Some scholars (*cf.* NEB) find further mention of constellations in verse 9, where they read *destruction* as Taurus (emending Heb. *šôd* to *šôr*), *strong* as Capella (emending Heb. *'āz* to *'ēz*), and *fortress* as Vintager (emending Heb. *mibṣār* to *mᵉbaṣṣēr*).[2] Though the present text has some difficulties in it, it is understandable without such emendations and suits better the context of judgment when left virtually as it is. Two slight emendations, both supported by the Septuagint, improve the poetic balance: read 'stronghold' (JB; NIV) instead of *strong* (RSV; NASB) and 'brings' (JB; NIV) instead of *comes* (RSV; NASB).

[1] See Coote, pp. 79–82, for comments on the structure and meaning of this passage.
[2] See G. Hoffman, 'Versuche zu Amos', *ZAW*, 3, 1883, p. 111, and Delcor, p. 211, for this theory which is also suggested in the critical apparatus of *BHS*. On the constellations and stars of the Old Testament see J. M. Everts, 'Astronomy', *ISBE*, rev., I, pp. 344–348, and M. T. Fermer, 'Stars', *IBD*, pp. 1214–1215.

The structure of these verses is chiastic, pushing into prominence the verbs with which the sentence begins and ends – verbs that highlight the fact that the Lord who controls the creation is able and ready to tackle any human situation that defies his will, no matter how well buttressed and fortified that situation may seem.[1] Once again (*cf*. 1:4, *etc*.; 3:9, 11; 4:3), Amos acknowledges God's special enmity against the human arrogance that thinks itself impregnable to divine judgment.

iv. Announcement of judgment for blatant injustice (5:10–13). The *gate* (*cf*. vv. 10, 12, where *gate* forms an envelope for the whole passage as second word from the beginning and second word from the end) is the setting for this direct and specific judgment speech, which combines accusation (vv. 10–11a, 12) and announcement (v. 11b). The *they* of verse 10 suggests that Amos here is talking *about* the culprits of the house of Israel, not *to* them. Judicial decisions for each community were taken at the gate of the city, where the heads of families and other elders assembled to hear witnesses, arbitrate disputes, decide controversies and generally dispense justice. The space on the inner side of the gate together with rooms or alcoves in the gate area itself were used as courtrooms.[2]

The accusation in verse 10 makes specific the more general indictment of verse 7 by describing some chief ways in which justice and righteousness were perverted. Its main subject is truth-telling, the giving of reliable and accurate testimony in any judicial hearing. Amos' accusation is made biting by another use of the chiastic pattern, which begins and ends with the verbs *they hate* and *they abhor*: what the divine commandments cherished (Ex. 20:16; Dt. 5:20) and what the wise men honoured (Pr. 6:19), the leaders of Israel despised (*cf*. Pr. 12:1; 15:10 for similar judgments on those who hate correction or reproof). No matter whether the elders tried to do their duty by rendering strong scoldings or sound corrective decisions to irresponsible acts of conduct, or whether witnesses spoke faithfully as to what they had seen and heard, the

---

[1]L. Zalcman. 'Astronomical Illusions in Amos', *JBL*, 100, 1982, pp. 53–58, suggests reading v. 9b as a quotation: As 'Destruction shall come on the fortress'. *Cf*. Is. 13:6; Joel 1:15.

[2]See L. Köhler, *Hebrew Man* (E.T., New York and Nashville: Abingdon Press, 1956), pp. 127–150.

result was the same: the utter contempt of the very persons chartered to guard the welfare of the social and legal life of Israel.

In the threat of judgment (v. 11) the culprits are once again addressed directly, and the case against them is amplified to include harsh practices of taxation of the peasant share-croppers. It is probably best to read the first two clauses in close parallelism. Both describe the greedy crime of charging tenant-farmers too much for the use of land which may well have been taken away from the rightful owners by fraud (in violation of the letter and spirit of Lv. 23:13–38). To support the close parallelism, we should not amend the first verb to *you trample* (Heb. *bûsᵉkem*; cf. RSV; NIV; JB) but should interpret it as a technical word meaning something like 'you receive rent from' (Heb. *bôsaskem* might then be a garbled form of the Akkadian verb *šabasu*; cf. Wolff; Mays; NEB; NASB).[1]

The wickedness of the greedy rich is made even more clear in the announcement of judgment (v. 11b) that depicts how they have used their ill-gotten gain: (1) for ostentatious living in houses not of clay-bricks, the ordinary building material (Is. 9:8–10), but of cut stone with all the expense of quarrying, transporting, shaping and applying mortar – a luxury intro-duced by Solomon (1 Ki. 5:13–18; 7:1–12) and abused by Samaria's elite, as Amos notes (3:15; 6:4); and (2) for the planting of lovely vineyards (*cf.* Is. 5:1–2) which not only symbolized their personal freedom and security (*cf.* Mi. 4:4) but also supported the carousing and debauchery which Amos so roundly denounced (4:1; 6:6). The prescribed judgment is exile, resulting in the ultimate loss of land. They who had looted the lands of the weak to sate their greed will undergo the total deprivation of living without house or vine.

Amos knows firsthand (v. 12) that the *transgressions* (*pᵉšā'îm*; cf. 2:6; 3:14; 4:4) and *sins* (Heb. root *ht'*; *cf.* 9:8, 10; Ho. 4:7, 8; 8:11; 10:9; 12:8; 13:2) of the Israelites are not occasional lapses but are so numerous ('countless', NEB; a better transla-tion of *ᵃṣumîm* than *great*, RSV; NIV) as to be the rule not the exception. In this verse, the prophet, who has been doing the speaking since verse 6 (God's words will conclude the speech in vv. 16–17), adds further accusations, as though to reinforce

---

[1]See H. Torczyner (Tur-Sinai) *Altbabylonische Tempelrechnungen*, Denkschrif-ten d. Kais. Akad d. Wiss. (Vienna: 1913), p. 130.

the need for the judgment that he has already announced. In so doing, he also returns to the failure of the legal system on which note he began in verses 7 and 10. As in verse 7 he folds the accusations into an address that begins with a participle and concludes with a finite verb, thus forming a chiastic structure that emphasizes the illicit actions of persecuting the 'innocent' (*cf.* 2:6 for this translation of *ṣaddîq*) and rejecting the valid claims of the poor (*cf.* 2:6), when those claims are presented in court (the *gate*). The heart of the matter here seems to be bribery, the specific means by which the innocent were harassed and the poor defrauded of their rights. Again, wealth and power have conspired to thwart the covenant insistence that every member of society should receive a fair hearing in litigation.

Therefore (v. 13) should ordinarily signal an announcement of judgment. Instead, we find what looks like a proverb. The silence referred to cannot be Amos'. That form of wisdom or prudence would contradict all that he says about the inescapable commission to prophesy and the folly of trying to muzzle it (2:11–12; 3:3–8; 7:10–17). One key to understanding the role of this verse is the timing. *In such a time* (*i.e.* 'in that time') must reach forward to the time of judgment by exile announced in verse 11. That time is called *evil* (*cf.* 3:6) because of its utter calamity, its total disaster; all of life is harshly uprooted and roughly transplanted to foreign soil. In that future time, the prudent person will quietly acquiesce to the judgment, since the prophetic word has so fully demonstrated both its certainty and its necessity. They who have silenced the claims of the innocent in court shall themselves be silenced by the inevitability of their own punishment.

v. Further admonitions of opportunity (5:14–15). For the third time in the speech (*cf.* vv. 4–5, 6–7), the prophet injects admonitions into the heart of a judgment speech. Though the form may be borrowed from priestly instruction (*tôrâ, cf.* 4:4–5), the focus is not on the shrines, whose evil end he has already announced (vv. 5–6), but on the *gate*. So great is his passion for justice and so closely does he identify justice with God's character, that he calls the people not to seek the Lord but to seek the *good*, the true obedience to God's will that demonstrates itself in the *setting up* (*establish*, RSV) of justice (contrast this with the *casting down* of righteousness in v. 7).

The *good* that is sought, even loved (v. 15) is much more than a rigid legal system; it is responsible and considerate social conduct warmed by a generosity akin to God's (*cf.* Ps. 23:6).

The posing of the opposites – *good* and *evil, hate* and *love* – as choices adds to the intensity of the exhortation. As in wisdom literature, this antithetical structure makes clear the life and death differences that such decisions entail (for similar language, see 1 Ki. 3:9; Is. 1:16–17; Pr. 1:22; 9:8; 11:27; 12:1; 13:24; *cf.* also Pss. 34:12–14; 37:3, 27–28).

Each verse is a kind of conditional sentence in which the imperatives – *seek, hate, love* – are to be understood as *if* clauses (protases); the conditional promises – 'the Lord . . . will be with you', 'perhaps the Lord . . . will be gracious' – are the *then* clauses (apodoses). The first conditional promise (v. 14) borrows its language from Israel's ancient traditions of divine provision (Gn. 26:3, 24; 28:15; 31:5) and protection in times of holy war (Nu. 14:43; 23:21; Dt. 31:8; Jdg. 6:12–13). *As you have said* points to the use of a formula like 'Yahweh is with us' in public worship, perhaps at Bethel. What Amos has judged to be presumption *could* become a fact, *if* the people would really dedicate themselves (*seek*) whole-heartedly to the practice of justice in all its forms and ramifications.

The second conditional promise is made even more tentative by the 'perhaps' (or *it may be that*; Heb. *'ûlay*). Here Amos' understanding of the stubborn will of the people and his consciousness of the Lord's freedom to decide on whom to shine his mercies (Ex. 33:19) combine to make the prophet couch the promise in the subjunctive mood. He dare offer no guarantee, only the slight possibility that God may extend grace (as a master would to a servant or a strong parent to a weak child). *Remnant* should be read in the light of Israel's weakness: it is not so much a promise of the future rescue of some faithful Israelites (*cf.* Is. 37:31–32) as it is a recognition of the present frailty of Joseph's sons and daughters in the Northern Kingdom, wracked as they have been by previous judgments (4:6–11) and small as they seem among the nations (7:1–6).

vi. Announcement of widespread lamentation (5:16–17). The final announcement of judgment, triggered by the usual *therefore* (*cf.* vv. 11, 13) and messenger formula, is delivered in the words of the Lord, who earlier in the speech had announced the devastation of Israel's armies and admonished the people to seek him by heeding the prophet's word (vv. 3–5). The tone of the announcement – voiced in weeping, wailing, woe and lamentation – takes us back to the funeral dirge with which Amos began this third judgment speech (vv. 1–2). *Therefore* connects these verses, not just to verse 12 as most commentators note, but to the entire passage, which contains both direct accusations (vv. 7, 10–11a, 12) and indirect accusations in the form of admonitions (vv. 4–6, 14–15). So patent is it to Amos that Israel will ignore the admonitions that he proceeds immediately with the announcement. Furthermore, the rejection of the admonitions becomes part of the indictment and thus paves the way for judgment.

Lamentation or *wailing* (Heb. *mispēd* occurs three times) dominates the city – Samaria seems to be in view though not actually mentioned – and the countryside as thoroughly as it does the first scenes in Joel, which are draped in calls to lament (Joel 1:8–13). The public plazas and the narrow streets alike ring with the cries of 'woe' (or *alas*; Heb. *hô*; more frequently *hôy*; cf. 1 Ki. 13:30; Je. 22:18; 34:5). So great is the grief that even the farmhands who had been forced to work the land for such meagre wages (v. 11) are mustered to help the professional mourners (cf. 2 Ch. 33:25; Ec. 12:5; Je. 9:17–22) in venting their public grief. Stylistic balance has led most translators and commentators to follow the Vulgate in placing the preposition *in* (Heb. *'el*) before *wailing* (end of v. 16) rather than before 'professional mourners' (*skilled in lamentation*), where it has stood in the MT, which reads literally (v. 16c):

> And they will call farmer(s) to mourning
> and wailing to those skilled in lamentation.

RSV's rendering preserves the parallelism,

> and to wailing those who are skilled in lamentation.

The ironic mention of the summoning of farmers to assist in the funeral (and perhaps burial) rites, reinforced by the specific mention of grief in the vineyards (v. 17; Is. 16:10), recalls, by way of contrast, the joyful singing of the workers in the happy times of harvest. These are the same vineyards, undoubtedly, in which Israel's rich had taken pride and of whose wine they had so freely imbibed (v. 11; *cf.* Introduction to Joel for the possibility that farms are singled out as sites of lamentation because their crop failure would be seen as the bankruptcy of their fertility cult).

The reason for the all-consuming grief becomes clear in the last line – the Lord himself threatens to pass through their midst as he had once passed through the land of Egypt and destroyed the first-born of Pharaoh's land (Ex. 12:12). God's people had become the enemy, defiling his name in their shrines, perverting justice and righteousness into bitter and worthless waste, robbing their countrymen of God-given land and despising his invitations to return to him. They have left Yahweh no choice but to pass through (Heb. *'br* with *b*) in devastating judgment and never again to pass by (Heb. *'br* with *l*; *cf.* 7:7; 8:2) in grace and forgiveness. What form this judgment may take is not stated. The context, especially verse 3, points to military invasion (*cf.* also 6:14), while the hint of the Lord's work in Egypt suggests a plague. The *how* of destruction is not Amos' subject here; it is enough for him to make clear the *who*. The collapse of justice and righteousness leads to more than social upheaval. It leads inevitably to divine retribution. Covenant righteousness and justice are not mere political conveniences to oil the social relations of Israel. They are divine necessities for a covenant people, whose very reason of being is to demonstrate the uniqueness of their just and righteous God. When justice and righteousness are moved out of Israel's midst, Yahweh can do nothing else but move in.

V. TWO WOE ORACLES AGAINST ISRAEL (5:18 – 6:14)

In two celebrated speeches Amos continued to inveigh against Israel's twin evils: ardent worship without a corresponding concern for justice (5:18–27) and opulent indolence without an appropriate awareness of pending calamity (6:14). The two sections begin by highlighting a common theme: Israel's misguided sense of security, whether in the supposed victories that the day of the Lord would bring (5:18) or the alleged impregnability of Mount Samaria (6:1). Both sections end by threatening a common fate: exile (5:27) and invasion (6:14).

Three different backgrounds have been suggested for the *woe* oracles found here and in other prophets (*cf.* Is. 5:8, 11,

18, 20–22; 10:1; 28:1; 30:1; 31:1; 33:1; Hab. 2:6, 9, 12, 15, 19): (1) the *curse*, where a powerful person pronounces doom upon an individual or group (*e.g.* Gn. 9:25; Jdg. 5:23); using Deuteronomy 27:15–26 as an illustration, Westermann holds that the prophetic woes are curses that have been adapted to the legal (cultic) practices of Israel in ways that brought them in close touch with the judgment speech;[1] (2) the funeral *lament*, where a mourner sobs in grief for a dead loved one (*e.g.* 1 Ki. 13:30; Je. 22:18; 34:5);[2] and (3) a form of *wisdom instruction*, sometimes used in opposition to 'blessed' (Heb. *'ašrê; cf.* Is. 3:10–11 and Ec. 10:16–17 in JB; NEB; *cf.* Lk. 6:20–26), where the disastrous results of bad conduct are dramatized; note JB's 'trouble for those' as a way of catching this wisdom nuance.[3] The strongest evidence seems to stand on the side of the third alternative, as has been strongly argued by J. W. Whedbee and H. W. Wolff.[4]

Though the terror and finality of the judgment predicted by Amos may be reminiscent of a curse, and though the passage just preceding this (5:1–17) is heavy with funereal language, Amos' aim in these woes appears to be a warning of trouble as a reward for Israel's foolish conduct rather than pronouncement of a curse or an expression of lament, as though Israel were already dead. The disputation questions (5:20, 25; 6:2–3, 12–13) and admonitions to change their ways (5:23–24) stamp the woes as warnings to which Israel must respond or else.

a. Woe oracle: misguided interpretation of the Day of Yahweh (5:18–27)

It seems best to treat this passage as a unified block of teaching

---

[1]C. Westermann, *Basic Forms of Prophetic Speech* (E.T., Philadelphia: Westminster Press, 1967), pp. 190–198.

[2]R. J. Clifford, 'The Use of Hoy in the Prophets', *CBQ*, 28, 1966, pp. 459ff.; D. E. Gowan, *The Triumph of Faith in Habakkuk* (Atlanta: John Knox Press, pp. 50–67. J. G. Williams, 'Irony and Lament: Clues to Prophetic Consciousness', *Semeia* 8, 1977, pp. 51–74: 'The alas-form does not focus on future calamity as much as it expresses a lament over a present loss. ... It is the bemoaning of a sickness unto death' (p. 55).

[3]E. Gerstenberger, 'The Woe-Oracles of the Prophets', *JBL*, 81, 1962, pp. 249–263.

[4]J. W. Whedbee, *Isaiah and Wisdom* (New York and Nashville: Abingdon Press, 1971), pp. 80–110; H. W. Wolff, *Prophet*, pp. 17–34.

on the Day of the Lord – the wrong and right understanding of it – despite the varied literary forms which occur: woe (v. 18a), accusing question (v. 18b), corrective answer (v. 18c), illustration in form of parable (v. 19), disputation question (v. 20), divine cultic response (vv. 21–22), negative and positive admonitions (vv. 23–24), disputation questions (vv. 25–56), announcement of judgment (v. 27). The unity of the paragraph is found in the description of public worship in which Israel anticipated the Day of Yahweh as a day of victory over all her enemies and yet which, to Israel's utter surprise, Yahweh hated. So empty was that worship when it had no impact on the social and personal righteousness of the people.

i. Description of the Day of Yahweh (5:18–20). The intensity with which Israel celebrated their anticipation of the Day of the Lord (v. 18) is conveyed in the word *desire* ('long for', NIV) which elsewhere describes sharp hunger or thirst (Nu. 11:34; 2 Sa. 23:15) and is denounced in Proverbs (11:23; 13:4; 21:25–26) as a greed akin to covetousness. The strength of the verb serves both to show how passionately the people yearned for God's deliverance and to set them up for the vast contrast between what they believed the day would be and how it would, indeed, turn out.

The confidence in the Day of Yahweh was for Israel a bridge between past and present. Though Amos' mention of it is the earliest that we can date in biblical literature, it is clear from the context that he was correcting an old misunderstanding, not introducing a new notion. The Day of Yahweh seems to have been linked to Israel's past wars in which the Lord miraculously intervened to bring victory to his people. The memory of victories like Gideon's over the Midianites (Jdg. 7) or David's over the Philistines (2 Sa. 5:17–25) sparked hope of the future conquest of God's enemies (Is. 9:4; 28:21). Such manifestations of divine intervention were called *the day* (*e.g.* day of Midian, Is. 9:4; day of vengeance, Is. 34:8; day of Yahweh, Is. 13:6, 9).[1]

These victories were not merely events of the past. Their

---

[1]For discussion of the 'holy war' as possible background to Israel's understanding of the Day of Yahweh, see G. von Rad, *OT Theology*, II, pp. 119–125.

significance was kept fresh in Israel's consciousness by the frequent celebration of them in public worship (*cf.* Ps. 136). That worship, in turn, increased Israel's expectations of future deliverance. In fact, prayer for such future blessing could be part of Israel's thanksgiving for the past (Ps. 118:21–25). And that very event of thanksgiving for past victory and petition for future intervention was heralded as 'the day which the Lord has made' (or 'on which he has acted') and in which 'he has given us light' (Ps. 118–24, 27). This combination of motifs – joy in past victory, hope for future intervention, celebration of a day in which God has given light – serves as a window into the meaning of Amos' paragraphs in 5:18–27. To put it briefly, Amos' pressing question about the significance of the Day of the Lord to the Israelites ('What really does the day of the Lord mean to you?') and his stinging answer ('darkness and not light') presuppose both a wrong *belief* about the purpose of the Day and a naive *practice* of worship that featured the celebration of the Day.[1]

Darkness is the state where clear sight is impossible and, therefore, where danger lurks, where enemies can hide, where pitfalls beckon; it symbolizes unexpected danger, disaster unforeseen (Jb. 18:6, 18; La. 3:2). *Light*, in contrast, depicts clarity of vision, ability to catch the full picture, see the way fully; it connotes safety, security, freedom from fear (*cf.* Ps. 27:1; Is. 9:2).

The illustrative parable (v. 19) makes it clear that darkness and light do not speak here of wickedness and righteousness (*cf.* Is. 5:20) but of disaster and safety. The movement of the parable is best understood as stages in one story, where each apparent moment of security is fraught with fresh danger. The climax is the ironic picture of a breathless fugitive leaning against the wall of his own house, panting in gratitude for the rescue from the *lion* and *bear*, only to have a snake pop its head from a crack between the mud bricks and bite his hand (*cf.* 9:3). The threat of lions (*i.e.* the Asiatic or Persian species, which lived in Palestine until about AD 1300) is well attested in the Old Testament, as the experiences of Samson (Jdg. 14:6),

---

[1]For a recent interpretation of the Day that combines von Rad's emphasis on holy war and S. Mowinckel's (*He That Cometh* [E.T., Oxford: Basil Blackwell, 1956], pp. 124–154) view that the Day originally referred to Yahweh's manifestations in Israel's public worship especially the autumn New Year festival, see A. J. Everson, 'Day of the Lord', *IDB Supp.*, 1976, pp. 209–210.

David (1 Sa. 17:34–36), and Benaiah (2 Sa. 23:20) show. Bears (*i.e.* Ursus Syriacus, kin to the Ursus Arctos of Europe and Asia) though usually herbivorous, could be viewed as even more ferocious, especially when their young were threatened (*cf.* 2 Sa. 17:8; Pr. 17:12; Ho. 13:8). Bears survived in northern Palestine into the beginning of the twentieth century. The *serpent* is assumed to be poisonous (*cf.* Ec. 10:8), although most of the identifiable Palestinian species of snakes both in ancient and modern times are not. Both *lion* (*cf.* 3:8; Ho. 11:10; 13:8) and *bear* (Ho. 13:8) serve as metaphors for God, but serpent does not. Used symbolically, serpent (*nāḥāš*) signals either evil (Ps. 58:4; 140:3) or dangerous craftiness (Gn. 49:17; Is. 14:29). We view, therefore, Amos' three figures as well-understood symbols of danger rather than as images with any deeper spiritual meaning.

Any lingering illusion that Israel cherished about the glories of the Day of Yahweh is shattered by the rhetorical questions with which Amos clinched his point (v. 20). What he had already declared to his hearers in verse 18 he reaffirmed: the Day entailed for rebellious Israel not the light and brightness (*nōgah* often described Yahweh's brilliant rescue of his people; *cf.* Ps. 18:12, 28; Is. 9:1; 13:10; Hab. 3:4, 11) which they imagined and sang about, but darkness and gloom, like the plague that shrouded Egypt in the Exodus (Ex. 10:21–29). The desperate, more detailed pictures of the Day in the prophets (*e.g.* Is. 13:6–16; Joel 2:1–2, 30–31; Zp. 1:7–16) take their dark colours from Amos' palette.

ii. Denunciation of cultic festivities (5:21–24). The lack of transition suggests a strong connection between these verses and the previous section. It was in public worship, probably at Bethel (5:5–6; 7:13), that the wrong conception of the Day of the Lord was perpetuated.

The intensity of the attack on Israel's cult is sustained in a number of ways. First, Yahweh himself begins to speak, as is clear from the content and the concluding messenger formula in verse 27. Second, the absence of an introductory formula (*e.g.* 'thus says Yahweh' or 'hear this word') points to an impatience, as though the prophet in Yahweh's name had interrupted the service to denounce it (Wolff). Third, the hatred and rejection of Israel's feasts is expressed in language as sharp and cutting as possible (*cf.* Ho. 4:6, against the priests; 9:15, 17, against the people themselves; Dt. 12:31, 16:22, against Canaanite religion to which level Israel's had now stooped). Fourth, God stamps his disapproval on the religious transactions by branding them *your* feasts, *your* gatherings (or 'assemblies'; *solemn assemblies* in RSV and AV gives the wrong impression; the gatherings were noisy and exuberantly joyful), *your* offerings, *your* fatted calves; this spate of religiosity is strictly the people's doing.

Fifth, the cluster of words used for various facets of religious ritual underscores the thoroughness of God's denunciation. The events themselves (feasts and assemblies) God despises, with all of their components, including: (1) *burnt offering* called '*ôlâ* because it goes up (Heb. *'lh*) to God in smoke, and was designed to express total (note *kālîl* = entire, as a frequent descriptor of the burnt-offering; Dt. 33:10; 1 Sa. 7:9; Ps. 51:21) homage to God and to effect atonement for sin (Lv. 1:3–4), or (2) *cereal* (grain) *offering*, called *minhâ* because it was a 'gift' in which the offerers paid tribute to Yahweh by returning to him part of his creation on which they were dependent (*cf.* Lv. 2:1–16); *minhâ* can also have the more general meaning of 'offering' and can describe animal sacrifice (*cf.* Abel's offering in Gn. 4:4; NEB, JB, Wolff, Mays take Amos' meaning in the more general sense, while RSV, NIV, NASB restrict it to cereal or grain offering), or (3) *peace offering*, in which the worshippers burnt part of the animal sacrifice on the altar, shared part with the priests and ate part themselves with family and friends, thus symbolizing their devotion to God and their communion with each other (Lv. 3:1–17).

Sixth, the verbs 'I cannot stand' (NIV; *despise*, RSV; Heb. *rwh*; literally, 'to savour the odour of'; *cf.* Lv. 3:5, 16, where the pleasant odour of the peace offering is featured) and 'I will have no regard' (NIV; Heb. *nbṭ*; literally, 'to gaze at') embrace this passage and convey the revulsion of God, who cannot stomach the stench nor sight of such flagrant abuse of worship. Seventh, the pivotal verb *I will not accept them* (Heb. *rṣh*) is a technical term (*cf.* Lv. 19:5) used to describe the purity of the sacrifice and its conformity to the levitical regulations. Here Yahweh, acting as his own priest, pronounces Israel's offerings as unfit for him, not because of ritual impurity but because they are unaccompanied by acts of justice and righteousness (v. 24).

Though the first line of verse 22, 'Even though you bring

181

me burnt offerings' (NIV) has no parallel clause, there is no evidence either that it has been added or its parallel line dropped out (*cf.* JB, Mays, Wolff). The approach of virtually all the versions which connect it with what follows is an adequate way of treating it.

The Lord has announced his decision about the failure of Israel's worship. Next he issues two admonitions (vv. 23–24) defining precisely what he demands of Israel in response to his condemnatory verdict.

The negative admonition (v. 23) calls for the removal of even the most fervent and celebratory expressions of worship – the music in which the praises of Yahweh were extolled. The more general term, *songs*, a frequent title in the Psalter (Heb. *šîr*; Pss. 30, 68, 83, 87, 92, 108, 120–134), may have been chosen in Amos to indicate that Israel's worship contained neither true prayer (Heb. *tĕpillâ*; *e.g.* Pss. 17, 86, 90) nor true praise (Heb. *tĕhillâ*; *e.g.* Ps. 145). Frequently in religious events, the songs were accompanied by *harps* (1 Sa. 10:5; 2 Sa. 6:5). The precise size and structure of the harp (Heb. *nēbel*) we cannot tell. It may have held ten or more strings (*cf.* Ps. 33:2) and probably had a curved yoke with a bulging, jar-like sound-chamber. Egyptian models were sometimes ten or twelve feet high.

The negative command in this verse contrasts dramatically with the call to worship in Psalm 33:2–3, which summons the people of God to strum their instruments and sing their festive songs. We can judge how incensed God must have been to shun what he usually desired. The grammar in verse 23 has suddenly turned singular, as though Amos is holding a single leader responsible or, more probably, as though the abuse of worship is so universal that the nation of Israel can be rebuked as if it were a single person.

The positive admonition (v. 24) also serves as the explanation of God's rejection of Israel's worship: it was not accompanied by an abundant (*roll down like waters*) and a consistent (*everflowing*) commitment to acts of *justice* and *righteousness* (see on 5:7 for discussion of these terms). The similes, whose chiastic structure gives prominence to them by beginning and ending with the mention of waters, were especially effective in a context where most streams were seasonal, abounding with life-giving water in the rainy seasons and bone-dry through the long, hot summer. The similes also served to show how utterly essential justice and righteousness were to Israel's life and faith. A society in covenant with Yahweh could no more live without them than without an adequate and steady water supply.

Despite the sternness of this passage, it has hidden in it a hint of hope: the admonition form suggests that change, however unlikely, is yet possible; in so doing, Amos' word contrasts somewhat with the cloud of utter hopelessness that hovers over the similar oracle of Isaiah (5:7). Once again Amos has drummed home his point that the cults of Bethel, Gilgal (*roll*, *yîggal*, in v. 24 may be a touch of Hebrew punning on the name Gilgal; *cf.* 5:5), and Beersheba miss the very heart of worship: those who seek to adore Yahweh's name must be those who honour Yahweh's character in deed as well as word. Concern for the rights and welfare of all his people flows, like a mighty river, from his own heart. Whoever would truly serve him must go with that flow.

iii. Announcement of judgment by exile (5:25–27). This brief prose paragraph contains a handful of problems. First, it seems a bit anticlimactic, given the powerful lines of verse 24, which could well have brought this woe to an impressive finale. To have done so, however, would have omitted the announcement of judgment (v. 27) with which virtually all of Amos' oracles conclude. That might have led to higher hopes than Amos intended to engender. It sounds as though Amos wanted to add another form of argument to reinforce his point about the danger and futility of Israel's worship. To do this, he used a type of rhetoric found frequently in the book: disputation questions, questions to which there can be only one answer (*cf.* 2:11c; 3:3–8; 5:20; 6:2d–3, 12–13; 7:2, 4; 9:7). Furthermore, the questions cause Israel to face their own history and see how out of phase their present worship is with what God intended at the beginning.

Second, taken at face value verse 25 seems to conflict with the accounts of Israel's wilderness experience in Exodus and Numbers: 'There is no way to reconcile this view with the extant Pentateuchal tradition which knows nothing of a period in Israel's beginnings when sacrifice was not offered' (Mays, p. 111). True, Exodus, Leviticus, Numbers and Deuteronomy contain substantial sections that outline *instructions* for sacrifices, but true also is the fact that apart from the ceremony of covenant ratification at Sinai (Ex. 24:1–8), virtually nothing is recounted about the *practice* of sacrifice in the wilderness. The laws of sacrifice (Heb. *zebaḥ*, the most general word for animal sacrifice; *cf.* Gn. 46:1; Ex. 10:25; Ho. 6:6) and offering (see on v. 22) anticipate the entry into the promised land either explicitly (*e.g.* Nu. 15:2ff., 17ff.; Dt. 12) or implicitly (*e.g.* Ex. 23:14–18, where the mention of fields and crops presupposes not the wilderness, but settlement in the land). Taken literally, Amos' mention of forty years (*cf.* Nu. 14:33; Dt. 2:7) begins with Israel's refusal to trust God to deliver the land into their hands and embraces the life-span of the entire generation of Israel, who were twenty years of age or older at the time of this rebellion (Nu. 14:29–30), except for Caleb and Joshua. On the use of sacrifices during that period, the Old Testament is notably silent.

Third, Amos' question seems to reflect a tendency, noted also in other prophets (*e.g.* Je. 2:2–3; Ho. 2:14–15), to picture the wilderness experience as a high point in Israel's covenant commitment to God (*cf.* 2:10), whereas both Numbers (*e.g.* Korah's rebellion, chapter 16 and Israel's murmurings, 21:5–9) and Deuteronomy (*e.g.* Israel's refusal to enter Canaan, 1:26–28) chronicle a history marked by conflict and disobedience. Amos was probably no more naive here than Hosea, who knew well the story of Israel's compromise with the Moabite worship of Baal of Peor (9:10; Nu. 25). The recounting of the wilderness relationship as the heyday of covenant harmony was not an idle act of nostalgia. It was a way of underscoring how deeply corrupted Israel's present life had become: in contrast to their wicked perversions of worship and ruthless breaches of justice, the old days, with whatever outbursts of complaint or rebellion they may have witnessed, were indeed golden. Devotion was high and distraction low. The commandments were harboured in the ark, and the relationship with God, though strained at times, was intimate.

Fourth, the connection of verse 26 to the rest of the paragraph is unclear. It can be read as part of the *announcement* of judgment with which this first woe ends. In that case the tenses will be translated as future, and verse 26 will be tightly linked to verse 27 (*cf.* RSV; JB; NEB). On the other hand, verse 26 can be read as part of the *accusation* along with verse 25 and translated in the past tense to describe something the people have already done (*cf.* LXX; Vulg; AV; NIV; NASB; Mays). A further possibility, the one assumed here, can read verse 26 as a second accusing question, following up on the question of verse 25 and asking whether in those golden days of the past Israel carried about with them the idolatrous emblems that violate their present relationship to God (Wolff). The implied answer to both of the questions is 'no'. And thus Israel is forced to acknowledge the necessity of the judgment promised in verse 27.

Fifth, the translation of verse 26 needs attention. How are we to understand the Heb. *sikkût malkᵉkem?* We can repoint the first word to *sukkat* and translate it 'shrine' or 'tabernacle' (LXX, Vulg; AV, NEB, NIV). The phrase would then read 'shrine of your king' or 'shrine of the Milcom', *i.e.* Molech, the name of an Ammonite deity (*cf.* Lv. 20:2–5; 1 Ki. 11:7; 2 Ki. 23:10; Je. 32:35). The other difficult word is Heb. *kiyyûn*, translated variously 'pedestal' (NIV; NEB) or as the name of a deity, Chiun (AV), Kiyyun (NASB), or *Kaiwan* (JB; RSV; Mays; Wolff). The mention of an astral deity (literally, 'star of your god', *i.e.* 'star-god') gives us the clue that proper names are meant by the Hebrew words. And Mesopotamian texts list the terms Sakkuth and Kaiwanu (which LXX and Acts 7:43 misspell as Rephan) as names of the planet Saturn. The Hebrew vowels in both words, *i* followed by *u*, are the result of a familiar device in which names of idols or pagan deities are deliberately misspelled to brand them as shameful or abominable: here the two vowels of *šiqqûṣ*, 'a detestable thing', often used to describe idols (*e.g.* Dt. 29:16; 2 Ki. 23:24; Je. 4:1) were substituted both to label and mock the foreign deities. One other suggestion about the text is warranted: we should probably transpose (*cf.* LXX) the Hebrew word for 'your images' with 'star-god' in order to get the best flow of meaning (*cf.* RSV).[1]

The entire verse, then, would read: 'And did you (in the wilderness; *cf.* v. 25) take up Sakkuth your king and Kaiwan your star-god, your images which you made for yourselves (as you are now doing)?'[2] Mesopotamian art has depicted effigies of the gods attached to standards and carried aloft. One such picture features an eight-pointed star above the

---

[1]On this verse and its meaning see C. D. Isbell, 'Another Look at Amos 5:26', *JBL*, 97, 1978, pp. 97–99; J. Gray, 'Sakkuth and Kaiwan', *IDB*, IV, p. 165; J. M. Everts, 'Astronomy', *ISBE*, rev., I, pp. 344–348.
[2]On the making of idols, see Ho. 8:4, 6; 13:2; 1 Ki. 14:9; 2 Ki. 17:29–31.

head of the deity.[1]

The final problem stems from this interpretation. If idolatry from the Tigris-Euphrates Valley infiltrated Israel to the extent the text suggests, why did Amos mention it only here? And why does Hosea, who constantly decried Israel's idolatry, focus only on the Canaanite cult of the Baals, not on worship imported from Assyria? These questions have led Wolff (pp. 265–66) to assign these verses to a 'Deuteronomist' who added them to Amos' text in order to describe the sharp spiritual decline that afflicted the northern territory when the Assyrians occupied and resettled it after 721 BC (2 Ki. 17).

It is not easy to bring concrete evidence to bear against Wolff's reasoning. The practice of idolatry seems to be in view in 8:14, although Wolff would disqualify this passage as evidence by crediting it, along with most of chapter 8, to a disciple of Amos (pp. 325–26). It is the assumption that lies behind Wolff's argument that should be questioned. If we deny a passage to a prophet largely on the ground that he does not mention the topic elsewhere, then it follows logically that no prophet could ever treat a major topic in just one place. He would be obliged to mention everything twice in order to deal with it once!

The upshot of this woe and its powerful elaborations is the Lord's personal pledge to see to Israel's judgment (v. 27). Worship was empty; justice had dried up. All that they had been brought to the land to accomplish was marked by abject failure. *Exile* was God's obvious response. Land abused will be land lost. The announcement of destination is deliberately vague, *beyond Damascus.* Assyrian might is given only a slight nod. Amos' largest gesture is directed toward the all powerful Lord of hosts, whose day Israel had craved (v. 18) but whose coming spells desolation.

Time was when denunciations of the cult like this one were interpreted as a prophet's desire to abolish all formal and ceremonial acts of worship. Words of Samuel (1 Sa. 15:22–23), the Psalmist (51:16–17), Isaiah (1:10–17), Hosea (6:6), Micah (6:6–8), and Jeremiah (7:21–26) all agree that sacrifice without obedience is a meaningless ritual, an insult to the grace and goodness of the covenant Lord. Rowley's summation captures well the way most contemporary scholars view the relationship

[1]*ANEP*, fig. 535.

between cultic worship and personal faith in this period: 'The pre-exilic prophets denounced sacrifices which were hollow and ineffective; but there is no reason to suppose that they held that no other sacrifices could be offered by men whose hearts were right with God.' Of Isaiah, whose call took place in the temple, Rowley concludes: 'It cannot be that he thought it wrong to tread the Temple courts, or supposed the altar to be a thing evil in itself.'[1]

Amos' quarrel with the cult seemed to stem from the following factors discoverable from this woe-oracle: (1) the cult propagated a false optimism about the Day of the Lord; (2) the cult put emphasis on mere ritual acts, as though sacrifices and songs were powerful in themselves, apart from the devotion and obedience of the worshippers;[2] and (3) the cult was susceptible to corruption from Canaanite and foreign elements, living as it did in deliberate isolation and protest against the Jerusalem temple (*cf.* 8:14; 1:2), which itself was not exempt from compromise. A non-cultic worship would probably have been unthinkable to a Hebrew prophet, especially one as firmly rooted in Israel's traditions as Amos was. Yet to get Israel's attention he had characteristically to overstate his position to make clear that Yahweh was more than prepared to destroy the present cult in order to enforce his claim to full obedience (*cf.* 9:1–6).

Stephen's speech to the Jewish leaders (Acts 7:2–53) uses Amos 5:25–27 as a pivotal proof text in his recital of salvation history and Israel's persistent rebellion throughout its course (Acts 7:42–43). Attributing the quotation to the 'book of the prophets', Stephen quotes the LXX and embellishes it, especially by citing 'beyond Babylon' not 'beyond Damascus' as the locale of the exile, thus adapting the text to the realities of Israel's history. Furthermore, in using the aorist (past) tenses of the LXX, he makes the descriptions of idol-worship part of a long-standing pattern that began with Aaron's calf and led to worship of the hosts of heaven (Acts 7:40–43). Finally, Stephen phrases the question of 7:42 (Am. 5:25) in such a way to suggest that Yahweh was not worshipped in the wilderness,

[1] H. H. Rowley, *The Unity of the Bible* (New York: Meridian Books, 1957), p. 48.

[2] J. A. Motyer, 'Amos', *NBC* rev., p. 735, reminds us that the Hebrew word order of verse 25 encourages a reading like 'was it sacrifices and offering (only) that you brought me . . .?'

but the pagan deities named by him Moloch (based on the Heb. 'your king') and Rephan, probably a corruption of Kaiwan. Though in many details Stephen departs from Amos' text, in the major thrust of the passage – the obdurate rebellion and idolatry of Israel which resulted inevitably in exile – the two preachers stand shoulder to shoulder.[1]

b. Woe oracle: misdirected sense of material security (6:1–14)

Technically speaking, the actual woe speech may end at verse 7. But the unity of themes – *indictment for arrogance* (v. 8) with its attendant evils like false security (vv. 1–2, 13), violence toward the weak (v. 3, 12), idle luxury (vv. 4–7, 11) and *threat of judgment by exile or invasion* (vv. 7–11, 14) – serves to stitch the passage together with sufficient cohesion for us to treat it as a single unit. As is the pattern in Amos, this oracle is an assembly of diverse literary forms: *woe* whose purpose is accusation (v. 1), *quotation* of an admonition and of disputation questions (v. 2), *addresses* to Israel, continuing the woe (vv. 3–6), *announcement* of judgment (v. 7), report of a *divine oath* pledging judgment (v. 8), *prose account* of the fear and devastation accompanying the judgment (vv. 9–10), *report* of the divine command that triggers the judgment (v. 11), *disputation questions* and an address to Israel to sum up the accusations (vv. 12–13), and *final announcement* of judgment (v. 14).

   i. Denunciation of the idle rich (6:1–7). Again the *woe* (see on 5:18) drives home the arch stupidity and clear consequences of Israel's pride in luxury, the wickedness of which complements the extravagance of the cult and shows how wrongheaded Israel was in both cases: perverted worship, which presumed on God's blessing at the Day of the Lord, was perfectly matched by an abuse of social and financial position. In short, there was nothing basic to Israel's life that Amos deemed worthy of commendation.
   1. The mention of *Zion, i.e.* Jerusalem, seems strange,

---

[1]For a discussion of Stephen's use of Amos, see E. Haenchen, *The Acts of the Apostles* (E.T., Philadelphia: Westminster Press, 1971), pp. 283–284. He notes that the Damascus Document (DCD, VII, 14ff.) removes the references to idolatry by interpreting Sikkuth as the book of Torah, Kinyun as the book of the Prophets, and the star as the true teacher.

particularly as the lead item in the sentence. The many suggested emendations have not proved successful, and it seems
best to see it as Amos' reminder that the rulers of the Northern Kingdom had no corner on sinful complacency and that
God is not a respecter of capitals when it comes to punishment
– two points well-documented in Amos' judgment speeches
against the nations (1:3 – 2:5). Judah is in view elsewhere in
the book: the title mentions Uzziah of Judah (1:1); the theme
verse refers to Zion and Jerusalem (1:2); Judah is denounced
in a judgment speech (2:4–5); 'the whole family' rescued in
the Exodus seems to include Judah (3:1); and the 'falling
booth of David' points to Judah's judgment prior to their
restoration (9:11; *cf.* the reference to Edom, Judah's southern
neighbour in 9:12). The least that one can infer from all these
allusions to Judah is that whoever was responsible for the final
composition of the book believed firmly that Amos included
prophecies about Judah in the midst of his primary concern
for Israel.

What the mountain capitals of the two kingdoms share is
leadership that is lulled into an irresponsible sense of *security*.
The cavalier carefreeness (or carelessness; *at ease*), of Zion's
nobles was matched by the naive feelings of security of Samaria's leaders (*cf.* Pr. 14:16 for similar use of Heb. *bōṭēaḥ*).
Amos' times were heady ones for the two kingdoms: Aram
had spent itself in anti-Assyrian intrigue; Egypt posed no
southern threat; Assyria itself was still consumed by its
struggles with Urartu; none of the smaller neighbours –
whether Philistia, Phoenicia, Ammon, Moab, or Edom – could
mount noteworthy assaults. And, above all, Yahweh's next
move was thought to be vindication and blessing, not invasion
and judgment.

The cult itself encouraged such complacency. That God
would move in disaster against those who kept the air reeking
with the smell of sacrificial smoke and the temple-courts
ringing with the sounds of celebrative song was beyond their
ken. At heart their false security was not in their military
might or fortified capitals, proud as they were of these (*cf.* v. 2,
8), but in their failure to believe that a day of *evil* (*i.e.* of divine
judgment) would ever come (v. 3).

Such complacent pomp invites Amos' sarcasm. He picks up
the excessive language with which they would describe themselves and hurls it at them. *Notable* (v. 1) means literally 'nailed

in a prominent position' whether of acclamation (Is. 62:2) or of blasphemy (Lv. 24:11, 16); *cf.* NEB's 'men of mark'. Sensitive ears would not have missed the fact that *first* (or 'first-fruits'; *cf.* Je. 2:3) of the nations describes a chauvinism earlier attributed by Balaam to Amalek in a prophecy that, like Amos', announced judgment (Nu. 24:20). The sarcasm climaxes in the final clause that pictures the house of Israel clamouring for advice and support and prestige by fawning over their leaders. Where else could they go?[1]

2. It seems best to read this verse as a quotation of these boastful, self-reliant leaders of Samaria. They based their security on the fact that no city in their entire region, even though they had been distinguished and ancient city-states, could now compare in pomp and circumstance with Samaria. Not *Calneh* (*cf.* Is. 10:9; probably Assyrian *Kullani*), whose specific site has not been identified but was most likely located in north-central Syria, north of Aleppo, south of Carchemish, about midway between the big bend of the Euphrates and the Mediterranean coast. Not *Hamath* (2 Ki. 14:28; Is. 10:9, where Hamath came under Jeroboam II's sway as it had earlier come under Solomon's [2 Ch. 8:4], modern Hama, on the Orontes, some 200 kilometres north of Damascus and about 170 kilometres south of the proposed site of Calneh), *the great* – Amos' description was well-deserved – Hittite city that became an independent state at the collapse of the Hittite empire, *c.* 1200 BC and remained a dominant political and commercial force on the main north-south trade route for several centuries thereafter. Not *Gath* (whose elusive site is now frequently pin-pointed as Tell 'esSafi, some 15 kilometres east of Ashdod and 10 kilometres south of Ekron, near the point where the Philistine plains end at the hill country of Judah), the only Philistine city not mentioned in Amos' earlier indictment (1:6–8; *cf.* Mi. 1:10).[2]

The admonitions of Israel's leaders, urging sceptics like

[1]Scholars have frequently viewed this clause as both ambiguous and trite. A noteworthy suggestion of emendation that makes the whole clause refer to the leaders of Israel comes from W. L. Holladay, 'Amos VI 1b: A Suggested Solution', *VT*, 22, 1972, pp. 107–110.

[2]For proposed locations of these cities, see *The Macmillan Bible Atlas* (1968), maps 145, 146. For discussions of the history of each city see R. K. Harrison, 'Calneh', *ISBE*, rev., I, p. 582; H. F. Vos, 'Hamath', *ISBE*, rev., II, pp. 602–603; A. F. Rainey, 'Gath', *ISBE*, rev., II, pp. 410–415.

AMOS 6:3

Amos to make the grand tour and see for themselves the greater glory of Samaria, are clinched by the rhetorical questions which close the verse, questions which evoke the answer 'No, of course not!' The failure to hear verse 2 as a quotation and instead to attribute it directly to Amos has meant either that the force of the questions has been blunted (*e.g.* NIV) or the pronouns of the last clause have had to be transposed (*e.g.* NEB). A direct way to handle the questions (*e.g.* RSV; JB) is to read them like this:

'Are they (*i.e.* Calneh, Hamath, Gath) better than these kingdoms (of yours)? Is their territory (lit. border) greater than your territory?'

To make Amos the speaker here calls not only for transposing the pronouns but presumes that the three cities had already been sacked by Assyria and shorn of all power and glory, when what we know of the history indicates that such catastrophes did not take place till a quarter of a century or so after Amos' time. Another advantage of interpreting verse 2 as a boast is that the verse is then part of the accusation, illustrating the complacent pride of Israel, and not an intimation of judgment which the author deliberately builds to and does not strongly announce ('therefore') until verse 7.

3. In keeping with his style (*e.g.* 5:7, 12b), Amos uses an address to the people as part of his accusation. The participial construction, *who put far away*, carries on the woe formula of verse 1. The contrast in the two clauses sustains the note of sarcasm. What they should face up to, *viz.* the Lord's intervention in judgment (5:18–20), they will fully ignore, *i.e.* they drive out (*put far away*; Heb. *ndh* means to 'exclude from fellowship' in Is. 66:5 and to 'excommunicate' in later Heb.). What they should purge from their midst, *viz.* the rule or reign (*seat* here should probably be understood as 'seat' of a throne; *cf.* 1 Ki. 10:19) of violent oppression and exploitation, they *bring near* to themselves as though it were a solemn sacrifice (Heb. *nāgaš*; *cf.* 5:25). So preoccupied are they with their acts of violence and the leisurely life which such violence supports that all thought of divine retribution is banished from their consciousness. They behave as though justice had been erased from the vocabulary of the universe.

191

4–6. Here the accusation becomes more detailed. Participles, usually translated as relative clauses, dominate the syntax and maintain the structure of the woe from verse 1, as Amos continues to denounce the wealthy ruling élite of Samaria. The point of the passage needs to be seen from different angles: (1) the mistaken sense of security of verses 1–2 expresses itself in the gluttony, drunkenness and luxury of verses 4–6; (2) that idle self-indulgence is itself a by-product of violence; it has to be subsidized by the ordinary citizens who are looted of their goods through exacting of bribes and levying of taxes, as is clear right the way through the book (*e.g.* 2:6–8; 3:11; 4:1; 5:11–12; 8:4–6); note how the 'ruling throne (*seat*) of violence' (v. 3) and 'those who lie on beds of ivory' (v. 4) are mentioned back to back, both to connect the one act with the other and to set them in contrast; and (3) the key to interpreting verses 4–6 may be found in verse 7 in 'revelry' (Heb. *marzēᵃḥ*; *cf.* Je. 16:5), whose meaning has been elucidated by recently published texts from Ugarit.

Amos seems to condemn not just ordinary carousing but some kind of religious rite that had drunkenness to the point of uncontrollable stupor as its purpose (*cf.* Is. 28:7–8). In both the Ugaritic text and Jeremiah, there seems to be some connection between the *marzēᵃḥ* and acts of mourning. This connection is sustained in rabbinic interpretations which tie the *marzēᵃḥ* to funeral feasts where inordinate drinking was a custom. M. Pope sums up the Ugaritic, biblical, rabbinic, and Palmyrene evidence and concludes that 'the *marzēᵃḥ* was a social and religious institution which included families, owned property, houses for meetings and vineyards for wine supply, was associated with specific deities, and met periodically . . . to celebrate for several days at a stretch with food and drink and sometimes . . . with sacred sexual orgies'.[1]

This description accords well with much of what Amos pictures: (1) the lying down and even sprawling (Heb. *sāraḥ* means overhanging; *cf.* Ex. 26:12) in verses 4 and 7 depict not just comfort but drunken torpor; in fact *marzēᵃḥ* itself probably is related to a root attested in Arabic meaning to fall from

[1]M. H. Pope, 'A Divine Banquet at Ugarit' in *The Use of the OT in the New and other Essays*, Fs. William Franklin Stinespring, ed. by J. M. Efird (Durham, North Carolina: Duke University Press, 1972), p. 193; *cf.* also Coote, pp. 36–39, for interpretation of the *marzēᵃḥ* in Amos.

fatigue or weakness;[1] (2) the vessels for wine-drinking were not the ordinary cups but *bowls* or basins (Heb. *mizrāq*, suggesting a vessel for throwing or tossing more than drinking) from which the revellers could gorge themselves; (3) the Israelites' apathy is expressed by the clause 'they have not become sick (*grieved*) over the shattering (*ruin*) of Joseph', *i.e.* their own Northern Kingdom; this may hint that they had become sick but for the wrong reasons: their lamentable drunkenness has made them sick, perhaps even sick in mourning for the dead, but what should have made them sick were the evils they had done to their own people and the crushing fate that yet awaited them; and (4) the difficult story in verses 9-10 may reflect some connection with a cult to lament the dead, describing as it does relatives obligated to search for the corpses of their loved ones and give them decent burial (see comments below).

Beds inlaid with *ivory* were part of the furnishings of the houses of ivory threatened with annihilation in the coming judgment (see on 3:12, 15). The eating of meat (*lambs*) with any regularity was the privilege of the wealthy. The general population lived on wheat and barley and whatever fruits and vegetables were at hand, and if they had meat at all, reserved it for times of high celebration (*cf.* Lk. 15:23). This was one reason that the peace offering (see on 5:22) was so highly valued by the common people. In contrast, Samaria's élite not only ate animals at random but put their *calves* in special *stalls* to fatten them, undoubtedly on grain wrested from the poor by cruel taxation (*cf.* 5:11).

The picture of idle self-satisfaction is enhanced by the presence of music (v. 5). The initial participle – *who sing idle songs* (Heb. *prt*) – occurs only here in the Old Testament and is thus difficult to translate with precision. 'Improvise carelessly, idly' (BDB) is probably as close as we can come with the help of an Arabic cognate and Amos' parallel verb, 'devise' (*invent*; Heb. *ḥšb*). Whatever creative energies the Israelites had, they were not channelled into care for the poor among their countrymen or regard for the future of the state but were poured out with luxurious abandon in music to sweeten their revelry. For *harp*, see on 5:23. *Instruments of music* (literally, 'implements of song') were probably stringed and

[1] M. H. Pope, *loc. cit.*

percussive instruments that could be developed in almost endless varieties (*cf.* the lists in 1 Ch. 15:16; 16:42; 2 Ch. 5:13) to accompany the riotous singing. (For David's role in instrumental music, see 1 Sa. 18:10; 1 Ch. 15:16; 2 Ch. 29:27.)

The lavish use of wine and oil, condemned by Amos, is documented in a set of inscriptions on potsherds discovered at Samaria in the Harvard University expeditions of 1908–10. These potsherds (*ostraca*) contain records of the delivery of jugs of old wine and purified olive oil. While the suggested dates of the ostraca range over about a century from Jehu's reign (841–14 BC) to Menahem's (752–42 BC), they seem to provide clear evidence of the wasteful opulence of Samaria's ruling class: both the old wine, having been stored for long periods of time, and the oil, described as purified by repeated and careful straining, would be especially expensive goods, a fact that Amos recognized in the phrase 'the first-fruit of the olive oils' (*the finest oils*) with which the wealthy smeared themselves for refreshment and fragrance.[1] For a depiction akin to Amos' whole scene, see the ivory carving from Megiddo where a noble quaffs her thirst from a bowl in the presence of a servant playing a lute.[2]

7. The woe itself now is brought to a stingingly quick conclusion with the announcement of judgment, introduced appropriately by *therefore*. The sarcastic tone continues: the proud élitism that made the Israelite leaders revel in their role as the 'first-fruit of the nations' (v. 1) and that made them celebrate that role with the 'first-fruit of the oils' (v. 6) will now see them slogging out of their fortress capital as the 'first (or head) of the exiles'. Moreover, though surrounded by death when the invaders come to transport them, they will not be able to carry out their customary revelries on behalf of the dead (see *marzēaḥ*, above at v. 4).

For the Northern Kingdom the exile was to make a vast difference in the lives of the people and, especially, their leaders. Only scattered fragments of the population ever returned in the persons of their descendants, since nearly two

---

[1]On the Samaritan ostraca, see W. F. Albright in *ANET*, p. 321; J. N. Schofield in *DOTT*, pp. 204–208; P. R. Ackroyd, 'Samaria', in *Archaeology and OT Study*, ed. by D. Winton Thomas (Oxford: Clarendon Press, 1967), pp. 346–347; Coote, pp. 36–37.

[2]J. B. Pritchard, *Archaeology and the OT* (Princeton University Press, 1958) pp. 34–35; fig 14.

centuries elapsed between the deportations under Shal-
maneser V and Sargon II and the return prompted by Cyrus.
Samaria as a political entity never again enjoyed any significant span of independence, and no offspring of its kings ever
rose to authority over it again. A poignant essay has described
what lay ahead of Israel's intransigent nobles. 'Exile is life led
outside habitual order. It is nomadic, decentred, contrapun-
tal; but no sooner does one get accustomed to it than its
unsettling force erupts anew.'[1]

ii. Divine oath of judgment (6:8). The theme of judgment
is now played with variations in form and content. The divine
oath (*cf.* on 4:2; 8:7) is an unusually strong introduction to an
announcement of judgment and is reinforced by the oracle
formula and the identification of Yahweh as *God of hosts* (literally 'armies'), *i.e.* sovereign of both the heavenly council and
of the troops of the invaders that will work the promised
havoc and trigger the announced exile. *By himself* can also be
translated as 'by his life' (literally 'by his throat') signifying that
Yahweh will stake his very life on the fulfilment of this deadly
promise. Wolff (pp. 281–282, n. 8) calls attention to the
record of the treaty between Hammurabi and Zimri-Lim in
which each king is reported to have clutched his own throat as
if to pledge his own strangulation if he failed to keep the
bargain.

The content of the oath is a summation of the woe in verses
1–7. God uses the strongest possible language to express his
wrath – the language of abhorrence (*cf.* Pr. 6:16–17; 16:5) and
hatred, underscored by the chiasm that placed these words at
the beginning and end of their Hebrew clauses.[2] Jacob, as
God calls the Northern Kingdom here (and in 3:13; 7:2, 5;
8:7; 9:8; *cf.* 9:8), could not have been more wrong-headed:
humility before Yahweh and trust in him were to be the
kingdom's crowning attitudes. These had been replaced by

[1] E. W. Said, 'The Mind of Winter', *Harpers*, September 1984, p. 55.
[2] The translation *abhor* (RSV) follows many of the ancient versions and is based
on an emendation of the Heb. root *t'b* to *t'b*. M. Dahood, *Bib*, 59, 1978,
pp. 265–266, has made a strong case for retaining the original *'alep* and
dividing the participle form into two words, 'surely' (*mt*) and 'enemy' (*'b*),
rendering the whole line: 'Truly the foe am I of Jacob's arrogance.' The
parallel between *hate* and *foe* is thus preserved, and the text can be handled
without emendation of any consonants.

pride (*cf.* Pr. 8:13; 16:18) – an apt term to summarize the complacency and false security which made for profligate living – and *strongholds* – the catch-word for empty trust in defences and military might which lulled Israel into his deceitful leisure (*cf.* on 1:4). The terseness of the final clause is matched by its comprehensiveness. In just three Hebrew words, Yahweh swore that the great capital and all its goods and people (literally, 'its fullness'; *cf.* Ps. 24:1) would be delivered up to an unnamed foe (Heb. *hisgîr*, from root *sgr*, may also mean 'imprison'; *cf.* Jb. 11:10).

iii. Illustration of the awesome devastation (6:9–10). This story highlights two main points in Amos' tale of woe: (1) death and destruction utterly decimate the populace; and (2) the Lord himself stands behind the judgment with such ferocity that the survivors dare not mention his name. Whole households of ordinary citizens are to be wiped out with the same thoroughness that would devastate the armies mentioned in 5:3. If ten people survive from a large clan, there can be no rejoicing about the future of that remnant, for the final ten are destined to die as well.

The present text of verse 10 is not easy to handle, especially the third Hebrew word, which the AV tradition (with the Vulgate) reads 'and he that burneth him' (*cf.* RSV; NIV). This translation assumes that the Hebrew word *śrp* was here misspelt *srp* (the letter *samech* replaced by *sin*) and that, contrary to normal practice in Israel, the body was to be burned not buried. Arguments that the extraordinary act of cremation, an act which Amos himself denounced (2:1) and which was reserved almost exclusively in the Old Testament for notorious criminals (Gn. 38:24; Lv. 20:14; 21:9; an exception should be noted in 1 Sa. 31:12), was to obliterate pestilence or plague do not carry weight. No such epidemic is mentioned and the following verse seems to imply earthquake as the means of devastation.

To dodge these problems some scholars and versions have suggested readings like 'embalmer' (NEB) or 'undertaker' (NASB).[1] The Old Testament instances of embalming (Jacob and Joseph) occur in specifically Egyptian contexts (Gn. 50:2–3). Still others, taking a cue from the LXX, have emended

---

[1]*Cf.* G. R. Driver, 'A Hebrew Burial Custom', *ZAW*, 66, 1955, pp. 314–315.

srp to *psr*, 'to urge', or 'press upon' as in Genesis 19:3, 9; 33:11 and Judges 19:7 (Wolff, p. 180). But the LXX itself is too problematic, seemingly reading 'and he shall lift up' both at the end of verse 9 and the beginning of verse 10, to bank on with assurance.

As reasonable a suggestion as any is that of T. H. Robinson (p. 94), followed by Mays and Delcor, reading *meṣārepô* as a synonym of *dôdô* – the former meaning 'maternal uncle' and the latter 'paternal uncle'. The line would then be read: 'And when a person's near relative, whether on his father's or his mother's side, shall carry him to bring his corpse out of the house, and shall say. . . .' Burial plots were part of the family property, especially among the landed. Access to that property and care for the dead would be the responsibility of the next of kin. Hence the reference to the uncles on both sides of the family, either one of whom would have felt obliged to discharge this duty.

Bones seems to stand for corpse, though the form in Hebrew is masculine instead of the more familiar feminine (*e.g.* Gn. 50:25; Ex. 13:19). The story assumes that the kinsman is not alone but calls to a fellow searcher who has penetrated (perhaps burrowed through rubble) to the innermost part of the house (*cf.* 1 Sa. 24:4; Ps 128:3 for similar meanings of Heb. *yarkâ*), asking him if anyone is still alive there. The other searcher answers in the negative but immediately goes on to silence the one who spoke first and to warn against even mentioning Yahweh's name, lest further disaster be sparked by that mention. The inference to be drawn from this story is that the death site is charged with the awesome presence of God, as though it were a shrine. The Hebrew word for *Hush*! occurs in cultic contexts, where silence before Yahweh is the appropriate response (*e.g.* 8:3; Hab. 2:20; Zp. 1:7; Zc. 2:17). To mention Yahweh's name would be to invoke further his presence and, hence, to court further death.[1]

iv. Announcement of judgment by invasion (6:11–14).

11. The appearance of Yahweh, feared in verse 10, takes place here in full view of all Israel. Yahweh is in charge, like a generalissimo issuing his sharp commands (the tense is

---

[1]On death and burial in the Old Testament, see R. de Vaux, *Ancient Israel*, pp. 56–61.

present, insisting that the promised judgment is about to begin and will not be stayed, as the visions in chs. 7–9 will display) and ordering the destruction of all the houses, whether *little* or *great.* The mention of the extremes in sizes seems to be a *merism,* in which the whole range of houses of every size and shape is included in the two extremes. Though the intent here is the same as in 3:15, no direct identification with the winter and summer houses can be drawn. *Smitten* and *fragments* (or 'crushed pieces') and *bits* (or 'pieces split off') suggest earthquake more than military invasion and harmonize well with both the direct activity of God described and the awareness of a pending quake which runs through the book of Amos (see on 1:1; 2:13; 8:8; 9:1–6).

12–13. Both tone and content change sharply here, as Amos makes one more attempt to chide Israel for the stupidity of their ways. His technique is to press them again with rhetorical questions (*cf.* 3:3–8; 5:25–26; 9:7), this time with questions that are patently absurd. Of course *horses* do not *run* on rocky terrain. Pulling their chariots of war or carrying their crack-troops of cavalry, they are confined to the smooth roads of the valleys or the coastal plains. The sharp, rocky footing of the hillsides has to be left to the sure-stepping donkeys; the horses hooves cannot take the beating. And of course one does not haul an ox down to the seaside to pull a plough through the pounding waves. This interpretation, followed by almost all scholars and translations for the past century, is based on dividing the Hebrew word for oxen into two words: *babbᵉqarîm* becomes *babbāqār yām,* with no change of consonants, thus heightening the note of absurdity sounded in the first clause.

As is typical in such wisdom questions (*e.g.* Jer. 13:23), based as they are on the common sense of everyday experience, Amos has set a trap for his hearers. He springs that trap by pointing out something in their lives far more absurd than rocky horsemanship or wet ploughing: deliberate perversion of justice and corruption of righteousness (*cf.* on 5:7, 24). The life-giving stability of *justice* has been turned, for the poor and the oppressed, into a death-dealing *poison,* the strongest word yet used by Amos (*cf.* on 5:7), a word which describes the danger of inedible berries (Dt. 32:24; Jb. 20:16). The sweetly nurturing *fruit of righteousness* (*cf.* Is. 5:7 and comments on Ho. 10:12) has been degraded to the bitter, sickening taste of *wormwood* (see on 5:7).

This emphasis on the absence of justice and righteousness is the glue that holds the two woes (5:18–27; 6:1–14) together. And the questions of absurdity with which the second woe closes match the parable of absurdity (5:19) with which the first woe began.

Amos concludes his indictment, again in address form like 6:3–6, by returning to the dominant theme of this second woe, the arrogant self-sufficiency of Israel's leaders. Ironically he turns their own words against them (*cf.* 2:12; 5:14; 6:2; 8:5, 14; 9:10). It is military might of which they boast, might demonstrated in the reconquest of two Transjordanian cities by Jeroboam II (*cf.* 2 Ki. 14:28). Amos, by punning, turns their boast into a joke. He deliberately misspells the first town as *Lô' dāḇār* to mean 'nothing'. Far from a military trophy, it is a place of no consequence at all. And of the other places that had been reconquered he deliberately chooses *Karnaim*, to make fun of the strength alleged in its name 'Double-Horned' (for 'horn' meaning 'strength' see Dt. 33:17; 1 Sa. 2:1, 10; 2 Sa. 22:3).

The site of Lo-debar, spelled variously *lô' dᵉḇār* (2 Sa. 17:27), *lô dᵉḇār* (2 Sa. 9:4–5), and *liḏbir* (Jos. 13:26), has not been identified with certainty but seems to have been in the Gilead area of Transjordan north of Mahanaim and northeast of Beth-shean;[1] Tell 'el-Hammeh, north of the Jabbok, is one site suggested.[2] Karnaim was even further north and east and, therefore, much more readily drawn into Damascus' orbit. Its site is located at *Šeh Saʻd*, four kilometres north of Ashtaroth in the area of the Yarmuk.[3]

The language of the quotation itself rings with the same arrogance alluded to in the accusations of false security (6:1) and named directly in the divine oath where Jacob's pride is abhorred (6:8): 'Have *we* not by *our own* strength captured Karnaim *for ourselves*?' All sense of divine providence has been squeezed from their thinking by the heady ease which their troops and weaponry engender.

14. No wonder Yahweh has to catch their attention (*Behold*) and direct it away from their hollow achievements to the

[1] See *Macmillan Bible Atlas*, map 109.
[2] M. Metzger, 'Lodebar und der *tell el-mghannije*', *ZDPV*, 1960, pp. 97–102.
[3] See *Macmillan Bible Atlas*, map 148.

reality of his judgment (*I will raise up*). With power he identifies himself as the Lord of all armies and with specificity he directs his announcement to the whole house of Israel, *i.e.* the entire Northern Kingdom, doomed to disaster by the complacency and corruption of their leaders to whom this entire woe has been directed. The means of the judgment will be political – a nation chosen to pluck 'the first-fruit of the nations' (6:1) and to *oppress* it, *i.e.* grind it into the ground with a savagery akin to Egypt's (*cf.* Ex. 3:9, where the identical Heb. root *lḥṣ* is used).

Israel's brief boasting in military success is utterly swamped by the broad tidal wave of invasion that will flood the entire country, from its northern-most point of influence at the edge of the territory controlled by Hamath (of the exact location and whether it was a city or a region we cannot be sure)[1] to the southern boundaries marked by one of the brooks (which one we do not know) that empty into the Dead Sea, also called the Sea of the Arabah (Dt. 3:17; 2 Ki. 14:25). Amos deliberately used the traditional boundaries that recall both the grandeur of Solomon's realm (1 Ki. 8:65; 'from the entrance of Hamath to the Brook of Egypt', the southern boundary appropriate to the larger, united kingdom) and the conquests of Jeroboam II (2 Ki. 14:25).

The two woes have brought to a climax the accusations of sin that dominate the first six chapters of Amos. From this point on, the focus is almost entirely on judgment, a judgment whose necessity, nearness and intensity Amos will learn first hand from the dramatic visions which are the core of the remaining chapters.

VI. FIVE JUDGMENT VISIONS AGAINST ISRAEL (7:1 – 9:10)

The back-bone of this section is the set of five vision reports (7:1–3, 4–6, 7–8; 8:1–2; 9:1) that chronicle the stages by which God reveals the terror, sweep, certainty and inescapability of his judgment on the Northern Kingdom. The message of the

---

[1]See *Macmillan Bible Atlas*, map 142, for the suggested site of Lebo (translated 'entrance' in rsv) at the southern edge of Hamath region. For more on Hamath, see comment at 6:2.

visions is complemented and interpreted by a series of brief oracles interspersed among them (7:9; 8:3, 4–14; 9:7–10), by a report of Amos' dispute with Amaziah, priest of Bethel (7:10–17), and by the final stanza of a hymn celebrating the sovereignty of Yahweh (9:5–6; *cf*. 4:13; 5:8–9).

In form, the five vision reports are autobiographical, recounted by Amos in the first person singular: 'Thus the Lord God showed *me*' (7:1, 4; 8:1); 'he showed *me*' (7:7); '*I* saw' (9:1). The first four resemble each other closely: (1) each is introduced by a formula in which God *showed* Amos the vision, thus affirming the authoritative, revelatory character of the experience; and (2) each contains a dialogue between Yahweh and the prophet, thus underscoring the personal nature of these encounters and demonstrating that they were not only visual but auditory experiences – a combination reflected in the title of the book, 'The words of Amos ... which he saw concerning Israel' (1:1).

A further look at the forms leads to a grouping of the first four visions two by two: (1) visions one and two picture events as their object – a locust plague and a fiery drought; visions three and four picture things – a plumb-line and a basket of ripe fruit; (2) the dialogue in visions one and two consists of Amos' pleas for God to *forgive* or *cease* because Israel is dependent on him and of Yahweh's promises to withhold the disasters; (3) the dialogues in visions three and four contain Yahweh's questions to Amos, *what do you see?* (7:8; 8:2) and Amos' succinct answers that target the central object of the vision; and (4) in the first two visions the threat of judgment is so clear that Yahweh brings no explanation of it; in the next two, Yahweh interprets the meaning of the symbol – in the case of the plumb-line with a simple explanation announcing that no forgiveness is available (7:8), in the case of the fruit basket with a play on words to declare that Israel's end is at hand (8:2; note the similarity to Jeremiah's two visions: the almond branch is a word-play, 1:11–12; the pot facing away from the north is a symbolic object, 1:13–14).

The final vision (9:1) differs from the others markedly: (1) its object is a person, Yahweh; (2) it contains no dialogue, the prophet remaining a silent spectator and auditor; and (3) its content is almost entirely auditory; the prophet sees no action but hears the Lord's command to destroy the shrine and his promise to pursue the fugitives (vv. 2–4).

201

The movement through the sequence of the visions should not be missed. The emphasis of the first two is on the utter devastation caused by the ravages of locust hordes and unquenchable fire; the two worst enemies of a people dependent on agriculture were set loose, and Amos, for whom agriculture was a profession (7:14–15), recoiled at the sight. No wonder Amos begged God first to forgive and then to cease from such punishment which the Northern Kingdom was too weak to survive. And both times Yahweh yielded to Amos' importunity and pledged that such judgment would not take place.

The third vision featured not merely the threat of judgment but the ground for it. The plumb-line, the only part of the vision voiced by Amos in response to God's query, symbolizes God's standards of righteousness and justice which Israel's leaders had so sorely violated (5:7, 24; 6:12). Measured by such accuracy and rectitude the wall of Israel's political and religious life was shown to be tilted beyond repair; it had to come down. The change in literary form matches the change in mood: vision three contains no word of prophetic intercession, as though the undeniable evidence of a plumb-line against a crooked wall has convinced the prophet that the time for mercy had passed.

The fourth vision, based on the verbal similarity between *qāyiṣ*, 'the ripened fruit of summer', and *qēṣ*, 'end', assumes the validity of the plumb-line's verdict and states no grounds for the judgment, only its nearness and inevitability.

The fifth vision cuts short all the formalities of formula and dialogue, and fixes attention on Yahweh's personal contempt for Israel's corrupt worship. Like the boss of a demolition squad or the commander of an invading enemy, he snaps his orders for the smashing of the temple and takes personal responsibility for seeing that the last offender is brought to justice.[1]

These first-hand reports of Amos' visions assume that he is already engaged in the prophetic task when he received them. They cannot readily, then, be viewed as accounts of his prophetic call. In contrast with the visions that mark the commissioning of Isaiah (ch. 6), Jeremiah (ch. 1), and Ezekiel (chs.

[1]For a somewhat different summary of the movement expressed in the visions, see Motyer, pp. 151–167.

1–3), Amos' visions contain no hint of a divine command, no direction about his message or ministry, no objection on the prophet's part, and no assurance of Yahweh's provision and protection. The spot-light is not on Amos at all but on Yahweh who forms the locusts, calls for the fire, stands above the wall, explains the basket of fruit and looms above the altar commanding its destruction. Amos' role is to remind the Lord of his covenant responsibility and to sharpen our awareness of judgment's terror by his intercession in the first two visions; then Amos fixes our attention on the central objects, plumbline and fruit basket, in the last two.

In form, these visions are akin to Zechariah's, where the prophetic function is already clear, rather than to the call-visions of Isaiah, Jeremiah and Ezekiel. Indeed, Amos' intercession itself is a clue that he was already exercising his prophetic ministry, a ministry whose closest parallel is Abraham's intervention on behalf of Sodom (Gn. 18:22–33; *cf.* 20:7, where God speaks of Abraham to Abimelech in a dream: 'For he is a prophet, and he will pray for you, and you shall live'). Some interpreters have gone so far as to assign to Amos in these first two visions a role of covenant-mediator, whose pleas virtually accuse Yahweh of breaking covenant with Jacob who was totally dependent on divine protection for survival.[1]

Since these visions did not seem to accompany the prophet's call, which was described tersely not in the vision reports but in the account of his dispute with Amaziah (7:15), what can be said about their setting? Very little, because the text itself elaborates on them not at all but simply records them in their compact and somewhat formulaic terms. Are they reports of Amos' early experiences as prophet and, therefore, responsible for the degree to which his message is dominated by doom? Perhaps, but there is no firm reason to assume that visions were limited to the beginnings of prophetic ministries. They may have occurred from time to time throughout a prophet's career, as indeed they did in Ezekiel's and Zechariah's cases. Why else would Amaziah have chosen the term 'seer' as his label of Amos (7:12)? What hints the text does give seem to point to Bethel as the site of the visions: (1) the oracle that expands the vision report of the plumb-line centres in the

---

[1] *Cf.* W. Brueggemann, 'Amos' Intercessory Formula', *VT*, 19, 1969, pp. 385–399.

destruction of the shrines as well as the household of Jeroboam (7:9); (2) the encounter with Amaziah, deliberately inserted between visions three and four, takes place at Bethel; (3) the oracle interpreting the vision report of the fruit basket focuses on temple singers and their wailing (8:3); and (4) the final vision pictures Yahweh above the altar (9:1). The preoccupation with the shrines, then, and the specific reference to Bethel seem to suggest that the visions were first received in that setting, just as the woe on the idle élite had been pronounced at Samaria (6:1–14).

This section of Amos is rich with theological insight. The *sovereignty of Yahweh* is one dominant theme. He towers as large in every paragraph as he does in the final vision, where he overshadows the altar and calls for the collapse of the temple. That sovereignty is symbolized in the name of God that dominates this section – *Lord God*, literally 'My Master Yahweh' (Heb. *'a dônāy yhwh*; 7:1, 2, 4–6; 8:1, 3, 9, 11; 9:8). It is expressed in the intimate connection between Yahweh and the acts of judgment portrayed. We have seen how his presence is the central feature of each vision. Moreover, his personal threat of judgment lies at the heart of most oracles: 'I will rise against the house of Jeroboam' (7:9); 'I will never again pass by them' (7:8; 8:2); 'I will never forget any of their deeds' (8:7); 'I will turn your feasts into mourning' (8:10); 'I will send famine on the land' (8:11); 'I will set my eyes upon them for evil and not for good' (9:4).

That sovereignty is the foundation of Amos' argument with Amaziah: Amos is not free 'to pick up stakes', move south and stop prophesying at Bethel. He is a man under orders, commandeered by the Lord who snatched him from his vocations in agriculture and commissioned him to prophesy (7:14–15). But not just the prophet, the whole creation yields to that sovereignty whether in earthquake (8:8; 9:5) or eclipse of the sun (8:9) or flood (9:6), a sovereignty also vast enough to manage the migrations of all the peoples, not Israel's alone (9:7). Small wonder that flight from his presence is impossible; from Sheol to heaven, from the summit of Carmel to the depths of the Great Sea, Yahweh is Master (9:2–4).

Yet that sovereignty is seasoned by *compassion*. Even in the face of needed judgment, God is mindful of Israel's special relationship to him: he calls them repeatedly 'My people Israel' (7:8, 15; 8:2; *cf.* 9:14). Twice he withholds a judgment which the vision had already launched, responding to the prophet's poignant plea. Note how compassion and sovereignty combine in the merciful fiat, 'It shall not be' (7:3, 6). Even after the plumb-line has etched its indelible message of justice on the prophet's heart, the note of compassion is yet present. 'I will not utterly destroy the house of Jacob' even though 'all the sinners of my people shall die by the sword' (9:8, 10).

Mediating such sovereignty and compassion is the *prophetic word* which is the very word of Yahweh. Equally feared by Amos, who begs God to blunt its terrorizing power, and Amaziah, who reports it to the king and connives to rid the land of it, that word continues to dominate this section of the book. Amos insisted that Amaziah hear it, though it spelled doom for the priest, his family and his kingdom (7:16–17). Refusal to hear that word was as unconscionable as refusal to preach it. Israel was to learn that the hard way – by a famine of the words of Yahweh which would send them running in panic to find them, but without avail (8:11–12).[1]

a. Vision report: locusts (7:1–3)

1. The divine initiative in bringing judgment seems to be highlighted here. The transition *he was forming* (*cf.* RSV; AV; NASB; NIV) is to be preferred to 'swarm' (*e.g.* NEB; JB), the basic difference being the vowels of the Hebrew word (MT reads the participle *yôṣēr* and is followed by Vulg; LXX reads a noun *yeṣer* and translated it by *epigonē*, brood or offspring, hence swarm). A participle describing God's activity is found in the similar place at the outset of four of the five visions, the exception being the 'basket of ripe fruit', where God's presence is not a direct part of the vision. Though Yahweh is not specifically named as the one doing the forming, there can be little doubt that the participle has God as the subject, since the Lord is specifically mentioned as the one doing the calling in the second vision, where the form is virtually identical to the first. Furthermore Amos' sharp plea for forgiveness (v. 2) seems to imply that the locusts are Yahweh's work. (For other instances

---

[1] For a full discussion of the literary structures and theological themes of the vision reports, see G. Bartczek, *Prophetie und Vermittlung: zur literarischen Analyse und theologischen Interpretation der Visionsberichte des Amos* (Frankfurt am Main: Peter D. Lang, 1980).

AMOS 7:2

where God's creative action is viewed as forming or shaping, see Gn. 2:7; Am. 4:13.)

The tragedy of the locust plague is sharpened by its timing. Swarming hordes of locusts seem to be in view (*cf.* Am. 4:9; Joel 1:4), and all coming at a time when Israel's crops were most vulnerable. The word for *latter growth* (JB, 'second crop') stems from a root 'to be late' (Heb. *lqš*) and refers to the late spring crop of cattle-feed which is further described as coming *after the king's mowings*, an apparent reference to the royal right to tax the lands of farmers for fodder to feed the live-stock maintained by the court (*cf.* 1 Ki. 18:5). If the first cutting went to the court and the second crop to the locusts, Israel would be left destitute indeed. The April rains would have passed and the long drought of summer, usually six months, would make further growth impossible.

2. The intensity of the threatened judgment is heightened here, as the locusts are pictured as completely devouring the herbage or vegetation (*grass*; Heb. *'ēśeb* as food for cattle is used in Dt. 11:15; Ps. 106:20) of the land. Before Amos' eyes the whole countryside is stripped clean (*cf.* on Joel 1:4, 7).

Stunned by the ravaging sight, Amos forcefully begs God to *forgive*; the grammatical form is an imperative strengthened by a Hebrew particle (*nā'*) which conveys urgency: 'please' or 'now'. Though the vision report contains no account of sin, Amos knows that the locusts are an enactment of judgment upon a disobedient Israel; hence the plea for forgiveness. The Hebrew word (*slḥ* whose Akkadian cognate means 'to sprinkle', and hence 'to clean') is used exclusively of God's pardon (*cf.* Nu. 14:20; 1 Ki. 8:30, 39; Is. 55:7; La. 3:42).

The ground for Amos' request is Israel's (here called *Jacob*; *cf.* 3:13; 6:8; 9:8) frailty and vulnerability. The people would never be able to *stand* up under such an onslaught. Amos' pity is so keen that he does not wait for Yahweh to answer his rhetorical question but supplies the answer himself, an answer in sharp contrast to all the boasting of invulnerability and military prowess which dominated the previous chapter (6:1–2, 13): Jacob is little. The argument is noteworthy. No direct appeal is made to God's reputation (*cf.* Ex. 32:11–13) or to the covenant between Yahweh and Israel (*cf.* Ps. 74:20) or to their historic relationship which elsewhere looms large in Amos (2:9–11; 3:2). Amos had already been reminded that for Yahweh the covenant relationship was ground for harsh

judgment not lavish grace. So in the face of the locusts' terror
he appeals to God's compassion for a feeble people and to that
compassion alone. Yet even here covenantal overtones may be
heard: Israel is called *Jacob*, a reminder that he was the
smaller, younger one to Esau in Isaac's family; God had
deliberately chosen him and therefore was obligated to stand
by him in his helplessness.[1]

3. The prophet almost gained his desired result, but not
quite. Amos had begged for forgiveness of sin; Yahweh
granted only withdrawal of judgment: *It shall not be.* This
change of direction on Yahweh's part the text calls repentance
(*cf.* Gn. 6:6; Ex. 32:14; 1 Sa. 15:35; Joel 2:13–14; Jon. 3:10;
4:2). Though often described as an anthropopathism – a
human emotion ascribed to God which is not really an integral
part of the divine character – God's repentance is something
more than that. It is a reminder that the Old Testament never
makes Yahweh 'an arbitrary despotic Ruler but always regards
Him as a God who sympathizes with man'.[2] Theologically,
then, God's repentance is an expression of his compassion, of
his commitment to covenant and of his freedom.

When God chose to work out his salvation in history by
calling human persons to covenant obedience to him, he
freely opened himself to the implications of their historical
actions in either turning toward him or away from him. 'In
biblical thought God is always free to repent of the evil that he
said he would do to Nineveh (or Israel!) and not do it. . . . For
every man's cry of repentance and call for mercy presupposes
this freedom of God to forgive and deliver from the judgment
of law.'[3] Even more remarkably in this passage (as in the
intercession of Moses for Israel at Sinai; Ex. 32:11–14), God
withholds his wrath not in reply to the people's call for mercy
but in response to the plea of the solitary prophet, as though
Yahweh is open to any feasible reason to stay the judgment.

[1]W. Brueggemann, *op. cit.*, pp. 386–390.
[2]Th. C. Vriezen, *An Outline of OT Theology* (E.T., Newton, Massachusetts:
Charles T. Branford Co., ²1970), p. 316. See also from the standpoint of
systematic theology, J. Moltmann, *The Trinity and the Kingdom* (E.T., San Francisco: Harper & Row, 1981), pp. 21–60.
[3]J. Daane, *The Freedom of God: A Study of Election and Pulpit* (Grand Rapids:
Eerdmans, 1973), p. 95.

b. Vision report: fire (7:4–6)

In the first report (7:1–3), we were left to assume that the Lord God was the subject of the act of *forming* the locusts. Here there is no doubt of Yahweh's role in *calling* for the fire; the act of judgment is his and his alone. Whether such judgment is actually mentioned in the text is an open question: MT, LXX, Vulg., AV, RSV, JB, NASB, NIV all assume that it is, reading *lārib* as *for judgment* (lit. contention or controversy) *by fire*. For decades commentators have noted, however, that the parallel line in verse 1 does not overtly mention judgment and has only the direct object 'locusts' after the participle. Two alternative readings are, therefore, worth noting: (1) 'flame of fire' as in NEB (Heb. emended to *lahebet 'ēš*; cf. Ps. 29:7, or to *lahab 'ēš*; cf. Is. 29:6; 30:30; Joel 2:5) or 'rain of fire' which requires no change in the consonantal text, only in the word division (Heb. *lārib bā'ēš* is read *lir*ᵉ*bîb 'ēš* by H. W. Wolff, pp. 292–293, n.1).[1] The image of rain not only preserves the consonantal text but accords well with the supernatural character of the scene where the fire not only consumes everything on the arable land (lit. the portions marked off for growing crops) but the *great deep* as well. *Deep* probably refers primarily to the underground water supply which nurtures growth and would ordinarily be drawn on to replenish crops after a fire. But here its resources are exhausted too. There may be in this passage a side-glance at the pagan religions of Canaan and Mesopotamia which deified the deep: God's sovereign judgment was so sweepingly powerful that it enveloped even the pagan deities who could provide no shelter from it.

Judgment by fire divinely dispatched is a familiar scene in Amos (1:4, 7, 10, 12, 14; 2:2, 5; 5:6) as well as in Hosea (8:14). For Amos the locusts and the fire, divided into two vision reports with introductory formulas and identical literary patterns, are two separate episodes whose very repetition reinforces the threat of judgment. For Joel, in contrast, the imagery of fire is used to highlight the scorched earth policy of the locusts who leave nothing green or moist behind them and who sear the land with a touch akin to

---

[1] See J. Limburg, *CBQ*, 35, 1973, pp. 346–349, for cogent arguments in support of MT, which is interpreted as a description of fire used in judgment as an act of 'holy war' which also, as frequently, has connections with 'cosmic war', viz., the *great deep*.

drought (Joel 1:19–20; 2:3).

Amos' second plea (v. 5) deliberately contains a different word from his first (v. 2). There he had begged for forgiveness, but God did not grant it but only a stay of execution. Now he seeks merely a further stay with his urgent *'cease, please!'* (*Cf.* Ex. 9:29, 33–34, for another instance of the cessation of judgment-curses where the same Hebrew root *ḥdl* is used.) Forgiveness seems out of the question. The Lord's response notes that he has granted Amos' petition for a second time: 'This *also* shall not be'.

c. Vision report: plumb-line (7:7–8)

The central feature of this vision is the plumb-line, mentioned four times in the two verses. Not events – divinely-formed locusts or heaven-called fire – but a simple metal object (the Akkadian cognate of *'aᵃnāk* means lead or tin) dominates the scene. Found only here in the Old Testament, the word has sometimes been interpreted as an instrument of judgment, whether a sword made of tin or a bucket of molten lead. The mention of the wall, however, and the hand holding the metal object have pointed most interpreters and virtually all translations to a device used in measurement or construction, therefore, a *plumb-line*.

This interpretation shifts the thrust of the visions from the fact of judgment to the necessity or ground of judgment. God is the Masterbuilder; the *plumb-line* is the covenant standard of obedience to his call for justice and righteousness, proclaimed and demonstrated by the prophet himself;[1] the wall is 'my people Israel' whose lives are being tested for conformity to that standard; Amos who appeared in visions one and two as intercessor, pleading for forgiveness from sin or at least cessation of judgment, now is called to bear witness with his own eye to the message of the plumb-line: Israel's life is too crooked to warrant either pardon or relief.

The change in form of the vision report signals a sharp change in emphasis. Yahweh now has taken the initiative.

[1] A. Szabo', *VT*, 25, 1975, p. 507, has called attention to a possible pun in the similarity of *'aᵃñak* and *'ānōkî* the first singular pronoun *I*, which Amos uses of himself three times in 7:14. His conclusion that 'the prophet may have understood himself to be the "plumbline"', grasped by God from sheep-raising and sent to prophesy of Israel's crookedness, is suggestive.

Amos, what do you see? put Yahweh in charge of the discussion. He grasped the lead and set the agenda. No longer would he respond to Amos' question, 'How can Jacob stand?' Amos had to respond to Yahweh's question. This change in form, then, set God free to declare the meaning of the plumb-line to the prophet in verse 8, a meaning not left to the prophet's own understanding as was the meaning of the first two visions. Yahweh was putting Israel to the test of the plumb-line. Forbearance was no longer possible. Whatever compassion or covenant obligations may have sparked God's repentance have been overwhelmed by the magnitude of Israel's rebellion. Judgment was now inevitable. This seems to be what God indicated by his promise *I will never again pass by them, i.e.* never again overlook their sins and give them additional opportunity to repent (*cf.* 8:2).

d. Judgment speech: collapse of religious and political structures (7:9)

This brief oracle elaborates on the implications of God's withdrawal of opportunity for forgiveness. The prime targets for destruction, a destruction highlighted by the chiastic structure of the verbs which begin and end the first two parallel clauses, are, of course, the two prime targets of Amos' denunciations: the shrines and the royal household. (For discussion of *high places* and their religious significance, see on Ho. 4:13; 10:8.) The objects to be destroyed – the *high places* with their pillars and altars, the *sanctuaries* with their walls, courts and porches, the kingly *house* (though used metaphorically here of the royal family) with its stately architecture and lavish decor (3:15; 6:4, 11) – will all be put to the sword by Yahweh himself. The plumb-line has judged them as edifices unfit for divine use or for human benefit.

The references to *Isaac* (*cf.* also v. 16) are the only places in the Old Testament where *Isaac* stands for the nation of his descendants rather than for the patriarch himself. Amos seems to have in mind the special veneration for Isaac which the members of the Northern Kingdom displayed in making pilgrimages south to Beersheba (*cf.* 5:5; 8:14), Isaac's birthplace (Gn. 21:31) and the site of a theophany which he duly commemorated by the construction of an altar (Gn. 27:23–25). Implicitly in his reference to the patriarchs Isaac and Jacob (*cf.* 7:2, 5), Amos may be announcing and lamenting the tragic break with the covenantal past.

e. Report of Amos' conflict with Amaziah (7:10–17)

The judgment speech against the household of Jeroboam (v. 9) serves as a bridge to this prose report which fans to a blaze what must have been a smoldering antipathy between Amos and the religious and political hierarchies of Israel. The account of the direct threat on the king became the occasion for the editor of Amos to recount this story of prophetic conviction and courage. And the resistance of the royal and priestly establishments to the divine word serve as irrefutable evidence that the plumb-line did not lie. Israel, at the core of its leadership, was ripe for demolition.

This report, in its present context, is not so much an interruption in the sequence of visions as it is a confirmation of the accuracy of vision three, which demonstrates the necessity of judgment, and of the cogency of vision four, which reveals the finality of judgment. In form, the report (whose intent resembles those of Jeremiah 26 and 28, which record conflicts between prophet and priests and prophet and prophet) is a mixture of literary components: (1) a prose report of Amaziah's message to Jeroboam, which states Amaziah's charge of conspiracy (v. 10) and quotes Amos' poetic judgment speech directly as though Amaziah were the prophet's messenger (v. 11); (2) a prose report of Amaziah's admonitions to Amos banishing him to Judah and forbidding him to prophesy in Bethel (vv. 12–13); (3) a prose report of Amos' response denying any material motivation for his work and claiming divine authority for his prophetic mission (vv. 14–15); and (4) a poetic judgment speech to Amaziah blaming him because he forbade the ministry of prophecy and announcing judgment on the priest and his family (vv. 16–17).

i. Amaziah's report to Jeroboam (7:10–11). While Amos had condemned the pilgrimages to Gilgal (4:4; 5:5) and Beersheba (5:5), it was surely Bethel that drew his fiercest fire (4:4; 5:5–6), as Israel's chief shrine and the probable site of the rites so rigorously renounced in 5:21–24. The whole struggle between the prophetic word and Israel's vapid religion takes the form of a personal encounter here as, without introduction, Amaziah (*i.e.* 'Yahweh has been mighty,' a fairly common Old Testament name: (1) son of Joash and king of Judah, 2 Ki. 14:1; (2) descendant of Simeon, 1 Ch. 4:34; (3) a Levite, 1 Ch. 6:30; (4) Amos' adversary), the presiding priest of Bethel's sanctuary, appears on the scene to send a message to Jeroboam, presumably in Samaria, reporting what he deemed to be conspiracy on Amos' part. The literal meaning of Heb. *qšr* is to 'bind', *e.g.* Gn. 38:28; the figurative meaning to 'league together' or 'conspire' is found frequently in the historical texts, *e.g.* 1 Sa. 22:8, 13; 1 Ki. 15:27; 16:9; 2 Ki. 10:9; in the last three passages the conspiracy appears not to be a joint activity, despite the etymology of the word, but a one-man-plot as was the case in Amaziah's accusation of Amos.

Amaziah's message is testimony to his relationship with the king to whom he apparently had ready access as befitting the chief priest of the king's sanctuary (v. 13). Even more, that message is tribute to the power of the prophetic word which had become unbearable (*cf.* Joel 2:11), literally 'uncontainable'; the same Hebrew form is used to describe the capacity of Solomon's molten sea and bronze lavers (1 Ki. 7:26, 38), suggesting that Amos' words had spilled throughout the land and threatened to flood it with their calls for justice and threats of judgment.

As specific evidence of conspiracy, Amaziah cited, purportedly verbatim as the introductory messenger-formula suggests, a brief oracle summarizing Amos' announcements of judgment on *Jeroboam*, death by sword, and on *Israel*, exile from their land. Ample record we have seen of Amos' threats of exile (4:2–3; 5:27; 6:7; 7:17; 9:4), but scarce mention of the use of the *sword* (4:10 is an account of past judgment not a threat of future). The *sword* of punishment is unsheathed only at 7:9 where it is directed not against Jeroboam himself but against his house. Yet the differences between 'house of Jeroboam' and *Jeroboam* (v. 11) should not be overplayed. Given Hebrew understandings of the close identity of a person and his family, each statement may actually include the other. Once that sword is drawn, its blade flashes with consistency through the rest of the book: thrusting at Amaziah's sons and daughters (7:17); cutting off the fugitives' escape from the collapsed sanctuary (9:1); seeking them in exile (9:4); executing the sinners who bask in false security (9:10). Though the first line of Amos' alleged oracle (v. 11) is a paraphrase or even an exaggeration, the second line – promising exile – is a quotation so accurate that Amos uses it again as the final word of irony to Amaziah himself (v. 17).

ii. Amaziah's attempt to banish Amos (7:12–13). The text contains no mention of Jeroboam's response to Amaziah's message. Whether the priest's commands for Amos to flee home to Judah were an echo of an order from Samaria, we cannot tell. If they were, an interval of several days has to be assumed between the events of verses 10–11 and those of verses 12–13. It is hard to believe that Amaziah would not cite his king's authority if he had received a response. It is possible, however, that absence of any such citation is tacet evidence of the pivotal role that the chief priest himself played in political and religious affairs. Though the ultimate argument against Amos' ministry at Bethel was that the sanctuary belonged to the king and was designed to serve the needs of his kingdom (v. 13), it is the priest who takes full responsibility for declaring that word to the prophet.

There need be no irony in Amaziah's address to Amos, *O seer*. The description fits both the title of the book (*cf.* ḥzh in 1:1) and the function performed by him throughout the vision sequence (though the visions consistently use the other verb for seeing, *rʾh*). Amaziah's approach was not motivated by lack of regard but by abundance of respect for the unsettling power of his adversary's oracles.

Something else may be involved in the interplay of words used to describe prophetic activity in this passage: *seer* (v. 12), *prophet* (v. 14), and *prophesy* (vv. 12–16). A recent study has suggested that *ḥōzeh*, seer, was the technical term for morality prophets in the Southern Kingdom (*cf.* Gad, 2 Sa. 24:11), since the prophetic texts that use the term all come from Judahite prophets – Amos, Micah (3:5–8), and Isaiah (28:15; 29:10; 30:10). In the Northern Kingdom, according to this view, morality prophets were labelled *nᵉbîʾîm*; note Amos' use of the term in 2:11–12, where he chides the Northern Tribes for muzzling the prophets sent to them as an act of God's grace. Both the *ḥōzeh* and the *nābîʾ* engaged in acts of prophesying as 2:11–12 and 7:12–15 indicate. The difference between these two titles, then, was that *ḥōzeh* described a person from Judah engaged in speaking to the moral issues of his day and that *nābî'* was used of an identical ministry in Israel.

While the data on prophetic roles and offices are both obscure and complex, the above interpretation seems to accord well with the evidence of this passage and seems to shed some light on it: (1) Amaziah calls Amos *ḥōzeh*, and Amos enters no objection to the title; (2) the mention of the title *ḥōzeh* is followed immediately by a command not to cease prophesying but to return to Judah and to continue a prophetic ministry there, as is appropriate for a *ḥōzeh* (v. 12); (3) Amos acknowledges that he is not a *nābî'* but that his authority to minister in the north comes directly from Yahweh's command to prophesy to Israel (vv. 14–15), so that his ministry in no way can be limited to Judah; and (4) Amos seems to renounce any concern for prophetic office, and more particularly for any possible income from such office – summarized in Amaziah's *eat bread there, i.e.* earn your living by acting as an official prophet in Judah.[1]

iii. Amos' rejection of the ban (7:14–15). Amos' answer to Amaziah focuses on two points: he is not and never has been a professional prophet whose livelihood depended on his ministry, but he had other occupations that fully supported him (v. 14); he ventured into Israel to prophesy for one reason only: he was snatched from his vocation and dispatched on his mission (v. 15). If the interpretation of this encounter with Amaziah outlined above (see on vv. 12–13) is reasonably accurate, the best way to solve the sticky problem of the tenses in verse 14 is to read them as present tenses. The sentences contain nouns only, and the translators have to choose whether to insert 'am' (*e.g.* Vulg; RSV; NEB; NASB; Wolff; Cripps), or 'was' (*e.g.* LXX; AV; JB; NIV; Mays; Rowley).[2] The present tense is most natural from the standpoint of grammar and suits best the overall context: Amos prophesies by divine authority not prophetic office and still considers agriculture

---

[1]For the evidence on which these conclusions about *nābî'* and *ḥōzeh* are based, see D. L. Petersen, *The Roles of Israel's Prophets, JSOT* suppl. 17 (Sheffield: JSOT Press, 1981), pp. 51–69. For a contrasting interpretation that finds in Amos 'a very serious inner conflict and . . . ambiguous feelings regarding his own identity', see Y. Hoffmann, *VT*, 27, 1977, pp. 209–212.

[2]H. H. Rowley, 'Was Amos a Nabi?', *Festschrift Otto Eissfeldt* (Halle: Niemeyer, 1947), pp. 191–198.

his occupation; he is not at all a prophet in the way that Amaziah, used to the cult prophets and the roaming bands of their disciples ('sons') that had functioned in the Northern Kingdom since the days of Elijah and Elisha (*e.g.* 1 Ki. 20:35–43; 2 Ki. 2:3, 5, 15; 6:1; 9:1), employed the term.[1]

Amos' precise occupation is hard to define. If we use 'sheep-raiser' (*nōqēd*, 1:1) and *flock* (*ṣō'n*, v. 15) as keys, then *herdsman* or 'shepherd' (*bôqēr*, v. 14, from *bāqār*, cattle) most likely means something like 'breeder of livestock' which may include large cattle (*i.e.* cows, oxen) and small cattle (*i.e.* sheep, goats; Wolff, pp. 306–307, n.e.). *Dresser of sycamore trees* (RSV; NEB) is even harder to pin down. The sycamore trees (*cf.* 1 Ki. 10:27; Ps. 78:47; Is. 9:10) seemed to thrive in the warmer climates of the Shephelah, the lowlands in western Judah on the edge of Philistine territory. They produced a mulberry fig, which dressers used to nick with a knife or nail to speed the ripening. The Greek translation suggests that this is what Amos meant by calling himself a *bôlēs*, a word akin to Semitic words for 'fig' but found only here in the Old Testament. Jewish interpretations vary: the Targum has Amos say, 'I have sycamores in the Shephelah', while Rabbi David Qimchi interprets *bôlēs* as meaning 'who seeks out sycamore fruit (for his food)'.[2] The more general translation, therefore, of the NIV may be preferable, given our lack of specific knowledge about Amos' ventures into horticulture: 'and I also took care of sycamore-fig trees.' An inference that some have drawn from this statement is that 'the concern of Amos with the sycamore was in providing fodder for those animals in his charge.'[3] Surely this double vocation[4] took Amos away from Tekoa seasonally and gave him ample opportunity to judge the spiritual and moral quality of places beyond his hometown.

[1]Debate over the tenses has sometimes obscured the fact that the stress is not upon *time* but 'upon what happened and that Yahweh acted and spoke in the call and commissioning of Amos.' G. M. Tucker, 'Prophetic Authenticity: A Form-Critical Study of Amos, 7:10–17', *Int*, 27, 1973, p. 432, n. 23, citing R. Knierim's unpublished conclusion.

[2]On Qimchi's interpretation, see J. J. Gluck, 'Three notes on the book of Amos', in *Studies on the Books of Amos and Hosea: Papers read at 7th and 8th meetings of the O. T. Werkgemeenskap in Suid-Afrika*, 1964–65, pp. 119–121.

[3]T. J. Wright, 'Amos and the Sycamore Fig', *VT*, 26, 1976, p. 368.

[4]L. Zalcman, *VT*, 30, 1980, pp. 252–253, reduces Amos' occupations to one, 'piercer and tender of sycamore figs', emending *bôqēr* to *dôqēr* in 7:14 and *nōqᵉdîm* to *nōqᵉrîm*, 'borers' or 'piercers' in 1:1.

Amos' account of his agricultural occupations was subordinate to that of his prophetic commission (v. 15). Yahweh's initiative which has loomed large in the vision reports was the towering theme of this verse. The verb *took* underscored this, whether one compares it with the 'took' of God's election (*e.g.* Dt. 4:20; 1 Ki. 11:37) or with the even harsher uses like the taking away of prisoners by the coalition of kings that plagued Abram (Gn. 14:12). *Took* connoted both strength and surprise. The command that accompanied it was patterned deliberately to show how Amaziah and Yahweh stood on opposite sides of the question of *where* Amos should prophesy. Both Amaziah and Yahweh prefaced their words with *go*. Both commanded Amos to *prophesy* (v. 12; v. 15). Yahweh's commission had as its object *my people Israel*; Amaziah's location was less personal, *the land of Judah*. This difference marked the summit of Amos' response to Amaziah's orders: mere prophesying was not his calling but prophesying to God's people in the Northern Kingdom. The call to prophesy and the assigned audience were of one piece. Amaziah's refusal to understand that 'the authentic prophet is the one who has responded to a divine commission'[1] would cost him his life.

iv. Amos' judgment speech against Amaziah (7:16–17). This is Amos' only judgment speech against an individual (*cf.* 2 Ki. 1:5–6); but in his challenge of priestly, indeed royal authority, he marks himself as worthy successor to Nathan (2 Sa. 12), Elijah (1 Ki. 21), Micaiah (1 Ki. 22), and Elisha (2 Ki. 9). Following a call to attention (*cf.* 3:1; 4:1; 5:1), the cardinal accusation was made in starkest terms: you commanded me not to prophesy to Israel. The indictment places Amaziah firmly in the camp of the ancient Israelites already condemned by the prophet (2:11–12).[2] Again both the act of prophesying and the audience were crucial, since the issue

[1]G. M. Tucker, 'Prophetic Authenticity: A Form-Critical Study of Amos 7:10–17', *Int*, 217, 1973, p. 434. Tucker's article is a valuable study of the form, setting and intent of this portion of Amos.
[2]See T. W. Overholt, *CBQ*, 41, 1979, pp. 517–532, for the alleged role that the people played in commanding the content and timing of the prophet's ministry. Though the parallels from other religions are probably overdrawn, the article is reminder of the vast difficulties endured by prophets like Amos unless the people accepted their right to prophesy.

with Amaziah turned on the 'to whom' of Amos' ministry. The prohibition against prophesying was reinforced here with a parallel verb, usually rendered *preach* (RSV; NASB; NIV). The Hebrew root (*nṭp*) suggests a flow of words, excitedly delivered (NEB, 'go drivelling on'), and may be used derogatorily (*e.g.* Ezk. 20:46 [MT 21:2]; 21:2 [MT 21:7]). Again *Isaac* is used as a synonym for Israel, the Northern Kingdom (*cf.* v. 9).

The announcement of judgment (v. 17) was fortified with the full strength of the messenger formula and reminds us of the heinousness of Amaziah's sin by the thoroughness and finality of the promised punishment. Amaziah's sin was two-fold: (1) stifling the prophetic word and consequently challenging Yahweh's authority (2:12; 3:7–8); and (2) failing in his priestly duties as Yahweh's servant by becoming the king's puppet. The punishments suited these crimes: (1) for Amaziah's wife to become a harlot in the city (*cf.* Dt. 22:23–24, for the difference between illicit intercourse in the city, where a woman could cry for help, and intercourse in the open fields, where it would be interpreted as rape not adultery) meant that she would be utterly unfit to be married to a priest (Lv. 21:7); (2) for Amaziah's offspring to be slain meant that his priestly line would be wiped out and his office perish; and (3) for Amaziah to die in an unclean, *i.e.* ceremonially defiled, non-kosher, land meant a stinging insult to all his priestly instincts.

The breach of covenant (*cf.* the biting indictment of priestly failure to keep covenant in Mal. 2:1–9) that Amaziah's sin and judgment implied is attested by the close parallels between Amos' prescriptions of judgment and those in Assyrian vassal treaties: harlotry, execution of children, dividing of land.[1] One other note may echo in this announcement of judgment: Yahweh cherishes his word as the expression of his person-hood as warmly as a man cherishes his children; rejection of that word can appropriately be judged only by the rejection of the sinner's children (*cf.* on Ho. 4:6) or by complete with-drawal of the life-giving word (Am. 8:11–12).

The announcement drives on to an ironic conclusion. Not only will the priest die an exile in a foreign land, stripped of his own land-holdings which he probably gained as a gift of

---

[1]D. R. Hillers, *Treaty-Curses and the OT Prophets. Biblica et Orientalia* 16 (Rome: Pontifical Biblical Institute, 1964), pp. 58–59.

his king, but Amos' key word, which the priest so sharply dreaded and so irately protested (v. 11), would yet come true – Israel's exile was as certain as yesterday's headlines. Like priest, like people (*cf.* Ho. 4:9). Their futures, Amaziah's and Israel's, were inextricably entwined. The fate of the one would be the fate of the other.[1] Failure to heed Yahweh's word delivered by a duly commissioned prophet was as heinous as any sin could be. Amos' followers who knew this story also knew its powerful significance for any time and place where the authentic prophet word is met with scepticism.

f. Vision report: basket of summer fruit (8:1–2)

With no transition at all, the reports were resumed, and the third-person biographical style of the conflict with Amaziah gave way again to the autobiographical style of 7:1–3, 4–6, 7–8. The vision could not be simpler. In contrast to the plumb-line, where Amos had to sort out what was central from what was peripheral – wall, hand, *etc.*, what Yahweh showed here was identical to what Amos saw: *a basket of summer fruit*. The Heb. *qāyiṣ* may mean 'summer season' (*e.g.* Gn. 8:22; Am. 3:15) or 'fruit that ripens in summer', probably either figs or pomegranates (*cf.* 2 Sa. 16:1–2). While the ripe fruit may have hinted that Israel was ripe for judgment or was going to be carried into exile as in a basket (*cf.* 4:2–3), the overt connection between the vision and Israel's fate was in the word-play based on the similar sounds (though different technical derivations) of *qāyiṣ* and *qēṣ*, which means *end*. The point of this vision, then, is the finality of judgment. All time for repentance was past. The plumb-line (7:7–8) and the encounter with Amaziah combined to prove that compassion could no longer be extended; the gavel of judgment must fall. The verdict was sealed by Yahweh's announcement, repeated from 7:8, that his mercy would no longer be available.

g. Judgment speech: death prevails (8:3)

Like the third vision report (7:7–8), the fourth (8:1–2) was expanded and interpreted by an oracle which amplified the

---

[1] On the relationship between Amaziah's deportation and Israel's, see A. J. Bjorndalen in *Werden und Wirken des Alten Testaments*, Fs. C. Westermann. Ed.

picture of judgment (*cf.* 7:9; 8:3). In keeping with the theme of the *end*, *i.e.* of death, the whole scene turned funereal: (1) the songstresses (the feminine form of the Heb. points to 'singers' – NEB; JB – not *songs* as in RSV; NASV; NIV) of the royal court (read 'palace' rather than *temple*; *cf.* 2 Sa. 19:35; 2 Ch. 35:25; Ec. 2:8) no longer entertained but became official mourners, wailing the grief of their patrons; (2) corpses were so numerous that they were tossed about everywhere and could not be dealt with decently; (3) the scene was so macabre that 'Hush!' was the only proper word to voice (JB; a better reading of the imperative form than the phrase *in silence*, RSV; NASB; NIV). The prophet has here picked up the themes of wailing (*cf.* 5:16–17; 8:8, 10) and of disposing of the carnage of judgment (6:9–10). The setting of this unspeakable event was *in that day*, an echo of Amos' dark words of the day of the Lord (5:18–20) and a preview of the eschatological gloom depicted in 8:9, 11, 13.

h. Judgment speeches: God remembers (8:4–14)

This cluster of five short oracles served several purposes within the book: (1) it delayed the fifth vision and thus added to the suspense in the sequence of vision reports, a suspense already tightened by the lengthy intrusion of Amaziah and his impossible proposal to Amos (7:10–17); (2) it prepared for the final vision by calling more attention to Israel's corruption and Yahweh's righteous wrath; (3) it recapitulated themes from earlier parts of the book as if to refresh our memories of what Amos had said about sin and judgment; and (4) it rang the changes on the singular theme of the terse report of vision four – *the end* – by recounting injustices to the poor and crooked market practices as grounds for bringing the covenant to an end (vv. 4–7), by describing the end as an earthquake (v. 8) and an eclipse of the sun (vv. 9–10), by signalling Yahweh's final withdrawal from his people with an absence (a *famine*) of his words (vv. 11–12), and by threatening a drought that even the choicest of young people cannot endure (vv. 13–14). The heart of the matter was the terror, scope and severity of the judgment, coming and certain. Yet the

---

by H. R. Albertz, *et al.* (Göttingen: Vandenhoeck and Ruprecht, 1980), pp. 236–251.

dominant accusations were also present, quiet but telling evidence that Yahweh is just, not arbitrary. The covenant retribution was at hand because the covenant stipulations had been violated: (1) the poor had been oppressed (vv. 4–6; *cf.* 2:6–8; 3:9; 5:11–12); (2) the word of Yahweh had been suppressed (vv. 11–12; *cf.* 2:11–12; 7:12–13); and (3) the worship of Yahweh had been compromised by pagan accretions in Israel's shrines (v. 14; *cf.* 5:26).

i. Sacrilegious oppression of the poor (8:4–7). In style, this oracle exhibited several features common in Amos: (1) use of *hear* in the call to attention (v. 4; *cf.* 3:1; 4:1; 5:1; 7:16); (2) an address in participial form, which is also an accusation – *you who trample* (v. 4; *cf.* 5:7; 6:3–6, 13); (3) Israel's own words quoted as part of the case against them (vv. 5–6; 2:12; 4:1; 5:14; 6:2, 13; 8:14; 9:10); and (4) the announcement of judgment fortified by an oath formula sworn by Yahweh (v. 7; *cf.* 4:2; 6:8).

In theme, the speech is a mixture of repetition and innovations. The trampling of the poor (v. 4) and the transactions of buying them at minimal cost (v. 6) recall Amos' first judgment speech against Israel (2:6–8), although there the emphasis was on selling slaves not buying them and the whole indictment here has a finality to it, as expressed in the strong verb *bring to an end*, literally 'cause to cease' or 'destroy' in verse 4.

New in this passage are: (1) the notes of impatience with the religious holidays when commerce was suspended (for *new moon* and *sabbath*, see on Ho. 2:11), a different angle on the cultic life of Israel from that of 5:21–23 and one that shows more clearly why worship was no substitute for justice (5:24); (2) mention of crooked weights and measures (v. 5), where the *volume* measure, the *ephah* – a dry measure of about 22 litres, *i.e.* slightly larger than a half bushel – was reduced, probably by lining the basket, and the *weight* measure – the *shekel*, a piece of metal of about 11 grams or 0.4 oz. – was enlarged so that it took more gold or silver to balance it on the scales;[1] moreover, the balance itself was bent out of kilter in favour of the seller so that the poor buyers, who could scarcely afford anything to begin with, ended by paying more than they

[1] D. J. Wiseman, 'Weights and Measures', *IBD*, III, pp. 1634–1639.

should have for less than they thought they had bought; it should not have taken prophetic oracles to remind people of how wrong all this was, since the wisdom prevalent in the clans had plenty to say about honest weights and measures (*cf.* Pr. 11:1; 16:11; 20:10, 23); the merchants' crookedness was compounded by the fact that the *wheat* they did sell in shrunken quantities and for inflated prices was not always wheat itself but sometimes *refuse* (verse 6), *i.e.* wheat swept up from the ground or threshing floor and therefore mixed with foreign materials; this clause now attached rather loosely to verse 6 may have been accidentally transposed by scribal lapse from the end of verse 5, where it would seem to fit better; (3) the form of the oath formula in which Yahweh swore not by his holiness (4:2) nor by himself (6:8) but by the *pride of Jacob* (v. 7), a phrase best understood as extreme sarcasm by which Yahweh used the constancy of Israel's horrible arrogance (*cf.* 6:8) as the measure of his own constancy in keeping his promises to judge (Wolff, p. 328); and (4) the more general form of the judgment announcement (v. 7), which lacked the blood and fire so frequently found in Amos yet contained its own quiet terror – the solemn oath that Yahweh would not forget these deeds but would hold them accountable for them all (*cf.* Ho 8:13).

ii. Judgment by earthquake (8:8). Just how terrifying Israel's accountability and Yahweh's inerasable memory could be was made clear in this verse. The rhetorical question presupposed the crimes described in the previous verses and continued the implied dialogue between prophet and people. Their own quotations had been used as evidence against them (vv. 5–6), and now they were asked by the question-form to confirm the rightness of the announced judgment. Yahweh, through the prophet, was saying in effect, 'What else can anyone expect? What else is the reasonable response to such flagrant injustice but the shaking of the very land which you have corrupted?' Previously Amos had used questions to seal his *indictments* (*cf.* 2:11; 5:18, 20, 25–26; 6:2–3, 12; 9:7) or to argue for his prophetic *authority* (3:3–8). Here it was the necessity of inescapable *judgment* that was his point – judgment demanded by divine logic and yet fully understandable to human reason. The question-form, demanding a positive answer, shut off all possibility of protest.

The question-form may have been chosen as a fitting complement to what seemed to be the quotation of lines from a hymn, as a parallel text in 9:5 suggests: the mourning of the inhabitants and the rising and sinking of the Nile are described in both passages in language that is almost verbatim. A possible reading of the rhetorical questions, then, would be, 'Are not the words of the hymn true – the hymn you sing about Yahweh's power to come in judgment and shake the land with the same ease which he employs in the flow and ebb of the Nile?'[1]

The earthquake is one of the dominant motifs of judgment in Amos (2:13; 3:14–15; 9:1, although the Hebrew word in 8:8, *rgz*, *cf.* Joel 2:10, is a synonym of *r'š* which is normally found in Amos). And undoubtedly his prophecies gained substantial credibility in Israel when the quake remembered in 1:1 actually took place. The terror struck by the quake threw the entire population into mourning, as Amos had already predicted (8:3). Amos' point in using the flood cycles of the *Nile* as illustration seems to be the extent of the motion (for the tossing action described in the Heb. *grš*, *cf.* Is. 57:20). It is true that the flooding of the Nile was more beneficial than calamitous and more gradual in its timing than the sudden rolls and thrusts of an earthquake, contrasts of which Amos would scarcely have been ignorant, but his point is *massiveness*. And where better could he go for analogy but to the most massive and life-changing natural phenomenon known to his part of the world, the mighty Nile that gives life to Egypt?

iii. Judgment by solar eclipse (8:9–10). The emphasis on catastrophic, grief-producing intervention continued with the description of an eclipse of the sun. The connection between the two terrifying experiences, the shaking of the earth and the darkening of the sun, was made clear by the time reference *and on that day*, which also pointed to the eschatological future of the Day of Yahweh, previously pictured as a day of darkness not light (5:18, 20). Two such eclipses have been calculated to have occurred in Amos' lifetime: one in 784 BC, the other in 763 BC. Since Yahweh is lord of all creation, the

---

[1] On the relationship between quake and theophany, see B. S. Childs, 'The Enemy From the North and The Chaos Tradition' in *A Prophet to the Nations: Essays in Jeremiah Studies*, ed. by L. G. Perdue and B. W. Kovacs (Winona Lake, Indiana: Eisenbrauns, 1984), pp. 152–154.

line between his supernatural and his natural actions was not a solid one. While this context seems to suggest an eclipse, the very presence of Yahweh was often accompanied by clouds of smoke that might obscure the sun (*cf.* 4:13; Joel 2:30–31 and the comments there; *cf.* also Is. 13:10).

The mood of awesome calamity was expressed in funereal language, each phrase of which expressed either a dramatic contrast (*feasts into mourning, songs into lamentation*; *cf.* 5:1, 16–17) or a customary expression of grief (*sackcloth upon all loins*; *cf.* Gn. 37:34 and the comment on Joel 1:8, 13; *baldness on every head*; *cf.* Je. 16:6 for the custom of shaving the head in time of disaster). The passage drove to its climax, when the whole event was shrouded by grief like that of a family or a widow lamenting the loss of *an only son*, and therefore saying goodbye to all hope of progeny and the continuation of the name and personhood that the son represented (*cf.* Je. 6:26; Zc. 12:10). *Bitter day* is a day utterly soaked in grief (*cf.* Ezk. 27:31) with overtones of death itself (1 Sa. 15:32), as though the mourners were lamenting their own fate as well as that of their loved ones – an experience that would be literally true in the death of an only son.

The interplay between Israel's sin and the well-being of the whole cosmos was a recurring theme in the prophets, whose doctrines of creation and covenant were intertwined, thanks, of course, to their conviction that Yahweh was Lord of all and that the creation served as setting and context for the covenant with Israel (*cf.* on Ho. 2:18; 4:1–3).

iv. Judgment by withdrawal of revelation (8:11–12).

The calamitous mood continued. The judgment announcements of quake and eclipse were followed by the threat of *famine* – not of food (*bread*; *cf.* 7:12) but of *hearing the words of the Lord*. The longer eschatological formula, *Behold, the days are coming*, occurs in Amos only here and in 9:13; Amos' more usual pointer was *in that day* (*cf.* 2:16; 3:14; 8:3, 9, 13). The longer formula was characteristic of Jeremiah (*e.g.* 7:32; 9:25; 16:14; 19:6; 23:5; 30:3; 31:27, 31, 38). In both Amos and Jeremiah, the formula may introduce announcements of judgment, as here, or promises of salvation (Am. 9:13).

The comparison of God's word to bread is a familiar biblical device (Dt. 8:3; Is. 55:1–3; Mt. 4:4; and by implication in Jn. 6:51). The indispensable, life-giving quality of the divine word is what the comparison conveyed. No-one could live without the power and guidance of the divine words any more than anyone could live without the nourishment of bread and the refreshment of water.

As usual in judgment speeches, the punishment here fitted the crime: rejection of the prophetic word (*cf.* 2:12; 7:12–13) forced withdrawal of that word. The seriousness of that withdrawal was indicated in the picture of frustration and panic that sent the population scurrying in search of Yahweh's word (the picture recalled the drought of 4:7–8 and used similar language) but to no avail. *Wander* (*nwʿ*; *cf.* 4:8; Je. 14:10; Is. 24:10; La. 4:14–15) and *run to and fro* (*šwṭ*; *cf.* the search for manna; Nu. 11:8; and the satan's itinerating in Jb. 1:7; 2:2) showed how out of control life would be and how desperate the behaviour of those who spurned the word yet knew they could not live without its counsel and hope. Absence of the word would indeed mark their *end* as Amos had already envisaged (8:2). The frantic quest was world-wide, *sea to sea* and *north to east* suggested absence of any geographical limits and embraced the whole earth (*cf.* Ps. 72:8 and Zc. 9:10), thus underscoring the terror and devastation of this judgment. (For another picture of Israel's seeking of Yahweh without success, see Ho. 5:6.)

v. Judgment by thirst (8:13–14). The litany of calamities concluded with a description of physical *thirst*, as the counterpart to the spiritual hunger and thirst of the previous oracle. The sequence of speeches makes its impact by covering the basic social and spiritual sins of the people and describing their attendant judgment in the most comprehensive terms: heaven and earth conspired against Israel and brought to an end their national existence in both its physical and spiritual expressions. The cream of the population was singled out for judgment, the beautiful *virgins* and the choice *young men* (*cf.* Zc. 9:17, where the same group was selected for blessing). What can this mean but the end of the nation, since those on whom its future population depended have collapsed in *faint* like Jonah in the searing heat of Nineveh (Jon. 4:8)?

These prized young persons were not helpless victims but represented a wayward people whose worship at the shrines of the land had led them astray from the God of the covenant (v. 14). Amos' language here is so compressed and difficult to understand that scholars have often felt the need to emend the text. First, if we take our cue from the second clause whose wording seems clear – 'And they say, "As your god lives, O Dan" ' – then it seems likely that both the Samaria and the Beersheba clauses contain references to swearing by a deity, especially the latter clause, whose language parallels the Dan clause. Second, to many scholars it has seemed preferable, then, to read the Hebrew word (*bᵉʾašmat*) translated 'by the shame of' Samaria (NIV, following LXX and Vulg.) as either *bᵉʾašimâ*, *i.e.* 'by Ashimah', the idol which the citizens of Hamath made in Samaria (RSV; NEB; JB; 2 Ki. 17:30) or *baʾᵃšērat*, *i.e.* by Asherah, Canaanite goddess and consort of El, though linked to Baal in the Old Testament (Jdg. 3:7; 1 Ki. 15:13, where an idol is described). If the original 'sin' or 'guilt' is allowed to stand, the reference must still be to a nameless image whose influence was so despicable that the prophet branded it 'shame' and refused to dignify it with a proper name. As to cultic practices in Samaria, Amos was otherwise silent, focusing instead on the economic and social corruptions of the capital (*e.g.* 4:1–3; 6:1–8). Third, the *way* (Heb. *derek*) *of Beersheba* has been interpreted literally as the 'pilgrimage' of Beersheba (*i.e.* the religious rites that were the purpose of that trek from north to south; *cf.* on 5:5). It has been connected with the Ugaritic word *drkt*, 'dominion' or 'might' (*i.e.* a mighty deity), and with Ashkelon's fish-goddess, *i.e.* Derketo. It has also been read as *dōrᵉkā*, 'your circle' or 'company' of gods, *i.e.* your pantheon, and it has been emended to *dōdᵉkā*, 'your kin god', *i.e.* the one who keeps you safe as a new relative (see options in Wolff, pp. 323–324).

When all these suggestions are weighed, it is hard to view any as an improvement over the present text. Samaria's 'guilt' or 'shame' is a readily understandable epithet for a deity, and 'Beersheba's way' could well be a succinct expression for all that the pilgrimage stood for.

What seems clear in all of this is that Israel was playing false with Yahweh by taking oaths and making promises in the names of alien deities. Though Amos did not choose to expand on such conduct, whose wretchedness should have been self-evident to any true Israelite, these cryptic references suggest that he had valid reasons for admonishing the people not to 'seek Bethel', which strangely he does not mention here, nor 'cross over to *Beersheba*', which he does mention (5:5). *Dan*, noted in Amos only here, was the northernmost Israelite city,

some 35 kilometres north of Lake Chinnereth and 45 kilometres east of Tyre. In seeking to placate the tribes of the far
north, Jeroboam I gave national status to its shrine (1 Ki.
12:29–30) which had been founded by Jonathan, grandson of
Moses (Jdg. 18:30). The combination of *Dan* and *Beersheba* was
Amos' way of tarring the entire land (Jdg. 20:1), far north to
deep south, with the brush of idolatry.

The final clauses of verse 14 brought to a close this chain of
oracles (vv. 4–14) which were a series of symphonic variations
on the theme, *the end* (8:2). The finest of youth, representa-
tions of the entire populace, would collapse of thirst and not
be able to get up again – the end, indeed! And these clauses
did even more: the reference to *virgins* harks back to 5:2
where the virgin Israel was lamented as one who had fallen,
never again to stand up. The last words of verse 14, then, were
an echo of the first words of chapter 5 and indicated that the
whole series of judgment speeches which began at 5:1 and
continued through the first four visions had reached its conclusion. No wonder that 9:1 featured a final separate vision
which would bring the theme of judgment to its shaking
climax.

i. Vision report: the Lord above the altar (9:1–6)

The pattern of visions begun in 7:1 is both completed and
broken in this passage. It is completed by its subject, the Lord
himself shouting his orders of judgment as commander-in-
chief. Since the quintet of visions is about judgment, what
further revelation is required? It is enough to see *the Lord*, as
terrifying a privilege as there can be (Is. 6:1; Jb. 42:5–6). The
pattern is broken by the drastic changes in form: (1) not 'thus
the Lord God showed me' (7:1, 4, 7 ['he showed me']; 8:1), but
I saw; (2) no plea of Amos, 'O Lord God, forgive' (7:2, 7:4
['cease']), but God's command to smite the sanctuary (9:1); (3)
no pledge of divine repentance (7:3, 6), but a detailed picture
of the judgment's thoroughness (9:1–4); and (4) no divine
query, 'What do you see?' (7:8; 8:2), but the direct affirmation
of Amos, without introduction or amplification, *I saw the Lord*
(9:1).

The break in pattern serves to thrust the content of the
vision into bold relief: the sovereignty of Yahweh is the theme
and that sovereignty is pictured and heard (the bulk of the

passage is audition more than vision) as acting with a finality that the third and fourth visions anticipated. Gone is the time for object lessons, pleas, repentance and dialogue. Come is the time for the fullness of the judgment, whose nature and need dominate the book, to be released.

The *vision* itself is found in 9:1a and immediately gives way to the *audition* in 9:1b, introduced by *and he said*. The first part of the audition is the double *command* 'smite' and 'shatter' (9:1b), which is immediately followed by the *threat* to the survivors (9:1c), introduced by *I will slay*. The threat is expanded in a series of concessive clauses marked by *though* (Heb. *'im*) and *from there* (Heb. *miššām*) which drum home the inescapable nature of God's judgment (9:2–4a). The audition closes with a *summary statement* reinforcing both the personal and the awful character of the punishment (9:4b). To seal the impact of the shattering vision and its terrifying audition, the passage climaxes in a *hymn-stanza* (9:5–6) that celebrates the cosmic majesty of Yahweh and his power to effect the promised judgment (*cf.* 4:13; 5:8–9).

In this vision report are clustered a number of motifs to which Amos has previously called attention. The *site* of the judgment is the sanctuary itself. Its dramatic collapse from top to bottom is the necessary result of the corrupting influence of the shrines that misled the Israelites (*cf.* 2:8; 4:4–5; 5:4–5, 21–26; 8:14) and is also the fulfilment of the prophecies both implied (5:6) and expressed (7:9). The *means* of the judgment are earthquake (9:1, 5) and exile (9:4), the two great threats that have hovered over the text from beginning to end: *earthquake* (1:1; 2:15; 3:14–15; 6:11; 8:8) is (1) an element in theophany, the powerful appearance of Yahweh to work blessing or destruction (*cf.* Jdg. 5:4; Ps. 18:7), (2) a sign that the basic order of creation has been unsettled and chaos is threatening to return (*cf.* Je. 4:23–26), and (3) a technical term for the chaos that accompanies the final judgment (*e.g.* Ezk. 38:19–20; Hg. 2:6, 7, 21; Joel 2:10; 3:16);[1] *exile* (3:11–12; 4:2–3; 5:27; 6:7; 7:11, 17; 9:9) is (1) the withdrawal of the grace God extended in the gift of the land, (2) the reversal of the Exodus in which he took the people from slavery to freedom, and (3) the King's ultimate curse on his rebellious people who failed to keep covenant with him.

[1]B. S. Childs, *loc. cit.*

The *thoroughness* of judgment, its utter inescapability (9:1b–4), is a theme that Amos has repeated (*cf.* 1:2 and 9:3, both of which mention Carmel as the most inaccessible point in the land, yet totally under God's sway; 2:14–16; 4:2, 'even the last of you'; 5:19; 6:9–10; 9:9–10) and here expands so as to bar any possibility of successful flight. From sheol to heaven, from sea floor to Carmel's summit, his judging hand holds sway. And serpents and swords abet his plan.

The *sovereignty* in judgment is made clear in the hymn-stanza with which the passage closes (9:5–6). Like its fellow stanzas (4:13; 5:8–9), this passage reinforces the divine power to judge by celebrating features of cosmic might so completely beyond human understanding, not to speak of competence, that they stagger the imagination. The One who controls the march of heavenly and earthly armies (*cf.* 1 Ki. 22:19–36) and is therefore called God of hosts can jolt the earth so that it rolls like the ebb and flow of the Nile (*cf.* 8:8), can build a habitat that spans the gulf between heaven and earth, and determine the seasons of drought and rain. That One can surely execute the promised judgment. And lest there linger any doubt as to Who can do all this, this stanza, like the other two, declares that the name of the sovereign deity is Yahweh. His majestic 'I wills', then, are not bravado or bluff. All that he has advertised in judgment he will produce (*cf.* 2:13; 3:14–15; 5:17, 27; 6:14; 7:9; 8:2, 9–11; 9:2–4, 8–9, for the divine 'I wills' of judgment which punctuate the book and come to a climax in this final chapter).

1. The shortened formula of vision report (see above) does not use the divine name Yahweh as had three of the preceding reports (7:1, 4; 8:1) but only *'ᵃdōnāy*, 'Master', though verses 5–6 make clear that the whole episode is Yahweh's work and words. What Amos saw precisely depends on the interpretation of the preposition *'al*, which can mean 'upon' (LXX; AV; Wolff) 'beside' or 'by' (RSV; NEB; JB; NASB; NIV; Mays) or 'above' (Vulg).[1] The overall tone of sovereignty, especially in the issuing of the commands of destruction, suggests the position of authority – 'above' or 'upon' – rather than *beside*, though there is no way we can be sure. Identical language, 'standing upon' or 'above', in 7:7 suggests a conscious connection

---

[1] Revelation 8:3 seems to borrow the language of the LXX to describe an angel's coming to stand at the altar.

between this vision and that of the plumb-line. The destruction of the high places and sanctuaries called for there, where they failed to measure up to God's standard, is implemented here. As the foci of the attacks on the political or social corruption were the gate (5:10, 15) and the citadels or strongholds (6:8), so the focus of religious corruption was the *altar* where sacrifices were offered (2:8; 3:14; 4:4–5; 5:22). The place where God had desired to meet his people in grace was now the site of his fierce and final judgment.

To whom are the divine commands *smite* and *shatter* addressed? To a heavenly servant like one of Isaiah's seraphim (6:2, 6–7)? To the prophet whose symbolic gesture or spoken word had the power to launch the destruction? We cannot be sure. It is more likely that the imperatives (both singular) are a dramatic way of announcing the pending devastation and are directed toward no specific agent. In any case emendation of either of them to make God the subject (so Wolff; NEB; JB) seems unnecessary (so LXX; AV; RSV; NASB; NIV).

The sanctuary is to collapse from top to bottom, from the dislodged capitals of the pillars to the loosened, shaky thresholds – a further sign that a divine act like an earthquake is in view rather than a military assault. Capitals and threshold together signify the completeness of the destruction: nothing survives from roof to floor, as Zephaniah 2:14 indicated in the graphic picture of Nineveh's desolation.

It is probably best (with RSV; NASB) to translate the second verb as *shatter* (Heb. *bṣ'*; lit. 'cut off' or 'shear') and to make its object the capitals of the temple pillars rather than the heads of the people (for the latter, see JB; NIV). The closest biblical parallel then would be the picture of Samson, 'eyeless in Gaza', collapsing the pillars on which he leaned, so that the sanctuary structure shattered apart and tumbled down on the heads of the Philistines (Jdg. 16:23–31). In the language of the audition, Amos made clear what he had previously admonished the people: to worship at Bethel instead of seeking the Lord by heeding the prophetic word was itself a form of death-wish (5:4).

Yahweh did not bank on the collapse of the sanctuary alone to work his punishment but promised to be at the ready with a *sword* to cut off all survivors. The word *'aḥªrîtām*, variously translated *what are left of them* or 'to the last man' (NEB), conveys the thoroughness of the judgment here as it did in 4:2, depicting the fate of the 'cows of Bashan' who were to be led into exile. The last two Hebrew lines underscore that thoroughness by their wording which leans toward redundancy to make its point strong: 'no fleer of them shall be able to flee; and no escaped one shall be able to escape.' The whole scene recalls an earlier one at Bethel, where Jehu slew the prophets and worshippers of Baal, posting armed guards to cut off the fugitives and using language that Amos almost mimics: 'Go in and slay them; let not a man escape' (2 Ki. 10:25). What it took eighty guards to do for Jehu, Yahweh would do by himself. Amos' point should not be missed: Yahweh's own people had become as corrupt as the followers of Baal and, thus, were doomed to a similar fate.

i. Pledge of divine pursuit (9:2–4). The theme of inescapability is expanded with specific illustrations couched in concessive clauses, 'Though ... from there', which are virtually *merisms*. By marking the extremes of God's sovereignty – Sheol and heaven (v. 2), the summit of Carmel and the Mediterranean sea-floor (v. 3) – they include everything in between. No place in all creation will afford shelter to the fugitives once God has set his judgment in motion.[1]

As *dig* (Heb. *ḥtr; cf.* Jb. 24:16; Ezk. 8:8) indicates, *Sheol* was viewed as a subterranean realm, occupied by the dead (Is. 14:9–11, 15–20) and popularly thought to be outside of Yahweh's sway of sovereignty (Jb. 10:20–22; 14:13). Amos, however, like the psalmist (Ps. 139:7–11), knew better. The God whose justice and power he had encountered was stranger to no part of his creation; his very dwelling embraced both heaven and earth (9:6). Nothing should be inferred about a Hebrew view of afterlife from this reference to Sheol. Its purpose is to state the length that persons will go to escape the divine wrath and the utter impossibility of such escape (*cf.* Ob. 4). The mention of the climb to heaven shows how hypothetical and hyperbolic Amos' language is. Could the fleeing Israelites do the impossible – ascend to the realm of heaven, home of sun, stars and planets – God, who made Pleiades and Orion (5:8), would be there to snatch them back to earth for

[1]For a summary of the movement of the five vision reports and their climax in this passage where 'the prophet expresses as never before the cosmic sweep of the (divine) presence', see S. Terrien, *The Elusive Presence: Toward a New Biblical Theology* (San Francisco: Harper & Row, 1978), pp. 237–241.

the judgment they deserve.

Carmel's summit (v. 3) symbolized the loftiest point in the land (*cf.* on 1:2). Its slopes, with wooden thickets (*cf.* Mi. 7:14) as well as caves and tombs, offered ample opportunity for hiding (Heb. *ḥbʾ*, as in Gn. 3:10) from human search parties but not from the divine Hunter (*cf.* Je. 16:16), who would leave no stone unturned to 'track them down' or *search* them *out* (Heb. *ḥpś* in intensive stem means to search thoroughly and systematically, as Laban did for Rachel's household gods in Gn. 31:35 or Joseph's steward did for his master's silver cup in Gn. 44:12).

The *bottom* (or 'floor'; *cf. qarqaʿ* in Nu. 5:17) *of the sea* is, of course, as inaccessible to human flight as Sheol or the heavens, so Amos continues the tone of hyperbole to emphasize his point as strongly as possible. As Jonah's story illustrated, Yahweh's sovereignty extended even there, though in both Jonah and Amos the Lord is pictured as using secondary agents to work his will. Though the sea was deified by both the Mesopotamians (Tiamat) and Canaanites (Yam), and though the Israelites may have sometimes pictured it as rebellious chaos (Jb. 7:12; Ps. 74:13–14; 93:3–4), yet it was Yahweh's domain. Even the *serpent* there took orders from him. The passage is all the more powerful if the serpent-servant is Leviathan, whose power and skill were celebrated and feared by the ancients (Jb. 41:1–34; Ps. 74:14; 104:26). The account of the serpent's bite seems deliberately to echo the punch-line of the parable in 5:19: no place is safe when the day of darkness has been decreed.

Nor would the people find refuge in *captivity* (v. 4). Foreign armies were instruments of divine judgment; their *sword* swung at Yahweh's command (*cf.* on 7:11). The final lines of verse 4 ring with the sound of a verdict, as though the King were rendering a final summation of his intended decision. He is not going to abandon them but to remain present with them not in the ritual of the cult but in the terror of judgment, wrought by the power of his gaze (*cf.* Ex. 14:24). The contrast between the *evil* (*i.e.* harm) that God promised and the *good* (*i.e.* blessing) that the Israelites expected was exactly the punishment that they merited. They had disregarded the admonitions 'seek good and not evil' and 'hate evil and love good' (5:14–15). Their love of evil (*i.e.* injustice and corrupt worship) was to be sated by the lavishness of God's judgment:

231

he would see to it personally that *evil* (*i.e.* disaster) and nothing else was their appointed lot (*cf.* Je. 24:6 for a positive promise phrased in similar form).

ii. Third hymn of divine sovereignty (9:5–6). The threats of inescapable judgment were reinforced with the celebration of Yahweh's cosmic power. The hymn-stanza recaptured the major themes of verses 1–4. The melting of the earth (theophanic language as in Ps. 46:6; Mi. 1:3–4) and the mourning of its inhabitants looked back to the earthquake of 9:1 (*cf.* Na. 1:5 where 'quake', *r'š*, and 'melt', *mwg*, are paralleled). God's access to both heaven and earth (9:2) was documented in the reference to the scope of his dwelling place (v. 6). His mastery over the sea (v. 3) was further explicated in the hymnic descriptions of the control of tides or rainfall (v. 6; *cf.* Ps. 104:3, 13). For the rising and falling of the Nile as an illustration of God's shaking of the earth, see on 8:8.

It is hard to catch the exact picture of what Yahweh is building in verse 6. The heavenly construction may be a 'staircase' (Heb. *ma'ªlâ*, *cf.* Ex. 20:26; 1 Ki. 10:19–20; LXX; Vulg; AV; NEB) or a 'roof-chamber' (*cf.* Jdg. 3:20, 23–25; 2 Sa. 19:1; 1 Ch. 28:11, reading Heb. *'ªliyyâ*, and omitting the initial *mem* as a duplication of the final *mem* of *heavens*; RSV; JB; NASB; NIV). The earthly component is even more difficult to define precisely. The Hebrew *'ªguddâ* (root *'gd* = bind) means (1) 'bundle' or 'sheaf' (*cf.* Ex. 12:23 Vulg); (2) 'rope' or 'thong' (Is. 58:6); and (3) 'band' of people (2 Sa. 2:25; so AV). The translations have used 'ceiling' (NEB), *vault* (RSV; JB), 'vaulted dome' (NASB), or 'foundation' (NIV), assuming that the basic meaning of *'ªguddâ* here is 'something bound together in construction'. Fortunately, we do not have to have a photographic image of Amos' scheme in order to catch its force. What counts is that God's presence is at home everywhere in the universe from top to bottom, and that presence is utterly dependable and permanently to be reckoned with as the verbs of construction, *builds* and *founds*, connote.

One of Amos' main concerns here was to make sure that all of this activity in judgment that he had witnessed in the visions was ascribed to Yahweh. He used, therefore, the divine name at the beginning and end of the hymn though he had used *'ªdônây* alone in verse 1. The title 'Lord Yahweh of hosts' (v. 5) is a variant form of the address usually found in Amos, 'Yahweh God of hosts' (3:13; 4:13; 5:16, 27; 6:8,14).

j. Judgment speech: the sieve and the sword (9:7–10)

The argumentative tone with which this passage begins suggests that Amos is either answering a protest or anticipating one. It is as though his audience arched their backs and rejected his message of judgment as totally unsuited to their privileged status as a covenant people who had been rescued by God's mighty arm in their Exodus from Egypt. The setting seems similar to that of 3:1–2, 3–8, where the people apparently denounced the threat of judgment and derided Amos' right to preach it (*cf.* 9:10). Here in 9:7–10 as there, Amos answered their objections with strong disputation questions and then went on to pound home his announcements of judgment (vv. 8–10), concluding them by quoting Israel's own words of foolish denial that God would ever dispatch disaster upon them (v. 10).

7. As in 5:25–26, Yahweh himself put the stabbing question to his people. They had staked their hopes on their unique relationship to God, established by an Exodus that distinguished them from all other peoples (*cf.* 2:9–11; 3:1–2). Now that hope was dashed by the very Lord on whom they had glibly counted and whose name they purported to honour. They were no more important to him than the *Ethiopians*, whom the Israelites regarded as a remote and insignificant people. Ethiopia (*i.e.* Cush; Heb. *kûš*, Gn. 10:6) was the name given by the LXX to the land of Nubia, whose kingdom ranged along the Nile from Aswan (Seveneh or Syene; *cf.* Ezk. 29:10; 30:6) south to the junction of the two branches of the Nile near Khartoum, a territory considerably north of modern Ethiopia.[1]

Even more stinging was the second question that forced them to recognize that God had managed the immigrations of their pagan, age-long opponents, the *Philistines* and the *Syrians* or Aramaeans. *Caphtor* is identified as Crete and recalls the movement of the Sea-peoples from the Aegean-Mediterranean area to the coasts of Palestine, whose very name is a Philistine

---

[1] See D. A. Hubbard, 'Ethiopia', *IBD*, I, p. 484.

legacy.[1] For *Kir*, see on 1:5. Two painful lessons were forced on Israel by Yahweh's questions: (1) God's sovereignty and care extended beyond their boundaries to distant and hostile peoples; and (2) their Exodus contained no uniqueness to protect them from judgment once they had ruptured the covenant. Any vestige of national pride, social smugness, or military security was snatched away by the divine interrogator.[2]

8. Again (*cf.* v. 4) Yahweh fixed his damning gaze on Israel, described here not only as in a class with the neighbour nations but even more bluntly, as *the sinful kingdom*, the ruling household (*cf.* 7:13) that had shattered God's law and missed the target (*cf.* Heb. *ḥṭ'* which literally means to 'miss the way' in Pr. 19:2) of justice and righteousness. This announcement of judgment stood in stark contrast to the Exodus note in verse 7: 'I brought up Israel from the land of Egypt' is paralleled by 'I will destroy it from the face of the earth' (NASB; NIV). The failure to live up to the meaning of the rescue could only result in the total loss of the land and of the political existence that were gifts of that rescue.

The interpretation of this verse turns on a distinction that must be drawn between: (1) Israel's political existence represented by the house of Jeroboam (*cf.* 7:9, 11, 13, where 'king's sanctuary' and 'temple of the kingdom' seem to be phrases that explain each other) and described here as *the sinful kingdom*; and (2) Israel's social existence as persons and families descended from Jacob, here called *the house of Jacob*. The *political* structures were to be toppled and even their rubble wiped away (*cf.* the similar reference in 1 Ki. 13:34). The *personal* survival of some Israelites was promised in line with the gracious admonitions of 5:14–15 and in expectation of the promise of salvation with which the book concluded. The clue to whether destruction or survival was to be the outcome was found in verse 10: 'the sinners ... shall die ...' To identify *sinful kingdom* with Israel, the Northern Kingdom, and *house of Jacob* with Judah, the Southern Kingdom, is both to introduce a

[1]On the Philistines, see K. A. Kitchen in *Peoples of Old Testament Times*, ed. by D. J. Wiseman (1973), pp. 53–78.
[2]W. Vogels, *VT* 22, 1972, pp. 223–239, has heard in Am. 9:7 an invitation for Israel to return to the covenant as his special children as well as a declaration of divine sovereignty over the destiny of all nations.

distinction not otherwise found in Amos and to use Jacob in a way that would have confused Amos' hearers (*cf.* 6:8; 8:7, where Jacob was clearly the Northern Kingdom).

9–10. Once more Yahweh was pictured as Commander-in-Chief (*cf.* 6:11; 9:1). What he ordered was a sifting. *Among* (Heb. *b*) *all the nations* has seemed for many commentators (Amsler, Cripps, Mays, Wolff) to be a later insertion to describe the dispersion of Israel in exile. It is possible that the preposition can also be rendered as 'together with' or 'along with' and be a reminder of God's universal sovereignty which holds all nations accountable, a theme enunicated at the beginning of the book (1:3 – 2:5) and a corollary of the claims to universal providence in 9:7.

The figure of sifting was an agricultural one, and its interpretation hinged on a knowledge of how grain was threshed. The *sieve*, a word found only here in the Old Testament, must have been used to separate the kernels of grain from the trash they had mingled with in the threshing: pebbles, twigs, etc. With its large mesh the sieve would allow the farmer to sift the useful kernels into a pot or sack while the strings of the sieve retained the unwanted trash (*cf.* Sir. 27:4). The *pebble* (*cf.* 2 Sa. 17:13) represents the sinful leaders of the house of Israel, none of whom would escape the sieve of God's judgment. That some good grain may be left can only be inferred both from the metaphor and its place in the text following the 'I will not utterly destroy' of verse 8. The spotlight, however, was not on the survivors but on the condemned and on the *sword* (which stands at the beginning of the Heb. text of verse 10) that wrought their judgment (*cf.* 7:9, 11, 17; 9:1, 4).

Their sin (*sinners* in v. 10 should be linked to *sinful kingdom* in verse 8 in the manner of catch-words) was compounded by their complacency, a theme amply dealt with earlier (5:18–27; 6:1–14). Like their later Judean counterparts in the days of Micah (3:5) and Jeremiah (6:13–15; 7:4; 23:17, the last line of which resembled the quotation with which Amos closed his announcements of judgment), Amos' Israelites felt themselves exempt from disaster and tried to muzzle the prophets who proclaimed it. Can there be a more fitting ground for judgment or more glaring evidence of apostasy than to defy God's will and then claim immunity from accountability? Where such sin is the style, death can be the only result, as biblical faith has acknowledged from the beginning (*cf.* Gn. 2:17).

VII. TWO FINAL SALVATION PROMISES (9:11–15)

The transition from verse 10 to verse 11 is the most abrupt and surprising in the entire book. The sword of judgment gives way to the trowel of reconstruction. The day of darkness which Amos had warned against (5:18–20) is replaced by a day of light. The *timing* is one key to understanding how a book that has been dominated by doom could end with such brilliant hope. The eschatological formulas 'in that day' (v. 11) and 'behold, the days are coming' (v. 13) must mean 'in that day when judgment has run its course' and 'the days are coming after the divine judgment has done its righteous work'. Otherwise, these last two oracles (vv. 11–12, describing the restoration of the united Davidic kingdom; vv. 13–15, depicting the unparalleled fertility and unassailable security of the land) would undercut much of what Amos has previously said.

A second key to understanding this ending is, of course, the *covenant*. In the beginning God had not chosen Israel as his people because of their justice and righteousness but because of his love (Dt. 4:37). He committed himself to Jacob's descendants long before they committed themselves to him. It was that commitment, pledged to Abraham (Gn. 12:1–3; 15:1–21; 17:1–14) and reaffirmed to Isaac (Gn. 26:24–25) and Jacob (Gn. 35:9–15), that prompted the grace of restoration bestowed in Amos' closing words. It was that commitment, expressed in political terms to David by Nathan the prophet (2 Sa. 7) that was in view in the oracle about the *booth of David* (v. 11). It was that commitment, appealed to by Amos after the shock of the first two judgment-visions (7:1–6), that determined these final promises. If, as we have held, the messages of Amos are laced together with the thongs of God's covenant commitment which makes Israel's crimes so unspeakable and God's judgment so necessary, then the following appraisal of the crucial character of these final speeches may be accurate:

> Perhaps the centre of Amos is not to be found in chapters iv and v where we have usually located it but in the promise of ix 11–15 where the fidelity of Yahweh is affirmed and therefore the future of Israel is secured. What had seemed to be

an embarrassing gloss, in light of the meaning of intercession of vii 2, 5, may be the central kerygma of the
tradition of Amos.[1]

A third key to understanding these two salvation promises is
their relationship of *continuity and contrast* with much of what
Amos has previously said. The continuity is found in the
careful and conscious use of language and themes from the
rest of the book; the contrast comes in the fact that the whole
tone has changed from negative to positive – a change
summed up in the promise of 9:14: 'I will restore the fortunes
of my people Israel.' If most of Amos has described Israel's
fate as the tragic and total reversal of Israel's lot from
covenant darling to humiliated outcast, the ending of Amos
has promised 'that this reversal will also be reversed' in what
can be called 'the healing reversal of tragic reversal'.[2]

The drama of this second reversal is conveyed in part by the
parallels drawn from the earlier chapter. First, the eschatological formulas, *in that day* (v. 11; *cf.* 2:16; 8:3, 9, 13) and *behold
the days are coming* (v. 13; *cf.* 8:11), introduce promises of
salvation instead of announcements of judgment, as if Yahweh
says 'there is more to the future than I have yet told you; there
is hope beyond despair'. Second, the themes of falling (Heb.
npl) and rising (Heb. *qwm*) or raising (Heb. *hqym*) are picked up
here and turned topsy-turvy: 'fallen no more to rise … with
none to raise her up' (5:2) and 'they shall fall, and never rise
again' (8:14) were poignant descriptions of Israel's lot; they
are implicitly reversed in the expectation that 'I will raise up
the booth of David that is fallen' (v. 11). Third, the cows of
Bashan were seen carted into exile through the breaches (in
the city walls; 4:3), while the picture of the future sees Yahweh
heaping up stones (Heb. *gdr*) to close the breaches (Heb.
pᵉrāṣîm; v. 11). Fourth, *Edom*, whose vicious anger was so
vividly portrayed in the judgment speeches against the nations
(1:11–12), is singled out as the prime example of how divine
sovereignty will embrace even the nations who were previously hostile (v. 12), so that the international mayhem

---

[1]W. Brueggemann, 'Amos' Intercessory Formula', *VT*, 19, 1969, p. 399.
Brueggemann's phrase 'embarrassing gloss' recalls Wellhausen's famous
dictum, to the effect that these verses smack of 'roses and lavender instead of
blood and iron.' Cited by Wolff, p. 352.
[2]W. Brueggemann, *The Land* (Philadelphia: Fortress Press, 1977), p. 133.

pictured in the book's opening is thoroughly quelled at the close. Fifth, even the phrase *my people Israel* (v. 14) is uttered here with a change of tone from its earlier context in the reports of the visions and the conflict with Amaziah (7:8, 15; 8:3; *cf.* 9:10, 'my people'); the poignant, even angry, sound of judgment has been overwhelmed by the joy of restoration prompted by God's covenant fidelity. Sixth, the promises of rebuilding cities to live in them and of planting vineyards to drink their wine (v. 14) are a deliberate about-face of the threat issued in 5:11, while the mention of fruitful gardens recalls the chiding words of 4:9, 'I laid waste your gardens . . . yet you did not return to me.' Finally, the pledge of planting Israel on their land (v. 15) counters all the fore-warnings of exile that dot the book (3:11; 4:2–3; 5:5, 27; 6:14; 7:11,17; 9:4) and especially the explicit threat of 9:8: 'And I will destroy (the sinful kingdom) from the surface of the ground' (RSV; Heb. preposition *mē'al*, 'from upon', and noun *'ªdāmâ*, 'ground' or 'land', occur in both passages).

We can add to the evidence from thematic and verbal ties, the arguments from the nature of prophetic ministry expressed by G. von Rad that the prophets 'addressed themselves to definite sacral traditions' and preached them so as to make them 'relevant for the prophet's own day and generation'. The presence, then, of a Davidic, Messianic reference in this concluding oracle should come as no surprise from Amos, a Judean.[1] What is surprising is how little Amos' southern perspective has coloured his message.

When all of this is put together, the assignment of 9:11–15 to exilic or post-exilic times by a host of commentators (*e.g.* Amsler, Coote, Cripps, Delcor, Mays, Robinson, Wolff) seems a little glib. Some other scholars like Hammershaimb (pp. 135–38), Kohler, Reventlow and Sellin have argued for the authenticity of most or all of this section on the basis of the Judean background of Amos, the hope of restoration after judgment grounded in the prophetic knowledge of God's mercy and grace, or a possible liturgical scheme of cursing and blessings. There is no easy truce to be found in this tug-of-war of opinions. But given the way in which Hosea, Isaiah, Micah and Jeremiah all found room for hope beyond

---

[1]G. von Rad, *Old Testament Theology*, II, p. 138.

judgment in their ministries, there is no essential reason why Amos should not have done the same (Hammershaimb, p. 137).

a. Salvation promise: restoration of David's realm (9:11–12)

In that day elsewhere in Amos signals judgment yet to come (2:16; 8:3, 9, 13). Its role here was not so much to connect the restoration with the acts of judgment announced in the previous oracles (vv. 8, 9–10) as to lift the eyes of the hearers to a more distant but undefined future. *Booth of David* has been interpreted in a number of different ways: (1) Judah's Davidic dynasty which had collapsed (*fallen*) at the hands of the Babylonians – a reading that requires a date after 586 BC (Robinson, p. 107); (2) the influence of that dynasty diminished for centuries due to the rending of the kingdom under Rehoboam (Hammershaimb, p. 138); (3) the city of Jerusalem, imitating Isaiah's (1:8) description of Judah desolate like 'a booth in a vineyard ... a lodge in a cucumber field' (Wolff, p. 353); and (4) a return to the premonarchic period *days of old* (*cf.* Mi. 7:14, 20), when David championed the cause of the peasantry before he captured Jerusalem (Coote, p. 123). The first two interpretations have to struggle to understand *booth*, since the Davidic dynasty would normally be called '*house* of David' (*cf.* 2 Sa. 7:11). The third interpretation hinges on a literal reading of the picture of breaches and ruins which are puzzling expressions to apply to anything as fragile and easy to collapse as a booth or hut; furthermore, the similar passage in Isaiah is not of great help, since its antecedent is 'country' (*'a̲dāmâ*) not a city.[1]

The fourth interpretation offers an interesting possibility. *Booth* may well be a figure of simplicity and dependence on God, a return to the life of the wilderness as the Feast of Booths (or Tabernacles) symbolized (Lv. 23:42; Ne. 8:16). It is an agricultural not an urban term; it describes the temporary shelter, constructed of poles and palm branches, that a farmer would build to provide occasional relief from the sun while he

---

[1]H. N. Richardson, *JBL*, 1973, pp. 375–381, tries to make a case for reading *skt* not as 'booth' but as Succoth (*skwt*) a city in Transjordan (Jos. 13:27; Jdg. 8:5; Pss. 60:6; 108:7) that may have been strategically important to David's military ambitions. *Cf.* 2 Sa. 11:11; 1 Ki. 20:12, where Y. Yadin and others have read *skwt* not as 'tents' but as Succoth, the city.

worked his fields. Amos would have been very familiar with such huts. The choice of *booth* rather than 'house' to describe the re-establishment of the golden days of David may have been influenced by the negative ways in which palaces (or strongholds) and elaborate houses are treated in the book (*cf.* on 1:4; 3:11, 15; 5:11; 6:11). The messianic age – though Amos did not use the term, his wording points to that era (*cf.* Is. 11; Je. 23:5–6) – will not feature citadels to display wealth or shield from enemies but a simple trust in a sovereign God, like David's before Saul and against Goliath. The agricultural and rural inferences of the *booth* are reinforced in verse 13 with its beautiful picture of joyful and abundant fertility in the land, especially in the hill-country. The closest biblical parallel to this may be the words of Micah, Amos' fellow Judean and probably a peasant himself, where the old Davidic town of Bethlehem is described as the source of a new ruler who will shepherd his people in 'the strength of the Lord', not like the oppressors who fleeced the peasantry of Judah (Mi. 5:2–4).

If this interpretation is near the mark, then *breaches* and *ruins* are to be read figuratively to describe the basic shambles which the descendants of David have made in their failure to work the justice and righteousness which were their chief concern (*cf.* Ps. 72:1–2). Only when these priorities, so dreadfully neglected in both kingdoms, are re-established by God's power (*cf.* Is. 11:4–5; Je. 23:5; Ezk. 34:16) – note that *he* does the raising, the repairing, the rebuilding – will the kingdom be extended to its ancient boundaries (v. 12; Ps. 72:8–11) and will the desired prosperity come to pass (vv. 13–14; *cf.* Ps. 72:3–4).

God's purpose (Heb. *lᵉmaʿan*; *that* or 'so that') for the restoration is cast in universal terms, embracing Edom and all the nations upon whom God's name was called (v. 12). We find here a positive expression of the sovereignty of Yahweh, in contrast to its negative expression in the judgment speeches on some of these same nations in 1:3 – 2:3. Though *possess* often connotes military conquest (*cf.* Am. 2:10; Gn. 15:7–8; Nu. 13:30; Dt. 1:8, 21, 39; Jos. 18:13; Jdg. 11:21–23; Is. 65:9), there is no hint here of the means, beyond the promise that all of this is God's doing. Whatever temptation to triumphalism the Israelites might have heard in the promise of a revival of Davidic hegemony over the neighbour nations (*cf.* 2 Sa. 8) would have been tempered by the solemn reminder of Yahweh's humiliating question a few verses earlier (9:7).

The remnant of Edom (v. 12) should be compared with the
remnant of the Philistines (1:8) and understood as meaning 'all
of Edom', 'Edom to the very last person'. So interpreted, the
phrase is not necessarily an allusion to the ravished state in
which Edom found herself after the incursions of Nebuchadrezzar in the sixth century. Rather it is possible that the
specific mention of Edom not only corresponds to Edom's
prominent role in the opening speeches (1:6, 9, 11; 2:1) but
also connects with the references to Jacob (esp. 7:2, 5), whose
older twin, Esau, the Edomites claimed as their illustrious
ancestor (Gn. 25:30; 36:1). In the fidelity to covenant that
marks Yahweh's character, Jacob's descendants, who include
David as a prominent member, will exercise sovereignty over
Esau's descendants. The smaller, younger, more vulnerable
twin is to be given prominence over the older thanks to the
constancy of the divine covenant (*cf.* Mal. 1:2–5; Ob. 15–21).[1]

How literally should we take *all the nations* (v. 12)? We can
restrict the list to those on the map of David's modest empire
(Mays) or we can expand it to embrace 'the coming global
reign of Yahweh' (Wolff, p. 353; *cf.* Mal. 1:11). The immediate context, which mentions Cush, Philistia, Aram and Edom
(vv. 7, 12), together with the notes of correspondence between
this blessed scene of sovereignty and its grim counterpart in
1:3 – 2:3, argues for the narrower interpretation. *Who are
called by my name* is literally 'upon (or over) whom my name is
called (or invoked)'. A special relationship is implied, a relationship that virtually spells out an identity: the panicky
women grasping for a husband in Isaiah 4:1; the prophet's
personal relation to God in Jeremiah 15:16; Israel's kinship
with Yahweh in Deuteronomy 28:10; Yahweh's ownership of
the ark in 2 Samuel 6:2, of the temple in 1 Kings 8:43, of
Jerusalem in Jeremiah 25:29. These last examples imply that
the relationship is virtually one of ownership. And that
ownership or suzerainty is made even more clear in Joab's
warning to David that, if the general not the king captures
Rabbah, the people will view the city as Joab's not David's
possession (2 Sa. 12:28).[2]

The closing oracle formula is unique in the Old Testament,
expanded as it is with what sounds like a hymn-fragment: *Says*

[1]W. Brueggemann, 'Amos' Intercessory Formula', *VT*, 19, 1969, p. 399.
[2]P. K. McCarter, Jr., *II Samuel*, AB (1984), p. 312.

241

the Lord who does (is doing) *this* (*cf.* Mal. 4:3 [Heb. 3:21] for the closest parallel). Uniqueness is a double-edged argument when it comes to deciding authorship. If the clause occurs only here in the whole Bible, how can one argue for or against attributing it to Amos?[1] Amos' ample use of participles as descriptions and addresses throughout the book, whether of Yahweh in the hymn stanzas or of Israel in the woes and elsewhere, should prevent us from any snap judgment that would deny this clause to him. It is entirely fitting that a tome that constantly faulted Israel for crass self-sufficiency and a failure to trust Yahweh rather than might or opulence (*cf.* 6:1–14) should include this firm reminder that the hope of a future alight with Davidic glory must be based on God's doing and his alone.

The importance of the first salvation promise (vv. 11–12) did not escape the New Testament writers. Luke credited James with its quotation as the chief evidence for ending the church's Jewish-Gentile controversy over circumcision and the keeping of the law (Acts 15:16–18). The argument was abetted by the use of the LXX instead of the Hebrew text, since the Greek version read *remnant of Edom* as 'the rest of men' ('*ādām* for '*e̜dôm*), making it the subject of the verb 'they shall seek' which they read for *they may possess* (Heb. *drš* for *yrš*). Whatever universal overtones there may have been in the Hebrew were thus amplified in the LXX and, so quoted, contributed to the stabilization and universalization of the church, at a time when it was utterly crucial that its door be flung open for the Gentile believers. As Haenchen has noted, it was the Jesus event that Luke saw as the fulfilment of Amos' prophecy.[2]

b. Salvation promise: return of material prosperity (9:13–15)

As the book pushes to its conclusion, the rays of hope grow even brighter. The eschatological formula here introduces a superlative picture of fertility in agriculture which would have

---

[1] Wolff (p. 353) notes that this clause and the concluding one in 9:15 are not found elsewhere and argues for a 'later level of redaction', in part, on the basis of their uniqueness. But, if such formulas are not used in later writings, the argument is reduced to a matter of personal opinion.
[2] E. Haenchen, *The Acts of the Apostles: A Commentary* (E.T., Philadelphia: Westminster Press, 1971), p. 448.

set to watering the mouths of all the ancient hearers whose survival, like that of many of their modern counterparts in the third world, depended literally on the season-by-season regularity of crops. The storage system was primitive, the arable land limited, the water supply unpredictable. It took virtually all the time and effort of those who worked the land just to survive, let alone to set aside a surplus for an unrainy day. No prophecy could have been more welcome. With its note of hyperbole, it trumpeted a future that was more than a happy *reversal* of a tragic one; it was an *advance* to a way of life unprecedented in their experience, not just a recovery of the best of their past as verses 11–12 had promised.

13. The fecundity of the land will be so abundant that those who toil at the various tasks will be breathless to keep up with it. *Ploughman* and *reaper* laboured separately: the one beginning after the autumn rains in October or November; the other, after the spring rains in March or April. But here they bump into each other, so abundant are the crops and so eager is the land to grow more. Similarly, grape-treading is a September task after the summer vintage, while 'drawing' or 'trailing' (*sows*; Heb. *mšk* is to 'drag'; the noun *mešek* in Ps. 126:6 seems to mean 'trail of seed' for sowing [BDB, p. 604], though KB, p. 575, reads it as 'seed-bag') *the seed* through the furrows was scheduled for November and December.

The incredible fertility was further accented by the portrayal of the *mountains* and hill-country awash with *wine*. Not just the valleys and lowlands yield to the vintner's art, but the more remote, steep and inaccessible places are made so tillable that grapes flow down them like waves. The power of Yahweh to 'melt' (Heb. *mwg*) the earth (9:5) is at work here to 'dissolve' (*flow*; Heb. *htmwgg*) the *hills* with the blood of grapes.

Water, though not mentioned, must be the key to this scene. Accelerated crop-cycles and harvest in inaccessible places are possible only where water is abundant. The parallel prophetic pictures of fecundity make this clear: Ezekiel's river (47:12); Joel's fountain (3:18 [Heb. 4:18]). Amos has said enough previously about the damaging absence of water (4:6–8; 8:13) and about God's powerful providence to send water (5:8; 9:6) that he does not have to state the obvious here.

14. On *restore the fortunes*, see comments at Joel 3:1. That verse 14 is the clear reversal of 5:11 has already been stated. What needs to be emphasized is that the stinging indictment of 5:11 was addressed to the wealthy or ruling class, who alone could afford stone houses and choice vineyards. Here the whole people, named as God's own covenant family, *my people* (Heb. *'ammî*; *cf.* Ho. 1 – 2, for the full implications of this), partake in the restoration. What the élite had lusted after and trusted in had to be destroyed as the wormwood of unrighteousness, the poison of injustice (6:12). The new prosperity (note the building of *cities* not just 'houses') will be shared by the entire populace in a setting of personal well-being akin to Micah's picture (4:4).

15. Not only will the impact of exile, so frequently threatened by Amos (4:2–3; 5:5, 27; 7:11, 17), be reversed, but all future threat of exile will be eliminated. *Pluck* and *plant* continues the agricultural language of verses 13–14 but applies it metaphorically to the people, who elsewhere are called God's vine (Ps. 80; Is. 5; 27). What is employed in Amos only here is a persistent theme in Jeremiah from his call-vision onward (1:10; 24:6; 31:28; 42:10). The metaphor of planting speaks of both permanence and fruitfulness, *i.e.* security and obedience, as Isaiah's vineyard song made clear in its call for justice and righteousness (5:7). What was blatantly and disastrously absent from Israel's life (Am. 5:7, 24; 6:12) before the judgment will be the expected result of the new divine planting.

The land which I have given them is a reminder of the continuity of God's promise and action in their history. Amos had featured that gift as part of his first indictment of Israel: they had not only broken God's law but had done so in the face of magnificent grace (2:9–11). Yet that grace would persist beyond the judgment to bind together Israel's past and Israel's future, a note also sounded in the phrase *as in the days of old* (9:11). The heart of that grace for Israel would be, as ever, the gift of the *land*, their home, their badge of identity, their refuge against incursion by or assimilation to nations that feared not their Lord. Again, we catch the contrast between the close of the book and its beginning. In the judgment speeches of 1:3 – 2:3 the Levant was ablaze with aggression – Damascus threshing Gilead (1:3), Gaza capturing people to sell to Edom (1:6), Tyre following suit (1:9), Edom pursuing Israel (and Judah), sword in hand (1:11), Ammon grasping for Gilead at the cost of innocent women and unborn babies (1:13), Moab violating the corpse of Edom's king (2:1). Each of these actions threatened directly or indirectly the safety of God's people. The closing verse describes a different kind of world in which, by the covenant grace and loyalty of Yahweh, his people dwell safe, secure and prosperous, unthreatened by their enemies, since those very enemies that badgered them through the centuries would be called by Yahweh's name (v. 12).

Fittingly, it is that name with which the text closes. The concluding messenger formula 'said Yahweh' (*cf.* 1:5, 8 [Lord Yahweh], 15; 2:1; 5:17, 27; 7:3, 6 [Lord Yahweh]) is repeated in support of the prophet's divinely assigned role as messenger to the people (1:1; 2:11–12; 3:7–8; 7:14–15). More than repeated, the formula is expanded to a unique form, 'Said Yahweh, *your God*'. The covenant relationship has the last word and is the appropriate complement to the *my people* of verse 14. Together these terms, 'your God' and 'my people', constitute a renewed pledge of commitment on the part of him who first established the covenant and alone has the grace and power to carry it on. (On the stages of fulfilment of prophecies like these, see note at Ho. 1:10 – 2:1.)